The Lake English Classics

General Editor

LINDSAY TODD DAMON

Professor of English, Brown University

The Lake English Classics—continued

IRVING—*Tales of a Traveller*—and parts of *The Sketch Book*
    —KRAPP
LAMB—*Essays of Elia*—BENEDICT
LONGFELLOW—*Narrative Poems*—POWELL
LOWELL—*Visions of Sir Launfal*—See Coleridge
MACAULAY—*Essays on Addison and Johnson*—NEWCOMER
MACAULAY—*Essays on Clive and Hastings*—NEWCOMER
MACAULAY—*Goldsmith, Frederic the Great, Madame D'Arblay*
    —NEWCOMER
MACAULAY—*Essays on Milton and Addison*—NEWCOMER
MILTON—*L'Allegro, Il Penseroso, Comus, and Lycidas*—
    NEILSON
MILTON—*Paradise Lost, Books I and II*—FARLEY
Modern Plays, A Book of—COFFMAN
Old Testament Narratives—RHODES
One Hundred Narrative Poems—TETER
PALGRAVE—*The Golden Treasury*—NEWCOMER
PARKMAN—*The Oregon Trail*—MACDONALD
POE—*Poems and Tales, Selected*—NEWCOMER
POPE—*Homer's Iliad, Books I, VI, XXII, XXIV*—CRESSY AND
    MOODY
READE—*The Cloister and the Hearth*—DE MILLE
RUSKIN—*Sesame and Lilies*—LINN
Russian Short Stories—SCHWEIKERT
SCOTT—*Lady of the Lake*—MOODY
SCOTT—*Lay of the Last Minstrel*—MOODY AND WILLARD
SCOTT—*Marmion*—MOODY AND WILLARD
SCOTT—*Ivanhoe*—SIMONDS
SCOTT—*Quentin Durward*—SIMONDS
Selections from the Writings of Abraham Lincoln—HAMILTON
SHAKSPERE—*The Neilson Edition*—Edited by W. A. NEILSON
    As You Like It   *Macbeth*
    Hamlet   *Midsummer-Night's Dream*
    Henry V   *Romeo and Juliet*
    Julius Cæsar   *The Tempest*
                Twelfth Night
SHAKSPERE—*The Merchant of Venice*—LOVETT
SOUTHEY—*Life of Nelson*—WESCOTT
STEVENSON—*Inland Voyage and Travels with a Donkey*—
    LEONARD
STEVENSON—*Kidnapped*—LEONARD
STEVENSON—*Treasure Island*—BROADUS
TENNYSON—*Selected Poems*—REYNOLD.
TENNYSON—*The Princess*—COPELAND
THACKERAY—*English Humorists*—CUNLIFFE AND WATT
THACKERAY—*Henry Esmond*—PHELPS
THOREAU—*Walden*—BOWMAN
Three American Poems—*The Raven, Snow-Bound, Miles Stand-
    ish*—GREEVER
Types of the Short Story—HEYDRICK
VIRGIL—*Æneid*—ALLINSON AND ALLINSON
Washington, Webster, Lincoln, Selections from—DENNY

SCOTT, FORESMAN AND COMPANY
CHICAGO   ATLANTA   DALLAS   NEW YORK

The Lake English Classics

REVISED EDITION WITH HELPS TO STUDY

ONE HUNDRED NARRATIVE POEMS

EDITED FOR SCHOOL USE

BY

GEORGE E. TETER, M.A.

HEAD OF THE ENGLISH DEPARTMENT IN THE
MILWAUKEE NORMAL SCHOOL

SCOTT, FORESMAN AND COMPANY

CHICAGO   ATLANTA   NEW YORK

FOREWORD

All the world loves a story, and many excellent stories have been embodied in narrative poetry. Unfortunately, however, in the crowding of our English courses, many of the best poems have been passed over. This volume is an attempt to put before our students some of these poems, and in addition to present some modern narratives. Many of the poems should be, but are not now, a common heritage. They are full of dramatic power, they present excellent pictures, and they are dominated by vigorous and frequently admirable characters. They make a strong appeal to the heroic. They are rich in human emotion, with a concreteness that brings these emotions home. It is safe to say that few indeed are the boys and girls who will not greatly enjoy reading narrative poetry.

Since the poems are so vigorously and sympathetically human, and since they are so strongly dramatic, they furnish excellent material for reading aloud. The book is designed to encourage this practice. For this reason, critical analysis is scarcely to be recommended here. To interrupt a good story by many explanations is to kill the joy. Few notes are given, and these are conveniently placed at the foot of the page. Surely it would be a mistake to turn "How They Brought the Good News" into a geography lesson, or to make "Sohrab and Rustum" the basis for a critical study of the tribes and customs of Central Asia. The story is the thing. Once pupils get the habit of reading the poems aloud with real enthusiasm, the rest will be easy.

The appeal to the physical, so strong with young people, is too often ignored in courses of study; but just as a boy admires and imitates the baseball pitcher who wins a game against seemingly hopeless odds, or the halfback who turns apparent defeat into glorious victory, so he will learn to admire Robin Hood, Paul Revere, Richard Grenville, and Sohrab, once he falls under the sway of their personalities. Unfortunately, boys are not always choice in the selection of their heroes. It would surely be worth while to replace the rakish tough, so often attractive to the thoughtless boy, with the heroic characters of narrative verse. This hero-worship, as characteristic of girls as of boys, will be brought about, not by sermonizing, but by such a vivid presentation as makes the characters alive and thus enables them to do their own winning. Such a presentation is frequently found in narrative poems.

The physical appeal, however, is not the only one. Few are the emotions not called into play in the following selections. The variety is great enough to furnish material for the most varied taste. Whatever the appeal may be, and whatever the method of presentation, it is hoped that the result of a reading of the following poems will be an increased appreciation of narrative verse, a greater open-mindedness for other lines of poetry, and a strengthening of character.

The editor desires to express his appreciation of the courtesies extended by the following publishers, periodicals, and authors in granting permission to use the poems indicated, rights in which are in each case reserved by the owner of the copyright:

Messrs. Barse and Hopkins: "Fleurette" and "Grandpère" from *The Rhymes of the Red Cross Man* by Robert W. Service, copyright 1916.

Messrs. Charles Scribner's Sons: "Keenan's Charge" from *Dreams and Days* by George P. Lathrop, copyright 1902.

"Spanish Waters" by John Masefield. Used by permission of the author and The Macmillan Company.

"Vive la France" by Charlotte H. Crawford, Scribner's Magazine. Copyright, 1916, by Charles Scribner's Sons.

The George H. Doran Company and The Outlook: "The Prayer" by Amelia Josephine Burr. Copyright, 1918, by the George H. Doran Company.

Messrs. G. F. Weber and Company: "The Battle Flag at Shenandoah" and "The Defense of the Alamo" by Joaquin Miller.

Messrs. Harper and Brothers: "Arnold at Stillwater" by Thomas D. English.

The Houghton Mifflin Company: "Pan in Wall Street," by Edmund C. Stedman is used by permission of, and by special arrangement with, Houghton Mifflin Company, authorized publishers of his works.

The John Lane Company: "He Fell among Thieves" and "Vitaï Lampada" by Henry Newbolt.

The Macmillan Company: "The Fight" by Percy Mac-Kaye, and "The Host of the Air" by William Butler Yeats.

The Paget Literary Agency: "The Highwayman" by Alfred Noyes.

Messrs. A. P. Watt and Company of London, and Messrs. E. P. Dutton and Company: "The Ballad of East and West" by Rudyard Kipling.

Miss Helen Gray Cone: "Greencastle Jenny."

Mr. Edwin Markham: "How Oswald Dined with God" and "How the Great Guest Came" from *The Shoes of Happiness*.

Mr. Horace Traubel: "Vigil Strange I Kept on the Field One Night" and "The Singer in the Prison" by Walt Whitman.

G. E. T.

CONTENTS

CONTENTS

CONTENTS

One Hundred Narrative Poems

1

ROBIN HOOD AND LITTLE JOHN[1]

When Robin Hood was about twenty years old,
  With a hey down, down, and a down,
He happend to meet Little John,
A jolly brisk blade, right fit for the trade,
  For he was a lusty young man.

Tho he was calld Little, his limbs they were large,
  And his stature was seven foot high;
Wherever he came, they quak'd at his name,
  For soon he would make them to fly.

How they came acquainted, I'll tell you in brief,
  If you will but listen a while;
For this very jest, amongst all the rest,
  I think it may cause you to smile.

Bold Robin Hood said to his jolly bowmen,
  "Pray tarry you here in this grove;
And see that you all observe well my call,
  While thorough the forest I rove.

1. **Robin Hood.** The famous outlaw whose deeds have been the theme of many tales. He is the hero of a number of ballads, of which this is a good example. Robin Hood is traditionally said to have lived in the reign of Richard I of England, 1189-1199. The Robin Hood Ballads were in circulation a good while before 1377. For an example of Robin Hood's appearance in later literature see *Ivanhoe*, where he goes by the name of Locksley.
   This ballad and the following, unless otherwise indicated, are taken from the Kittredge-Sargent edition of *English and Scottish Popular Ballads.*

"We have had no sport for these fourteen long days,
  Therefore now abroad will I go;
Now should I be beat, and cannot retreat,
  My horn I will presently blow."

Then did he shake hands with his merry men all,
  And bid them at present good b'w'ye;
Then, as near a brook his journey he took,
  A stranger he chanced to espy.

They happened to meet on a long narrow bridge,
  And neither of them would give way;
Quoth bold Robin Hood, and sturdily stood,
  "I'll show you right Nottingham play." [2]

With that from his quiver an arrow he drew,
  A broad arrow [3] with a goose-wing;
The stranger reply'd, "I'll liquor thy hide,
  If thou offer'st to touch the string."

Quoth bold Robin Hood, "Thou dost prate like an ass,
  For were I to bend but my bow,
I could send a dart quite thro thy proud heart,
  Before thou couldst strike me one blow."

"Thou talk'st like a coward," the stranger reply'd;
  "Well armed with a long bow you stand,
To shoot at my breast, while I, I protest,
  Have nought but a staff in my hand."

"The name of a coward," quoth Robin, "I scorn,
  Wherefore my long bow I'll lay by;
And now, for thy sake, a staff will I take,
  The truth of thy manhood to try."

2. **Right Nottingham play.** Such fighting as is done in Nottingham. Sherwood forest, one of the haunts of Robin Hood, is about ten miles north of Nottingham.

3. **A broad arrow.** An arrow with a forked or barbed head.

Then Robin Hood stept to a thicket of trees,
   And chose him a staff of ground oak;
Now this being done, away he did run
   To the stranger, and merrily spoke:

"Lo! see my staff, it is lusty and tough,
   Now here on the bridge we will play;
Whoever falls in, the other shall win
   The battel, and so we'll away."

"With all my whole heart," the stranger reply'd;
   "I scorn in the least to give out";
This said, they fell to't without more dispute,
   And their staffs they did flourish about.

And first Robin he gave the stranger a bang,
   So hard that it made his bones ring:
The stranger he said, "This must be repaid,
   I'll give you as good as you bring.

"So long as I'm able to handle my staff,
   To die in your debt, friend, I scorn":
Then to it each goes, and follow'd their blows,
   As if they had been threshing of corn.

The stranger gave Robin a crack on the crown,
   Which caused the blood to appear;
Then Robin, enrag'd, more fiercely engag'd,
   And followed his blows more severe.

So thick and so fast did he lay it on him,
   With a passionate fury and ire,
At every stroke, he made him to smoke,
   As if he had been all on fire.

O then into fury the stranger he grew,
　　And gave him a damnable look,
And with it a blow that laid him full low,
　　And tumbld him into the brook.

"I prithee, good fellow, O where art thou now?"
　　The stranger, in laughter, he cry'd;
Quoth bold Robin Hood, "Good faith, in the flood,
　　And floating along with the tide.

"I needs must acknowledge thou art a brave soul;
　　With thee I'll no longer contend;
For needs must I say, thou hast got the day,
　　Our battel shall be at an end."

Then, unto the bank he did presently wade,
　　And pulld himself out by a thorn;
Which done, at the last, he blowd a loud blast
　　Straitway on his fine bugle-horn.

The eccho of which through the vallies did fly,
　　At which his stout bowmen appeared,
All cloathed in green, most gay to be seen;
　　So up to their master they steered.

"O what's the matter?" quoth William Stutely;
　　"Good master, you are wet to the skin":
"No matter," quoth he; "the lad which you see,
　　In fighting, hath tumbld me in."

"He shall not go scot-free," the others reply'd;
　　So strait they were seizing him there,
To duck him likewise; but Robin Hood cries,
　　"He is a stout fellow, forbear.

"There's no one shall wrong thee, friend, be not afraid;
 These bowmen upon me do wait;
There's threescore and nine; if thou wilt be mine,
 Thou shalt have my livery strait,

"And other accoutrements fit for a man.
 Speak up, jolly blade, never fear;
I'll teach you also the use of the bow,
 To shoot at the fat fallow-deer."

"O here is my hand," the stranger reply'd;
 "I'll serve you with all my whole heart.
My name is John Little, a man of good mettle;
 Nere doubt me, for I'll play my part."

"His name shall be altered," quoth William Stutely,
 "And I will his godfather be;
Prepare then a feast, and none of the least,
 For we will be merry," quoth he.

They presently fetchd in a brace of fat does,
 With humming strong liquor likewise;
They lovd what was good; so, in the greenwood,
 This pretty sweet babe they baptize.

He was, I must tell you, but seven foot high,
 And, may be, an ell in the waste;
A pretty sweet lad; much feasting they had;
 Bold Robin the christening gracd,

With all his bowmen, which stood in a ring,
 And were of the Notti[n]gham breed;
Brave Stutely comes then, with seven yeomen,
 And did in this manner proceed.

"This infant was called John Little," quoth he,
  "Which name shall be changed anon;
The words we'll transpose, so wherever he goes,
  His name shall be calld Little John."

They all with a shout made the elements ring,
  So soon as the office was ore;
To feasting they went, with true merriment,
  And tippld strong liquor gillore.

Then Robin he took the pretty sweet babe,
  And cloathd him from top to the toe
In garments of green, most gay to be seen,
  And gave him a curious long bow.

"Thou shalt be an archer as well as the best,
  And range in the greenwood with us;
Where we'll not want gold nor silver, behold,
  While bishops have ought in their purse.

"We live here like squires, or lords of renown,
  Without ere a foot of free land;
We feast on good cheer, with wine, ale, and beer,
  And evry thing at our command."

Then musick and dancing did finish the day;
  At length, when the sun waxed low,
Then all the whole train the grove did refrain,
  And unto their caves they did go.

And so ever after, as long as he livd,
  Altho he was proper and tall,
Yet nevertheless, the truth to express,
  Still Little John they did him call.

2

ROBIN HOOD'S DEATH AND BURIAL[1]

When Robin Hood and Little John
  Down a down, a down, a down,
Went oer yon bank of broom,
  Said Robin Hood bold to Little John,
"We have shot for many a pound,
  Hey, down, a down, a down.

"But I am not able to shoot one shot more,
  My broad arrows will not flee;
But I have a cousin lives down below,
  Please God, she will bleed me."

Now Robin he is to fair Kirkly gone,
  As fast as he can win;
But before he came there, as we do hear,
  He was taken very ill.

And when that he came to fair Kirkly-hall,
  He knockd all at the ring,
But none was so ready as his cousin herself
  For to let bold Robin in.

"Will you please to sit down, cousin Robin," she said,
  "And drink some beer with me?"
"No I will neither eat nor drink,
  Till I am blooded by thee."

1. There are conflicting accounts in the ballads as to the details of the death of Robin Hood. All agree, however, that he was basely betrayed by his cousin, who practically bled him to death.

"Well, I have a room, cousin Robin," she said,
　"Which you did never see,
And if you please to walk therein,
　You blooded by me shall be."

She took him by the lily-white hand,
　And led him to a private room,
And there she blooded bold Robin Hood,
　While one drop of blood would run down.

She blooded him in a vein of the arm,
　And locked him up in the room;
Then did he bleed all the live-long day,
　Until the next day at noon.

He then bethought him of a casement there,
　Thinking for to get down;
He was so weak he could not leap,
　He could not get him down.

He then bethought him of his bugle-horn,
　Which hung low down to his knee;
He set his horn unto his mouth,
　And blew out weak blasts three.

Then Little John, when hearing him,
　As he sat under a tree,
"I fear my master is now near dead,
　He blows so wearily."

Then Little John to fair Kirkly is gone,
　As fast as he can dree;[2]
But when he came to Kirkly-hall,
　He broke locks two or three:

2. **Can dree.** Is able.

Until he came bold Robin to see,
  Then he fell on his knee;
"A boon, a boon," cries Little John,
  "Master, I beg of thee."

"What is that boon," said Robin Hood,
  "Little John, [thou] begs of me?"
"It is to burn fair Kirkly-hall,
  And all their nunnery."

"Now nay, now nay," quoth Robin Hood,
  "That boon I'll not grant thee;
I never hurt woman in all my life,
  Nor men in woman's company.

"I never hurt fair maid in all my time,
  Nor at mine end shall it be;
But give me my bent bow in my hand,
  And a broad arrow I'll let flee
And where this arrow is taken up,
  There shall my grave digged be.

"Lay me a green sod under my head,
  And another at my feet;
And lay my bent bow by my side,
  Which was my music sweet;
And make my grave of gravel and green,
  Which is most right and meet.

"Let me have length and breadth enough,
  With a green sod under my head;
That they may say, when I am dead,
  Here lies bold Robin Hood."

These words they readily granted him,
  Which did bold Robin please:
And there they buried bold Robin Hood,
  Within the fair Kirkleys.

3

JOHNIE ARMSTRONG[1]

There dwelt a man in faire Westmerland,
  Ionnë Armestrong men did him call,
He had nither lands nor rents coming in,
  Yet he kept eight score men in his hall.

He had horse and harness for them all,
  Goodly steeds were all milke-white;
O the golden bands an about their necks,
  And their weapons, they were all alike.

Newes then was brought unto the king
  That there was sicke a won[2] as hee,
That livëd lyke a bold out-law,
  And robbëd all the north country.

The king he writt an a letter then,
  A letter which was large and long;
He signëd it with his owne hand,
  And he promised to doe him no wrong.

When this letter came Ionnë untill,
  His heart it was as blythe as birds on the tree:
"Never was I sent for before any king,
  My father, my grandfather, nor none but mee.

---

1. This ballad is founded upon fact. John Armstrong was such a famous outlaw knight that in 1530 James V of Scotland levied an army to suppress him. Armstrong, evidently having little hope for himself, rode with his company into the presence of the king, hoping to win favor. In this he failed. Some accounts say that he was lured to the king by treachery, as in the ballad. For a full account see *English and Scottish Ballads* by Child, Vol. III, page 362.

2. Sicke a won. Such a one.

"And if wee goe the king before,
  I would we went most orderly;
Every man of you shall have his scarlet cloak,
  Laced with silver laces three.

"Every won of you shall have his velvett coat,
  Laced with sillver lace so white;
O the golden bands an about your necks,
  Black hatts, white feathers, all alyke."

By the morrow morninge at ten of the clock,
  Towards Edenburough gon was hee,
And with him all his eight score men;
  Good lord, it was a goodly sight for to see!

When Ionnë came befower the king,
  He fell downe on his knee;
"O pardon, my soveraine leige," he said,
  "O pardon my eight score men and me!"

"Thou shalt have no pardon, thou traytor strong,
  For thy eight score men nor thee;
For tomorrow morning by ten of the clock,
  Both thou and them shall hang on the gallow-tree."

But Ionnë looke'd over his left shoulder,
  Good Lord, what a grievious look looked hee!
Saying, Asking grace of a graceles face—
  Why there is none for you nor me.

But Ionnë had a bright sword by his side,
  And it was made of the mettle so free,[3]
That had not the king stept his foot aside,
  He had smitten his head from his faire boddë.

3. **Free.** Excellent in any way.

Saying, Fight on, my merry men all,
  And see that none of you be taine;
For rather then men shall say we were hange'd,
  Let them report how we were slaine.

Then, God wott, faire Eddenburrough rose,
  And so besett poore Ionnë rounde,
That fowerscore and tenn of Ionnës best men
  Lay gasping all upon the ground.

Then like a mad man Ionnë laide about,
  And like a mad man then fought hee,
Untill a falce Scot came Ionnë behinde,
  And runn him through the faire boddee.

Saying, Fight on, my merry men all,
  And see that none of you be taine;
For I will stand by and bleed but awhile,
  And then will I come and fight againe.

Newes then was brought to young Ionnë Armestrong,
  As he stood by his nurses knee,
Who vowed if ere he live'd for to be a man,
  O the treacherous Scots revenged hee'd be.

4

SIR PATRICK SPENCE[1]

The king sits in Dumferling toune,[2]
    Drinking the blude-reid wine:
"O whar will I get guid sailor,
    To sail this schip of mine?"

Up and spak an eldern knicht,
    Sat at the kings richt kne:
"Sir Patrick Spence is the best sailor
    That sails upon the se."

The king has written a braid letter,[3]
    And signd it wi his hand,
And sent it to Sir Patrick Spence,
    Was walking on the sand.

The first line that Sir Patrick red,
    A loud lauch lauched he;
The next line that Sir Patrick red,
    The teir blinded his ee.

"O wha is this has don this deid,
    This ill deid don to me,
To send me out this time o' the yeir,
    To sail upon the se!

1. This ballad may or may not have a historical basis. In 1290 a deputation was sent to bring the Princess Margaret, heir to the crown of Scotland, from Norway to England to marry the eldest son of Edward I, but she died on the voyage. According to one account she perished in a storm. The ballad may be based upon this voyage.

2. Dumferling toune. Fifteen miles northwest of Edinburgh.

3. Braid letter. Either a letter on a broad sheet, or a long letter.

"Mak hast, mak haste, my mirry men all,
    Our guid schip sails the morne:"
"O say na sae, my master deir,
    For I feir a deadlie storme.

"Late late yestreen I saw the new moone,
    Wi the auld moone in hir arme,
And I feir, I feir, my deir master,
    That we will cum to harme."

O our Scots nobles wer richt laith
    To weet their cork-heild schoone;
Bot lang owre a' the play wer playd,
    Thair hats they swam aboone.[4]

O lang, lang may their iadies sit,
    Wi thair fans into their hand,
Or eir they se Sir Patrick Spence
    Cum sailing to the land.

O lang, lang may the ladies stand,
    Wi thair gold kems in their hair,
Waiting for thair ain deir lords,
    For they'll se thame na mair.

Haf owre, haf owre to Aberdour,
    It's fiftie fadom deip,
And thair lies guid Sir Patrick Spence,
    Wi the Scots lords at his feit.

4. **Thair hats they swam aboone.** Floated on the water, the men
being drowned.

5

YOUNG WATERS[1]

About Yule, when the wind blew cule,
   And the round tables [2] began,
A [3] there is cum to our king's court
   Mony a well-favord man.

The queen luikt owre the castle-wa,
   Beheld baith dale and down,[4]
And there she saw Young Waters
   Cum riding to the town.

His footmen they did rin before,
   His horsemen rade behind;
And mantel of the burning gowd
   Did keip him frae the wind.

Gowden-graithed [5] his horse before,
   And siller-shod [6] behind;
The horse Young Waters rade upon
   Was fleeter than the wind.

Out then spack a wylie lord,
   Unto the queen said he,
"O tell me wha's the fairest face
   Rides in the company?"

1. This ballad has no certain historical foundation.
2. Round tables. A game.
3. A. Ah.
4. Dale and down. Valley and upland.
5. Graithed. Shod.
6. Siller. Silver.

"I've sene lord, and I've sene laird,
  And knights of high degree,
Bot [7] a fairer face than Young Waters
  Mine eyne did never see."

Out then spack the jealous king,
  And an angry man was he:
"O if he had bin twice as fair,
  You micht have excepted me."

"You're neither laird nor lord," she says,
  "Bot the king that wears the crown;
There is not a knight in fair Scotland
  But to thee maun bow down."

For a' that she coud do or say,
  Appeasd he wad nae bee,
Bot for the words which she had said,
  Young Waters he maun die.

They hae taen Young Waters,
  And put fetters to his feet;
They hae taen Young Waters,
  And thrown him in dungeon deep.

"Aft I have ridden thro Stirling town [8]
  In the wind bot [9] and the weit;
Bot I neir rade thro Stirling town
  Wi fetters at my feet.

"Aft I have ridden thro Stirling town
  In the wind bot and the rain;
Bot I neir rade thro Stirling town
  Neir to return again."

7. Bot. But.
8. Stirling. Thirty-five miles northwest of Edinburgh.
9. Bot. Both.

They hae taen to the heiding-hill [10]
   His young son in his craddle,
And they hae taen to the heiding-hill
   His horse bot and his saddle.

They hae taen to the heiding-hill
   His lady fair to see,
And for the words the queen had spoke
   Young Waters he did die.

6

THE DOWIE DENS OF YARROW [1]

(Sir Walter Scott's Version)

Late at e'en, drinking the wine,
   And ere they paid the lawing,[2]
They set a combat them between,
   To fight it in the dawing.

"O stay at hame, my noble lord!
   O stay at hame, my marrow![3]
My cruel brother will you betray,
   On the dowie [4] houms [5] of Yarrow." [6]

"O fare ye weel, my ladye gay!
   O fare ye weel, my Sarah!
For I maun gae, though I ne'er return
   Frae the dowie banks o' Yarrow."

10. **Heiding-hill.** Heading-hill; place of execution.

1. In all the various versions of this ballad there is an ill feeling between the family of the woman and the man. This explains the treachery. Evidently the brother-in-law remained in the background until the man was well nigh slain.

2. **Lawing.** Tavern reckoning.

3. **Marrow.** Mate.

4. **Dowie.** Doleful, sad, wretched.

5. **Houms.** Level low ground on a river bank.

6. **Yarrow.** A small stream in southeastern Scotland.

She kiss'd his cheek, she kaim'd his hair,
    As oft she had done before, O;
She belted him with his noble brand,
    And he's awa' to Yarrow.

As he gaed up the Tennies bank,
    I wot he gaed wi' sorrow,
Till, down in a den,[7] he spied nine arm'd men,
    On the dowie houms of Yarrow.

"O come ye here to part your land,
    The bonny forest thorough?
Or come ye here to wield your brand,
    On the dowie houms of Yarrow?"

"I come not here to part my land,
    And neither to beg nor borrow;
I come to wield my noble brand,
    On the bonnie banks of Yarrow.

"If I see all, ye're nine to ane;
    And that's an unequal marrow;[8]
Yet will I fight, while lasts my brand,
    On the bonny banks of Yarrow."

Four has he hurt, and five has slain,
    On the bloody braes of Yarrow,
Till that stubborn knight came him behind,
    And ran his body thorough.

"Gae hame, gae hame, good-brother John,
    And tell your sister Sarah,
To come and lift her noble lord!
    He's sleepin sound on Yarrow."

7. **Den.** Small valley.
8. **Marrow.** Match.

"Yestreen I dream'd a dolefu' dream;
   I fear there will be sorrow!
I dream'd I pu'd the heather green,
   Wi' my true love, on Yarrow.

"O gentle wind, that bloweth south,
   From where my love repaireth,
Convey a kiss from his dear mouth,
   And tell me how he fareth!

"But in the glen strive armed men;
   They've wrought me dole [9] and sorrow;
They've slain—the comeliest knight they've slain—
   He bleeding lies on Yarrow."

As she sped down yon high, high hill,
   She gaed wi' dole and sorrow,
And in the den spied ten slain men,
   On the dowie banks of Yarrow.

She kiss'd his cheek, she kaim'd his hair,
   She search'd his wounds all thorough,
She kiss'd them, till her lips grew red,
   On the dowie houms of Yarrow.

"Now, haud your tongue, my daughter dear!
   For a' this breeds but sorrow.
I'll wed ye to a better lord,
   Than him ye lost on Yarrow."

"O haud your tongue, my father dear,
   Ye mind me but of sorrow;
A fairer rose did never bloom
   Than now lies cropp'd on Yarrow."

9. Dole. Grief.
2

7

THE BATTLE OF OTTERBURN[1]

(Sir Walter Scott's Version)

It fell about the Lammas tide,[2]
  When the muir-men win their hay,
The doughty Douglas bound him to ride
  Into England, to drive a prey.[3]

He chose the Gordons and the Graemes,
  With them the Lindesays, light and gay;
But the Jardines wald not with him ride,
  And they rue it to this day.

And he has burned the dales of Tyne,
  And part of Bamb'rough shire;
And three good towers on Reidswire fell,[4]
  He left them all on fire.

And he marched up to Newcastle,
  And rode it round about;
"O wha's the lord of this castle,
  Or wha's the lady o't?"

But up spake proud Lord Percy then,
  And O but he spake hie!
"I am the lord of this castle,
  My wife's the lady gay."

1. Otterburn is a brook in Northumberland, about thirty miles northwest of Newcastle and not many miles from the Scotch border. The battle of Otterburn was fought in 1388. The ballad aptly illustrates the border raids so common in early Scotch and English history. The two chief characters are Lord Douglas, Scotch, and Lord Percy, English. The other names are those of notable clans or lords, or near localities.
2. **Lammas tide.** August 1.
3. **Drive a prey.** To make a raid.
4. **Fells.** Highland.

"If thou'rt the lord of this castle,
   Sae weel it pleases me!
For, ere I cross the Border fells,
   The tane [5] of us shall die."

He took a lang spear in his hand,
   Shod with the metal free,
And for to meet the Douglas there,
   He rode right furiouslie.

But O how pale his lady looked,
   Frae aff the castle wa',
When down before the Scottish spear
   She saw proud Percy fa'.

"Had we twa been upon the green,
   And never an eye to see,
I wad hae had you, flesh and fell; [6]
   But your sword sall gae wi me."

"But gae ye up to Otterburn,
   And wait there dayis three;
And, if I come not ere three dayis end,
   A fause knight ca' ye me."

"The Otterburn's a bonny burn; [7]
   'Tis pleasant there to be;
But there is nought at Otterburn,
   To feed my men and me.

"The deer rins wild on hill and dale,
   The birds fly wild from tree to tree;
But there is neither bread nor kale, [8]
   To fend [9] my men and me.

5. **Tane.** One.
6. **Flesh and fell.** Flesh and skin.
7. **Burn.** Brook.
8. **Kale.** Colewort, used for green.
9. **Fend.** To provision, to feed.

"Yet I will stay at Otterburn,
  Where you shall welcome be;
And, if ye come not at three dayis end,
  A fause lord I'll ca' thee."

"Thither will I come," proud Percy said,
  "By the might of Our Ladie!"
"There will I bide thee," said the Douglas,
  "My troth I plight to thee."

They lighted high on Otterburn,
  Upon the bent [10] sae brown;
They lighted high on Otterburn,
  And threw their pallions [11] down.

And he that had a bonny boy,
  Sent out his horse to grass;
And he that had not a bonny boy,
  His ain servant he was.

But up then spake a little page,
  Before the peep of dawn:
"O waken ye, waken ye, my good lord,
  For Percy's hard at hand."

"Ye lie, ye lie, ye liar loud!
  Sae loud I hear ye lie:
For Percy had not men yestreen
  To dight [12] my men and me.

10. **Bent.** Coarse, reedy grass.
11. **Pallions.** Pavilions.
12. **Dight.** To equip, dress.

"But I have dreamed a dreary dream,
  Beyond the Isle of Sky; [13]
I saw a dead man win a fight,
  And I think that man was I."

He belted on his guid braid sword,
  And to the field he ran;
But he forgot the helmet good,
  That should have kept his brain.

When Percy wi' the Douglas met,
  I wat [14] he was fu' fain!
They swakked [15] their swords, till sair they swat,
  And the blood ran down like rain.

But Percy with his good broad sword,
  That could so sharply wound,
Has wounded Douglas on the brow,
  Till he fell to the ground.

Then he called on his little foot-page,
  And said, "Run speedilie,
And fetch my ain dear sister's son,
  Sir Hugh Montgomery.

"My nephew good," the Douglas said,
  "What recks the death of ane!
Last night I dreamd a dreary dream,
  And I ken the day's thy ain.

"My wound is deep; I fain would sleep;
  Take thou the vanguard of the three,
And hide me by the braken bush,
  That grows on yonder lilye lee.

13. **Isle of Sky.** An island of the Hebrides.
14. **Wat.** Know.
15. **Swakked.** Smote.

"O bury me by the braken-bush,
    Beneath the blooming brier,
Let never living mortal ken,
    That ere a kindly Scot lies here."

He lifted up that noble lord,
    Wi' the saut tear in his ee;
He hid him in the braken bush,
    That his merry men might not see.

The moon was clear, the day drew near,
    The spears in flinders flew,
But mony a gallant Englishman
    Ere day the Scotsmen slew.

The Gordons good, in English blood
    They steeped their hose and shoon; [16]
The Lindsays flew like fire about,
    Till all the fray was done.

The Percy and Montgomery met;
    That either of other were fain;
They swapped swords, and they twa swat,
    And aye the blood ran down between.

"Now yield thee, yield thee, Percy," he said,
    "Or else I vow I'll lay thee low;"
"To whom must I yield," quoth Earl Percy,
    "Now that I see it must be so?"

"Thou shalt not yield to lord nor loun, [17]
    Nor yet shalt thou yield to me;
But yield thee to the braken bush,
    That grows upon yon lilye lee!"

16. Shoon. Shoes.
17. Loun. Person of low rank.

"I will not yield to a braken-bush,
  Nor yet will I yield to a brier;
But I would yield to Earl Douglas,
  Or Sir Hugh the Montgomery, if he were here."

As soon as he knew it was Montgomery,
  He struck his sword's point in the gronde;
The Montgomery was a courteous knight,
  And quickly took him by the honde.

This deed was done at Otterburn
  About the breaking of the day;
Earl Douglas was buried [18] at the braken bush,
  And the Percy led captive away.

8

THE BELL OF ATRI

Henry Wadsworth Longfellow

At Atri in Abruzzo,[1] a small town
Of ancient Roman date, but scant renown,
One of those little places that have run
Half up the hill, beneath a blazing sun,
And then sat down to rest, as if to say,
"I climb no farther upward, come what may,"—
The Re Giovanni,[2] now unknown to fame,
So many monarchs since have borne the name,
Had a great bell hung in the market-place,
Beneath a roof, projecting some small space

18. **Buried.** Earl Douglas was really buried in Melrose Abbey. where his tomb is still to be seen.

1. **Abruzzo.** A former division of central Italy.
2. **Re Giovanni.** King John.

By way of shelter from the sun and rain.
Then rode he through the streets with all his train,
And, with the blast of trumpets loud and long,
Made proclamation, that whenever wrong
Was done to any man, he should but ring
The great bell in the square, and he, the King,
Would cause the Syndic [3] to decide thereon.
Such was the proclamation of King John.

How swift the happy days in Atri sped,
What wrongs were righted, need not here be said.
Suffice it that, as all things must decay,
The hempen rope at length was worn away,
Unravelled at the end, and, strand by strand,
Loosened and wasted in the ringer's hand,
Till one, who noted this in passing by,
Mended the rope with braids of briony,
So that the leaves and tendrils of the vine
Hung like a votive garland at a shrine.

By chance it happened that in Atri dwelt
A knight, with spur on heel and sword in belt,
Who loved to hunt the wild-boar in the woods,
Who loved his falcons with their crimson hoods,
Who loved his hounds and horses, and all sports
And prodigalities of camps and courts;—
Loved, or had loved them; for at last, grown old,
His only passion was the love of gold.

He sold his horses, sold his hawks and hounds,
Rented his vineyards and his garden-grounds,
Kept but one steed, his favorite steed of all,
To starve and shiver in a naked stall,
And day by day sat brooding in his chair,
Devising plans how best to hoard and spare.

3. **Syndic.** Chief Magistrate.

At length he said: "What is the use or need
To keep at my own cost this lazy steed,
Eating his head off in my stables here,
When rents are low and provender is dear?
Let him go feed upon the public ways;
I want him only for the holidays."
So the old steed was turned into the heat
Of the long, lonely, silent, shadeless street;
And wandered in suburban lanes forlorn,
Barked at by dogs, and torn by brier and thorn.

One afternoon, as in that sultry clime
It is the custom in the summer time,
With bolted doors and window-shutters closed,
The inhabitants of Atri slept or dozed;
When suddenly upon their senses fell
The loud alarm of the accusing bell!
The Syndic started from his deep repose,
Turned on his couch, and listened, and then rose
And donned his robes, and with reluctant pace
Went panting forth into the market-place,
Where the great bell upon its cross-beams swung,
Reiterating with persistent tongue,
In half-articulate jargon, the old song:
"Some one hath done a wrong, hath done a wrong!"

But ere he reached the belfry's light arcade
He saw, or thought he saw, beneath its shade,
No shape of human form of woman born,
But a poor steed dejected and forlorn,
Who with uplifted head and eager eye
Was tugging at the vines of briony.
"Domeneddio!" cried the Syndic straight,
"This is the Knight of Atri's steed of state!
He calls for justice, being sore distressed,
And pleads his cause as loudly as the best."

Meanwhile from street and lane a noisy crowd
Had rolled together like a summer cloud,
And told the story of the wretched beast
In five-and-twenty different ways at least,
With much gesticulation and appeal
To heathen gods, in their excessive zeal.
The Knight was called and questioned; in reply
Did not confess the fact, did not deny;
Treated the matter as a pleasant jest,
And set at naught the Syndic and the rest,
Maintaining, in an angry undertone,
That he should do what pleased him with his own.

And thereupon the Syndic gravely read
The proclamation of the King; then said:
"Pride goeth forth on horseback grand and gay,
But cometh back on foot, and begs its way;
Fame is the fragrance of heroic deeds,
Of flowers of chivalry and not of weeds!
These are familiar proverbs; but I fear
They never yet have reached your knightly ear.
What fair renown, what honor, what repute
Can come to you from starving this poor brute?
He who serves well and speaks not, merits more
Than they who clamor loudest at the door.
Therefore the law decrees that as this steed
Served you in youth, henceforth you shall take heed
To comfort his old age, and to provide
Shelter in stall, and food and field beside."

The Knight withdrew abashed; the people all
Led home the steed in triumph to his stall.
The King heard and approved, and laughed in glee,
And cried aloud: "Right well it pleaseth me!
Church-bells at best but ring us to the door:

But go not in to mass; my bell doth more:
It cometh into court and pleads the cause
Of creatures dumb and unknown to the laws;
And this shall make, in every Christian clime,
The Bell of Atri famous for all time."

9

GOD'S JUDGMENT ON HATTO [1]

Robert Southey

The summer and autumn had been so wet,
That in winter the corn was growing yet.
'T was a piteous sight to see all around
The grain lie rotting on the ground.

Every day the starving poor
They crowded round Bishop Hatto's door;
For he had a plentiful last-year's store,
And all the neighborhood could tell
His granaries were furnished well.

At last Bishop Hatto appointed a day
To quiet the poor without delay;
He bade them to his great barn repair,
And they should have food for the winter there.

Rejoiced the tidings good to hear,
The poor folks flocked from far and near;
The great barn was full as it could hold
Of women and children, and young and old.

---

1. "Hatto, Archbishop of Mentz, in the year 914 barbarously murdered a number of poor people to prevent their consuming a portion
of the food during that year of famine. He was afterwards devoured
by rats in his tower on an island in the Rhine."—Old Legend,
W. C. Bryant, *Library of Poetry and Song.*

Then, when he saw it could hold no more,
Bishop Hatto he made fast the door;
And whilst for mercy on Christ they call,
He set fire to the barn, and burnt them all.

"I' faith 't is an excellent bonfire!" quoth he;
"And the country is greatly obliged to me
For ridding it, in these times forlorn,
Of rats that only consume the corn."

So then to his palace returned he,
And he sat down to supper merrily,
And he slept that night like an innocent man;
But Bishop Hatto never slept again.

In the morning, as he entered the hall,
Where his picture hung against the wall,
A sweat like death all over him came,
For the rats had eaten it out of the frame.

As he looked, there came a man from his farm,—
He had a countenance white with alarm:
"My lord, I opened your granaries this morn,
And the rats had eaten all your corn."

Another came running presently,
And he was as pale as pale could be.
"Fly! my lord bishop, fly!" quoth he,
"Ten thousand rats are coming this way,—
The Lord forgive you for yesterday!"

"I'll go to my tower in the Rhine," replied he;
"'Tis the safest place in Germany,—
The walls are high, and the shores are steep,
And the tide is strong, and the waters deep."

Bishop Hatto fearfully hastened away;
And he crossed the Rhine without delay,
And reached the tower in the island, and barred
All the gates secure and hard.

He laid him down and closed his eyes,
But soon a scream made him arise;
He started, and saw two eyes of flame
On his pillow, from whence the screaming came.

He listened and looked,—it was only the cat;
But the Bishop he grew more fearful for that,
For she sat screaming, mad with fear
At the army of rats that were drawing near.

For they have swum over the river so deep,
And they have climbed the shores so steep,
And now by thousands up they crawl
To the holes and the windows in the wall.

Down on his knees the bishop fell,
And faster and faster his beads did he tell,
As louder and louder, drawing near,
The saw of their teeth without he could hear.

And in at the windows, and in at the door,
And through the walls, by thousands they pour;
And down from the ceiling and up through the **floor**,
From the right and the left, from behind and before,
From within and without, from above and below,—
And all at once to the bishop they go.

They have whetted their teeth against the stones,
And now they pick the bishop's bones;
They gnawed the flesh from every limb,
For they were sent to do judgment on him!

10

THE WRECK OF THE HESPERUS [1]

HENRY WADSWORTH LONGFELLOW

It was the schooner Hesperus,
  That sailed the wintry sea;
And the skipper had taken his little daughtër,
  To bear him company.

Blue were her eyes as the fairy-flax,[2]
  Her cheeks like the dawn of day,
And her bosom white as the hawthorn buds,
  That ope in the month of May.

The skipper he stood beside the helm,
  His pipe was in his mouth,
And he watched how the veering flaw did blow
  The smoke now West, now South.

Then up and spake an old sailör,
  Had sailed to the Spanish Main,[3]
"I pray thee, put into yonder port,
  For I fear a hurricane.

"Last night, the moon had a golden ring,
  And tonight no moon we see!"
The skipper, he blew a whiff from his pipe,
  And a scornful laugh laughed he.

---

1. It will be noted that in many respects this poem is like "Sir Patrick Spence."
2. **Fairy-flax.** The blossom of the flax is blue.
3. **Spanish Main.** The portion of the Caribbean Sea along the northern coast of South America; at first the name was applied to the land.

Colder and colder blew the wind,
  A gale from the Northeast,
The snow fell hissing in the brine,
  And the billows frothed like yeast.

Down came the storm, and smote amain
  The vessel in its strength;
She shuddered and paused, like a frighted steed,
  Then leaped her cable's length.

"Come hither! come hither! my little daughter,
  And do not tremble so;
For I can weather the roughest gale
  That ever wind did blow."

He wrapped her warm in his seaman's coat
  Against the stinging blast;
He cut a rope from a broken spar,
  And bound her to the mast.

"O father! I hear the church bells ring;
  Oh, say, what may it be?"
"'Tis a fog bell on a rock-bound coast!"—
  And he steered for the open sea.

"O father! I hear the sound of guns;
  Oh, say, what may it be?"
"Some ship in distress, that cannot live
  In such an angry sea!"

"O father! I see a gleaming light;
  Oh, say, what may it be?"
But the father answered never a word,
  A frozen corpse was he.

Lashed to the helm, all stiff and stark,
  With his face turned to the skies,
The lantern gleamed through the gleaming snow
  On his fixed and glassy eyes.

Then the maiden clasped her hands and prayed
  That savëd she might be;
And she thought of Christ, who stilled the wave,
  On the Lake of Galilee.

And fast through the midnight dark and drear,
  Through the whistling sleet and snow,
Like a sheeted ghost, the vessel swept
  Tow'rds the reef of Norman's Woe.[4]

And ever the fitful gusts between
  A sound came from the land;
It was the sound of the trampling surf
  On the rocks and the hard sea sand.

The breakers were right beneath her bows,
  She drifted a dreary wreck,
And a whooping billow swept the crew
  Like icicles from her deck.

She struck where the white and fleecy waves
  Looked soft as carded wool,
But the cruel rocks, they gored her side
  Like the horns of an angry bull.

Her rattling shrouds, all sheathed in ice,
  With the masts went by the board;
Like a vessel of glass, she strove and sank,
  Ho! ho! the breakers roared!

4. Norman's Woe. A reef in West Gloucester Harbor, Mass.

At daybreak on the bleak sea beach,
   A fisherman stood aghast,
To see the form of a maiden fair,
   Lashed close to a drifting mast.

The salt sea was frozen on her breast,
   The salt tears in her eyes;
And he saw her hair, like the brown seaweed
   On the billows fall and rise.

Such was the wreck of the Hesperus,
   In the midnight and the snow!
Christ save us all from a death like this,
   On the reef of Norman's Woe!

11

LOCHINVAR

Sir Walter Scott

Oh, young Lochinvar is come out of the west,
Through all the wide Border his steed was the best;
And save his good broadsword he weapons had none.
He rode all unarmed, and he rode all alone.
So faithful in love, and so dauntless in war,
There never was knight like the young Lochinvar.

He stayed not for brake,[1] and he stopped not for stone;
He swam the Eske river where ford there was none;
But, ere he alighted at Netherby gate,
The bride had consented, the gallant came late;
For a laggard in love, and a dastard in war,
Was to wed the fair Ellen of brave Lochinvar.

1. **Brake.** Thicket; brushwood.

So boldly he entered the Netherby hall,
'Mong bridesmen and kinsmen and brothers and all:
Then spoke the bride's father, his hand on his sword
(For the poor craven bridegroom said never a word),
"Oh, come ye in peace here, or come ye in war,
Or to dance at our bridal, young Lord Lochinvar?"

"I long wooed your daughter, my suit you denied;—
Love swells like the Solway, but ebbs like its tide;
And now I am come, with this lost love of mine
To lead but one measure, drink one cup of wine.
There are maidens in Scotland more lovely by far
That would gladly be bride to the young Lochinvar."

The bride kissed the goblet; the knight took it up:
He quaffed off the wine, and he threw down the cup.
She looked down to blush, and she looked up to sigh,
With a smile on her lips and a tear in her eye.
He took her soft hand ere her mother could bar,—
"Now tread we a measure!" said young Lochinvar.

So stately his form, and so lovely her face,
That never a hall such a galliard [2] did grace;
While her mother did fret, and her father did fume,
And the bridegroom stood dangling his bonnet and plume;
And the bride-maidens whispered, " 'Twere better by far
To have matched our fair cousin with young Lochinvar."

One touch to her hand, and one word in her ear,
When they reached the hall door and the charger stood
    near;
So light to the croupe [3] the fair lady he swung,
So light to the saddle before her he sprung!

2. **Galliard.** An old gay and lively dance.
3. **Croupe.** The portion of a horse's back behind the saddle.

"She is won! we are gone, over bank, bush, and scaur![4]
They'll have fleet steeds that follow!" quoth young Lochin-
    var.

There was mounting 'mong Græmes of the Netherby clan;
Forsters, Fenwicks, and Musgraves, they rode and they
    ran;
There was racing and chasing on Cannobie Lee;
But the lost bride of Netherby ne'er did they see.
So daring in love, and so dauntless in war,
Have ye e'er heard of gallant like young Lochinvar?

12

LADY CLARE

ALFRED TENNYSON

It was the time when lilies blow
And clouds are highest up in air,
Lord Ronald brought a lily-white doe
To give his cousin, Lady Clare.

I trow they did not part in scorn;
Lovers long-betroth'd were they;
They two will wed the morrow morn;
God's blessing on the day!

"He does not love me for my birth,
Nor for my lands so broad and fair;
He loves me for my own true worth,
And that is well," said Lady Clare.

4. **Scaur.** A steep cliff or a rocky place on the side of a hill or
mountain.

In there came old Alice the nurse,
Said, "Who was this that went from thee?"
"It was my cousin," said Lady Clare;
"Tomorrow he weds with me."

"O, God be thank'd!" said Alice the nurse,
"That all comes round so just and fair;
Lord Ronald is heir of all your lands,
And you are not the Lady Clare."

"Are ye out of your mind, my nurse, my nurse?"
Said Lady Clare, "that ye speak so wild?"
"As God's above," said Alice the nurse,
"I speak the truth; you are my child.

"The old Earl's daughter died at my breast;
I speak the truth, as I live by bread!
I buried her like my own sweet child,
And put my child in her stead."

"Falsely, falsely have ye done,
O mother," she said, "if this be true,
To keep the best man under the sun
So many years from his due."

"Nay now, my child," said Alice the nurse,
"But keep the secret for your life,
And all you have will be Lord Ronald's,
When you are man and wife."

"If I'm a beggar born," she said,
"I will speak out, for I dare not lie.
Pull off, pull off, the brooch of gold,
And fling the diamond necklace by."

"Nay now, my child," said Alice the nurse,
"But keep the secret all ye can."
She said, "Not so; but I will know
If there be any faith in man."

"Nay now, what faith?" said Alice the nurse,
"The man will cleave unto his right."
"And he shall have it," the lady replied,
"Tho' I should die tonight."

"Yet give one kiss to your mother dear!
Alas, my child, I sinn'd for thee."
"O mother, mother, mother," she said,
"So strange it seems to me.

"Yet here's a kiss for my mother dear,
My mother dear, if this be so,
And lay your hand upon my head,
And bless me, mother, ere I go."

She clad herself in a russet gown,[1]
She was no longer Lady Clare;
She went by dale,[2] and she went by down,[3]
With a single rose in her hair.

The lily-white doe Lord Ronald had brought
Leapt up from where she lay,
Dropt her head in the maiden's hand,
And follow'd her all the way.

Down stept Lord Ronald from his tower:
"O Lady Clare, you shame your worth!
Why come you drest like a village maid,
That are the flower of the earth?"

---

1. **Russet gown.** Russet, to denote low social position.
2. **Dale.** A valley.
3. **Down.** A hill.

"If I come drest like a village maid,
I am but as my fortunes are;
I am a beggar born," she said,
"And not the Lady Clare."

"Play me no tricks," said Lord Ronald,
"For I am yours in word and in deed.
Play me no tricks," said Lord Ronald,
"Your riddle is hard to read."

O and proudly stood she up!
Her heart within her did not fail;
She look'd into Lord Ronald's eyes,
And told him all her nurse's tale.

He laugh'd a laugh of merry scorn;
He turn'd, and kiss'd her where she stood:
"If you are not the heiress born,
And I," said he, "the next in blood—

"If you are not the heiress born
And I," said he, "the lawful heir,
We two will wed tomorrow morn,
And you shall still be Lady Clare."

13

LORD ULLIN'S DAUGHTER

Thomas Campbell

A chieftain, to the Highlands bound,
  Cries, "Boatman, do not tarry!
And I'll give thee a silver pound
  To row us o'er the ferry."—

"Now who be ye, would cross Lochgyle,
  This dark and stormy water?"
"Oh, I'm the chief of Ulva's isle,
  And this Lord Ullin's daughter.—

"And fast before her father's men
  Three days we've fled together,
For should he find us in the glen,
  My blood would stain the heather.

"His horsemen hard behind us ride;
  Should they our steps discover,
Then who will cheer my bonny bride
  When they have slain her lover?"

Out spoke the hardy Highland wight,[1]
  "I'll go, my chief—I'm ready:—
It is not for your silver bright,
  But for your winsome lady:

"And by my word! the bonny bird
  In danger shall not tarry;
So though the waves are raging white
  I'll row you o'er the ferry."—

1. **Wight.** A man.

By this the storm grew loud apace,
    The water-wraith [2] was shrieking;
And in the scowl of heaven each face
    Grew dark as they were speaking.

But still as wilder blew the wind,
    And as the night grew drearer,
Adown the glen rode armèd men,
    Their trampling sounded nearer.—

"O haste thee, haste!" the lady cries,
    "Though tempests round us gather;
I'll meet the raging of the skies,
    But not an angry father."—

The boat has left a stormy land,
    A stormy sea before her,—
When, oh! too strong for human hand,
    The tempest gather'd o'er her.—

And still they row'd amidst the roar
    Of waters fast prevailing:
Lord Ullin reach'd that fatal shore,
    His wrath was changed to wailing.

For, sore dismay'd, through storm and shade,
    His child he did discover:—
One lovely hand she stretch'd for aid,
    And one was round her lover.

"Come back! come back!" he cried in grief,
    "Across this stormy water:
And I'll forgive your Highland chief,
    My daughter!—oh, my daughter!"—

2. **Wraith.** A specter.

'Twas vain: the loud waves lash'd the shore,
  Return or aid preventing:—
The waters wild went o'er his child,
  And he was left lamenting.

14

AMY WENTWORTH

John Greenleaf Whittier

Her fingers shame the ivory keys
  They dance so light along;
The bloom upon her parted lips
  Is sweeter than the song.

O perfumed suitor, spare thy smiles!
  Her thoughts are not of thee;
She better loves the salted wind,
  The voices of the sea.

Her heart is like an outbound ship
  That at its anchor swings;
The murmur of the stranded shell
  Is in the song she sings.

She sings, and, smiling, hears her praise,
  But dreams the while of one
Who watches from his sea-blown deck
  The icebergs in the sun.

She questions all the winds that blow,
  And every fog wreath dim,
And bids the sea birds flying north
  Bear messages to him.

She speeds them with the thanks of men
   He perilled life to save,
And grateful prayers like holy oil
   To smooth for him the wave.

Brown Viking of the fishing smack!
   Fair toast of all the town!
The skipper's jerkin ill beseems
   The lady's silken gown!

But ne'er shall Amy Wentworth wear
   For him the blush of shame
Who dares to set his manly gifts
   Against her ancient name.

The stream is brightest at its spring,
   And blood is not like wine;
Nor honored less than he who heirs
   Is he who founds a line.

Full lightly shall the prize be won,
   If love be fortune's spur;
And never maiden stoops to him
   Who lifts himself to her.

Her home is brave in Jaffrey Street,
   With stately stairways worn
By feet of old Colonial knights
   And ladies gentle born.

Still green about its ample porch
   The English ivy twines,
Trained back to show in English oak
   The herald's carven signs.

And on her, from the wainscot old,
  Ancestral faces frown,—
And this has worn the soldier's sword,
  And that the judge's gown.

But, strong of will and proud as they,
  She walks the gallery floor
As if she trod her sailor's deck
  By stormy Labrador!

The sweetbrier blooms on Kittery-side,
  And green are Elliot's bowers;
Her garden is the pebbled beach,
  The mosses are her flowers.

She looks across the harbor bar
  To see the white gulls fly;
His greeting from the Northern sea
  Is in their clanging cry.

She hums a song, and dreams that he,
  As in its romance old,
Shall homeward ride with silken sails
  And masts of beaten gold!

O rank is good, and gold is fair,
  And high and low mate ill;
But love has never known a law
  Beyond its own sweet will!

15

MAUD MULLER [1]

John Greenleaf Whittier

Maud Muller on a summer's day
Raked the meadow sweet with hay.

Beneath her torn hat glowed the wealth
Of simple beauty and rustic health.

Singing, she wrought, and her merry glee
The mock-bird echoed from his tree.

But when she glanced to the far-off town,
White from its hill-slope looking down,

The sweet song died, and a vague unrest
And a nameless longing filled her breast,

A wish, that she hardly dared to own,
For something better than she had known.

The Judge rode slowly down the lane,
Smoothing his horse's chestnut mane.

He drew his bridle in the shade
Of the apple-trees, to greet the maid,

---

1. "The poem had no real foundation in fact; though a hint of it may have been found in recalling an incident, trivial in itself, of a journey on the picturesque Maine seaboard with my sister some years before it was written. We had stopped to rest our tired horse under the shade of an apple tree, and refresh him with water from a little brook which rippled through the stone wall across the road. A very beautiful girl in scantiest summer attire was at work in the hayfield, and as we talked with her we noticed that she strove to hide her bare feet by raking hay over them, blushing as she did so, through the tan of her cheek and neck."—Whittier.

And asked a draught from the spring that flowed
Through the meadow across the road.

She stooped where the cool spring bubbled up,
And filled for him her small tin cup,

And blushed as she gave it, looking down
On her feet so bare and her tattered gown.

"Thanks!" said the Judge; "a sweeter draught
From a fairer hand was never quaffed."

He spoke of the grass and flowers and trees,
Of the singing birds and the humming bees;

Then talked of the haying, and wondered whether
The cloud in the west would bring foul weather.

And Maud forgot her brier-torn gown,
And her graceful ankles bare and brown;

And listened, while a pleased surprise
Looked from her long-lashed hazel eyes.

At last, like one who for delay
Seeks a vain excuse, he rode away.

Maud Muller looked and sighed: "Ah me!
That I the Judge's bride might be!

"He would dress me up in silks so fine,
And praise and toast me at his wine.

"My father should wear a broadcloth coat;
My brother should sail a painted boat.

"I'd dress my mother so grand and gay,
And the baby should have a new toy each day.

"And I'd feed the hungry and clothe the poor,
And all should bless me who left our door."

The Judge looked back as he climbed the hill,
And saw Maud Muller standing still.

"A form more fair, a face more sweet
Ne'er hath it been my lot to meet.

"And her modest answer and graceful air
Show her wise and good as she is fair.

"Would she were mine, and I today,
Like her, a harvester of hay:

"No doubtful balance of rights and wrongs,
Nor weary lawyers with endless tongues,

"But low of cattle and song of birds,
And health and quiet and loving words."

But he thought of his sisters proud and cold
And his mother vain of her rank and gold.

So, closing his heart, the Judge rode on,
And Maud was left in the field alone.

But the lawyers smiled that afternoon,
When he hummed in court an old love-tune;

And the young girl mused beside the well
Till the rain on the unraked clover fell.

He wedded a wife of richest dower,
Who lived for fashion as he for power.

Yet oft, in his marble hearth's bright glow,
He watched a picture come and go;

And sweet Maud Muller's hazel eyes
Looked out in their innocent surprise.

Oft, when the wine in his glass was red,
He longed for the wayside well instead;

And closed his eyes on his garnished rooms
To dream of meadows and clover-blooms.

And the proud man sighed, with a secret pain,
"Ah, that I were free again!

"Free as when I rode that day,
Where the barefoot maiden raked her hay."

She wedded a man unlearned and poor,
And many children played round her door.

But care and sorrow, and childbirth pain,
Left their traces on heart and brain.

And oft, when the summer sun shone hot
On the new-mown hay in the meadow lot,

And she heard the little spring brook fall
Over the roadside, through the wall,

In the shade of the apple-tree again
She saw a rider draw his rein.

And, gazing down with timid grace,
She felt his pleased eyes read her face.

Sometimes her narrow kitchen walls
Stretched away into stately halls;

The weary wheel to a spinnet [2] turned,
The tallow candle an astral [3] burned,

And for him who sat by the chimney lug,
Dozing and grumbling o'er pipe and mug,

A manly form at her side she saw,
And joy was duty and love was law.

Then she took up her burden of life again,
Saying only, "It might have been."

Alas for maiden, alas for Judge,
For rich repiner and household drudge.

God pity them both! and pity us all,
Who vainly the dreams of youth recall.

For of all sad words of tongue or pen,
The saddest are these: "It might have been!"

Ah, well! for us all some sweet hope lies
Deeply buried from human eyes;

And, in the hereafter, angels may
Roll the stone from its grave away!

2. **Spinnet.** A musical instrument of the harpsichord class.
3. **Astral.** A fine lamp which casts no shadow directly under the blaze.

16

THE LORD OF BURLEIGH

ALFRED TENNYSON

In her ear he whispers gaily,
  "If my heart by signs can tell,
Maiden, I have watch'd thee daily,
  And I think thou lov'st me well."
She replies, in accents fainter,
  "There is none I love like thee."
He is but a landscape-painter,
  And a village maiden she.
He to lips, that fondly falter,
  Presses his without reproof:
Leads her to the village altar,
  And they leave her father's roof.
"I can make no marriage present:
  Little can I give my wife.
Love will make our cottage pleasant,
  And I love thee more than life."
They by parks and lodges going
  See the lordly castles stand:
Summer woods, about them blowing,
  Made a murmur in the land.
From deep thought himself he rouses,
  Says to her that loves him well,
"Let us see these handsome houses
  Where the wealthy nobles dwell."
So she goes by him attended,
  Hears him lovingly converse,
Sees whatever fair and splendid
  Lay betwixt his home and hers;
Parks with oak and chestnut shady,
  Parks and order'd gardens great,

3

Ancient homes of lord and lady,
  Built for pleasure and for state.
All he shows her makes him dearer:
  Evermore she seems to gaze
On that cottage growing nearer,
  Where they twain will spend their days.
O but she will love him truly!
  He shall have a cheerful home;
She will order all things duly,
  When beneath his roof they come.
Thus her heart rejoices greatly,
  Till a gateway she discerns
With armorial bearings stately,
  And beneath the gate she turns;
Sees a mansion more majestic
  Than all those she saw before:
Many a gallant gay domestic
  Bows before him at the door.
And they speak in gentle murmur,
  When they answer to his call,
While he treads with footstep firmer,
  Leading on from hall to hall.
And, while now she wonders blindly,
  Nor the meaning can divine,
Proudly turns he round and kindly,
  "All of this is mine and thine."
Here he lives in state and bounty,
  Lord of Burleigh, fair and free,
Not a lord in all the county
  Is so great a lord as he.
All at once the color flushes
  Her sweet face from brow to chin:
As it were with shame she blushes,
  And her spirit changed within.
Then her countenance all over
  Pale again as death did prove:

But he clasp'd her like a lover,
　And he cheer'd her soul with love.
So she strove against her weakness,
　Tho' at times her spirit sank:
Shaped her heart with woman's meekness
　To all duties of her rank:
And a gentle consort made he,
　And her gentle mind was such
That she grew a noble lady,
　And the people loved her much.
But a trouble weigh'd upon her,
　And perplex'd her, night and morn,
With the burthen of an honor
　Unto which she was not born.
Faint she grew, and ever fainter,
　And she murmur'd, "Oh, that he
Were once more that landscape-painter,
　Which did win my heart from me!"
So she droop'd and droop'd before him,
　Fading slowly from his side:
Three fair children first she bore him,
　Then before her time she died.
Weeping, weeping late and early,
　Walking up and pacing down,
Deeply mourn'd the Lord of Burleigh,
　Burleigh-house by Stamford-town.
And he came to look upon her,
　And he look'd at her and said,
"Bring the dress and put it on her,
　That she wore when she was wed."
Then her people, softly treading,
　Bore to earth her body, drest
In the dress that she was wed in,
　That her spirit might have rest.

17

LUCY GRAY

WILLIAM WORDSWORTH

Oft I had heard of Lucy Gray:
And when I cross'd the wild,
I chanced to see at break of day
The solitary child.

No mate, no comrade Lucy knew;
She dwelt on a wide moor,
The sweetest thing that ever grew
Beside a human door!

You yet may spy the fawn at play,
The hare upon the green;
But the sweet face of Lucy Gray
Will never more be seen.

"Tonight will be a stormy night—
You to the town must go;
And take a lantern, Child, to light
Your mother through the snow."

"That, Father! will I gladly do:
'Tis scarcely afternoon—
The minster-clock has just struck two,
And yonder is the moon!"

At this the father raised his hook,
And snapp'd a faggot-band;
He plied his work;—and Lucy took
The lantern in her hand.

Not blither is the mountain roe:
With many a wanton stroke
Her feet disperse the powdery snow,
That rises up like smoke.

The storm came on before its time:
She wander'd up and down;
And many a hill did Lucy climb:
But never reach'd the town.

The wretched parents all that night
Went shouting far and wide;
But there was neither sound nor sight
To serve them for a guide.

At day-break on a hill they stood
That overlook'd the moor;
And thence they saw the bridge of wood
A furlong from their door.

They wept—and, turning homeward, cried
"In heaven we all shall meet!"
—When in the snow the mother spied
The print of Lucy's feet.

Then downwards from the steep hill's edge
They track'd the footmarks small;
And through the broken hawthorn hedge,
And by the long stone-wall:

And then an open field they cross'd:
The marks were still the same;
They track'd them on, nor ever lost;
And to the bridge they came:

They follow'd from the snowy bank
Those footmarks, one by one,
Into the middle of the plank;
And further there were none!

—Yet some maintain that to this day
She is a living child;
That you may see sweet Lucy Gray
Upon the lonesome wild.

O'er rough and smooth she trips along,
And never looks behind;
And sings a solitary song
That whistles in the wind.

18

THE SINGING LEAVES

James Russell Lowell

I

"What fairings [1] will ye that I bring?"
Said the King to his daughters three;
"For I to Vanity Fair am boun,[2]
Now say what shall they be?"

Then up and spake the eldest daughter,
That lady tall and grand:
"Oh, bring me pearls and diamonds great,
And gold rings for my hand."

1. **Fairing.** A present, especially one bought at a fair.
2. **Boun.** Bound.

Thereafter spake the second daughter,
  That was both white and red:
"For me bring silks that will stand alone,
  And a gold comb for my head."

Then came the turn of the least daughter,
  That was whiter than thistle-down,
And among the gold of her blithesome hair
  Dim shone the golden crown.

"There came a bird this morning,
  And sang 'neath my bower eaves,
Till I dreamed, as his music made me,
  'Ask thou for the Singing Leaves.'"

Then the brow of the King swelled crimson
  With a flush of angry scorn:
"Well have ye spoken, my two eldest,
  And chosen as ye were born;

"But she, like a thing of peasant race,
  That is happy binding the sheaves;"
Then he saw her dead mother in her face,
  And said, "Thou shalt have thy leaves."

II

He mounted and rode three days and nights
  Till he came to Vanity Fair,
And 't was easy to buy the gems and the silk,
  But no Singing Leaves were there.

Then deep in the greenwood rode he,
  And asked of every tree,
"Oh, if you have ever a Singing Leaf,
  I pray you give it me!"

But the trees all kept their counsel,
  And never a word said they,
Only there sighed from the pine-tops
  A music of seas far away.

Only the pattering aspen
  Made a sound of growing rain,
That fell ever faster and faster,
  Then faltered to silence again.

"Oh, where shall I find a little foot-page
  That would win both hose and shoon,[3]
And will bring to me the Singing Leaves
  If they grow under the moon?"

Then lightly turned him Walter the page,
  By the stirrup as he ran:
"Now pledge you me the truesome word
  Of a king and gentleman,

"That you will give me the first, first thing
  You meet at your castle-gate,
And the Princess shall get the Singing Leaves,
  Or mine be a traitor's fate."

The King's head dropt upon his breast
  A moment, as it might be;
" 'T will be my dog," he thought, and said,
  "My faith I plight to thee."

Then Walter took from next his heart
  A packet small and thin,
"Now give you this to the Princess Anne;
  The Singing Leaves are therein."

3. Shoon. Shoes.

III

As the King rode in at his castle-gate,
  A maiden to meet him ran,
And "Welcome, father!" she laughed and cried
  Together, the Princess Anne.

"Lo, here the Singing Leaves," quoth he,
  "And woe, but they cost me dear!"
She took the packet, and the smile
  Deepened down beneath the tear.

It deepened down till it reached her heart,
  And then gushed up again,
And lighted her tears as the sudden sun
  Transfigures the summer rain.

And the first Leaf, when it was opened,
  Sang: "I am Walter the page,
And the songs I sing 'neath thy window
  Are my only heritage."

And the second Leaf sang: "But in the land
  That is neither on earth nor sea,
My lute and I are lords of more
  Than thrice this kingdom's fee." [4]

And the third Leaf sang, "Be mine! Be mine!"
  And ever it sang, "Be mine!"
Then sweeter it sang and ever sweeter,
  And said, "I am thine, thine, thine!"

At the first Leaf she grew pale enough,
  At the second she turned aside,
At the third, 't was as if a lily flushed
  With a rose's red heart's tide.

4. **Fee.** Wealth.

"Good counsel gave the bird," said she,
　"I have my hope thrice o'er,
For they sing to my very heart," she said,
　"And it sings to them evermore."

She brought to him her beauty and truth,
　But and [5] broad earldoms three,
And he made her queen of the broader lands
　He held of his lute in fee.

19

IN SCHOOL-DAYS [1]

JOHN GREENLEAF WHITTIER

Still sits the schoolhouse by the road,
　A ragged beggar [2] sunning;
Around it still the sumachs grow,
　And blackberry vines are running.

Within, the master's desk is seen,
　Deep scarred by raps official;
The warping floor, the battered seats,
　The jack-knife's carved initial;

5. **But and.** But also.
1. "Holmes calls this 'the most beautiful school-boy **poem in the** English language.' "—Pickard, *Life and Letters of Whittier.*
"Many years ago the little schoolhouse commemorated in 'School Days' was sold, and it was to be removed by its purchaser. It had hardly started on its journey when one of the wheels on which it was placed broke down and the building was left standing in the middle of the road, where it was burned by the boys. Mr. Whittier never himself indicated that the poem was other than imaginative except by including it in his collected works under the head of 'subjective and reminiscent.' "—Pickard, *ibid.*
2. **Beggar.** The schoolhouse is no longer in use; hence the poet calls it a beggar.

The charcoal frescos on its wall;
  Its door's worn sill, betraying
The feet that, creeping slow to school,
  Went storming out to playing!

Long years ago a winter sun
  Shone over it at setting;
Lit up its western window-panes,
  And low eaves' icy fretting.

It touched the tangled golden curls,
  And brown eyes full of grieving,
Of one who still her steps delayed
  When all the school were leaving.

For near her stood the little boy
  Her childish favor singled:
His cap pulled low upon a face
  Where pride and shame were mingled.

Pushing with restless feet the snow
  To right and left, he lingered;—
As restlessly her tiny hands
  The blue-checked apron fingered.

He saw her lift her eyes; he felt
  The soft hand's light caressing,
And heard the tremble of her voice,
  As if a fault confessing.

"I'm sorry that I spelt the word:
  I hate to go above you,
Because,"—the brown eyes lower fell,—
  "Because, you see, I love you!"

Still memory to a gray-haired man
   That sweet child-face is showing.
Dear girl! the grasses on her grave
   Have forty years been growing!

He lives to learn, in life's hard school,
   How few who pass above him
Lament their triumph and his loss,
   Like her,—because they love him.

20

WE ARE SEVEN

WILLIAM WORDSWORTH

—A simple child,
That lightly draws its breath,
And feels its life in every limb,
What should it know of death?

I met a little cottage girl:
She was eight years old, she said;
Her hair was thick with many a curl
That clustered round her head.

She had a rustic, woodland air,
And she was wildly clad:
Her eyes were fair, and very fair;
—Her beauty made me glad.

"Sisters and brothers, little maid,
How many may you be?"
"How many? Seven in all," she said,
And wondering looked at me.

"And where are they? I pray you tell."
She answered, "Seven are we;
And two of us at Conway dwell,
And two are gone to sea.

"Two of us in the church-yard lie,
My sister and my brother;
And, in the church-yard cottage, I
Dwell near them with my mother."

"You say that two at Conway dwell,
And two are gone to sea,
Yet ye are seven!—I pray you tell,
Sweet maid, how this may be."

Then did the little maid reply,
"Seven boys and girls are we;
Two of us in the church-yard lie,
Beneath the church-yard tree."

"You run about, my little maid,
Your limbs they are alive;
If two are in the church-yard laid,
Then ye are only five."

"Their graves are green, they may be seen,"
The little maid replied,
"Twelve steps or more from my mother's door,
And they are side by side.

"My stockings there I often knit,
My kerchief there I hem;
And there upon the ground I sit,
And sing a song to them.

"And often after sunset, sir,
When it is light and fair,
I take my little porringer,
And eat my supper there.

"The first that died was sister Jane;
In bed she moaning lay,
Till God released her of her pain;
And then she went away.

"So in the church-yard she was laid;
And, when the grass was dry,
Together round her grave we played,
My brother John and I.

"And when the ground was white with snow,
And I could run and slide,
My brother John was forced to go,
And he lies by her side."

"How many are you, then," said I,
"If they two are in heaven?"
Quick was the little maid's reply,
"O master! we are seven."

"But they are dead; those two are dead!
Their spirits are in heaven!"
'Twas throwing words away; for still
The little maid would have her will,
And said, "Nay, we are seven!"

21

THE INCHCAPE ROCK [1]

Robert Southey

No stir in the air, no stir in the sea,
The ship was still as she could be;
Her sails from heaven received no motion;
Her keel was steady in the ocean.

Without either sign or sound of their shock,
The waves flowed over the Inchcape Rock;
So little they rose, so little they fell,
They did not move the Inchcape Bell.

The Abbot of Aberbrothok
Had placed that Bell on the Inchcape Rock;
On a buoy in the storm it floated and swung,
And over the waves its warning rung.

When the Rock was hid by the surge's swell,
The mariners heard the warning Bell;
And then they knew the perilous Rock,
And blest the Abbot of Aberbrothok.

The Sun in heaven was shining gay;
All things were joyful on that day;
The sea-birds screamed as they wheeled **round,**
And there was joyance in their sound.

The buoy of the Inchcape Bell was seen,
A darker speck on the ocean green:
Sir Ralph the Rover walked his deck,
And he fixed his eye on the darker speck.

1. Inchcape Rock. A reef just off the coast of Scotland, near the Firth of Tay.

He felt the cheering power of spring;
It made him whistle, it made him sing:
His heart was mirthful to excess,
But the Rover's mirth was wickedness.

His eye was on the Inchcape float:
Quoth he, "My men, put out the boat,
And row me to the Inchcape Rock,
And I'll plague the Abbot of Aberbrothok."

The boat is lowered, the boatmen row,
And to the Inchcape Rock they go;
Sir Ralph bent over from the boat,
And he cut the Bell from the Inchcape float.

Down sunk the Bell with a gurgling sound;
The bubbles rose and burst around:
Quoth Sir Ralph, "The next who comes to the Rock
Won't bless the Abbot of Aberbrothok."

Sir Ralph the Rover sailed away;
He scoured the seas for many a day;
And now, grown rich with plundered store,
He steers his course for Scotland's shore.

So thick a haze o'erspreads the sky,
They cannot see the Sun on high:
The wind hath blown a gale all day;
At evening it hath died away.

On the deck the Rover takes his stand;
So dark it is, they see no land.
Quoth Sir Ralph, "It will be lighter soon,
For there is the dawn of the rising Moon."

"Canst hear," said one, "the breakers roar?
For methinks we should be near the shore."
"Now where we are I cannot tell,
But I wish I could hear the Inchcape Bell."

They hear no sound; the swell is strong;
Though the wind hath fallen, they drift along,
Till the vessel strikes with a shivering shock:
"O Christ! it is the Inchcape Rock!"

Sir Ralph the Rover tore his hair,
He curst himself in his despair:
The waves rush in on every side;
The ship is sinking beneath the tide.

But, even in his dying fear,
One dreadful sound could the Rover hear,—
A sound as if, with the Inchcape Bell,
The Devil below was ringing his knell.

22

THE WITCH'S DAUGHTER [1]

JOHN GREENLEAF WHITTIER

It was the pleasant harvest time,
    When cellar-bins are closely stowed,
    And garrets bend beneath their load,

1. "The only foundation for this charming ballad is the fact that Goody Martin, who lived at the place so graphically described by the poet, was hanged as a witch, during the prevalence of the dreadful delusion, being the only woman who suffered death on a charge of witchcraft on the north side of the Merrimac."—Pickard, *Life and Letters of Whittier.*

And the old swallow-haunted barns—
   Brown-gabled, long, and full of seams
   Through which the moted sunlight streams,

And winds blow freshly in, to shake
   The red plumes of the roosted cocks,
   And the loose hay-mow's scented locks—

Are filled with summer's ripened stores,
   Its odorous grass and barley sheaves,
   From their low scaffolds to their eaves.

On Esek Harden's oaken floor,
   With many an autumn threshing worn,
   Lay the heaped ears of unhusked corn.

And thither came young men and maids,
   Beneath a moon that, large and low,
   Lit that sweet eve of long ago.

They took their places; some by chance,
   And others by a merry voice
   Or sweet smile guided to their choice.

How pleasantly the rising moon,
   Between the shadows of the mows,
   Looked on them through the great elm-boughs!—

On sturdy boyhood sun-embrowned,
   On girlhood with its solid curves
   Of healthful strength and painless nerves!

And jests went round, and laughs that made
   The house-dog answer with his howl,
   And kept astir the barn-yard fowl;

And quaint old songs their fathers sung,
    In Derby dales and Yorkshire moors,
    Ere Norman William [2] trod their shores;

And tales, whose merry license shook
    The fat sides of the Saxon thane,[3]
    Forgetful of the hovering Dane!

But still the sweetest voice was mute
    That river-valley ever heard
    From lip of maid or throat of bird;

For Mabel Martin sat apart,
    And let the hay-mow's shadow fall
    Upon the loveliest face of all.

She sat apart, as one forbid,
    Who knew that none would condescend
    To own the Witch-wife's child a friend.

The seasons scarce had gone their round,
    Since curious thousands thronged to see
    Her mother on the gallows-tree;

And mocked the palsied limbs of age,
    That faltered on the fatal stairs,
    And wan lip trembling with its prayers!

Few questioned of the sorrowing child,
    Or, when they saw the mother die,
    Dreamed of the daughter's agony.

2. **Norman William.** William of Normandy conquered England at the battle of Hastings in 1066.

3. **Saxon thane.** Saxon lord. The Saxons held England previous to the Norman Conquest, but their power was frequently threatened by the Danes.

They went up to their homes that day,
  As men and Christians justified:
  God willed it, and the wretch had died!

Dear God and Father of us all,
  Forgive our faith in cruel lies,—
  Forgive the blindness that denies!

Forgive thy creature when he takes,
  For the all-perfect love thou art,
  Some grim creation of his heart.

Cast down our idols, overturn
  Our bloody altars; let us see
  Thyself in thy humanity!

Poor Mabel from her mother's grave
  Crept to her desolate hearth-stone,
  And wrestled with her fate alone;

With love, and anger, and despair,
  The phantoms of disordered sense,
  The awful doubts of Providence!

The school-boys jeered her as they passed,
  And, when she sought the house of prayer,
  Her mother's curse pursued her there.

And still o'er many a neighboring door
  She saw the horseshoe's curvéd charm,
  To guard against her mother's harm;—

That mother, poor, and sick, and lame,
  Who daily, by the old arm-chair,
  Folded her withered hands in prayer;—

Who turned, in Salem's dreary jail,
　　Her worn old Bible o'er and o'er,
　　When her dim eyes could read no more!

Sore tried and pained, the poor girl kept
　　Her faith, and trusted that her way,
　　So dark, would somewhere meet the day.

And still her weary wheel went round
　　Day after day, with no relief;
　　Small leisure have the poor for grief.

So in the shadow Mabel sits;
　　Untouched by mirth she sees and hears,
　　Her smile is sadder than her tears.

But cruel eyes have found her out,
　　And cruel lips repeat her name,
　　And taunt her with her mother's shame.

She answered not with railing words,
　　But drew her apron o'er her face,
　　And, sobbing, glided from the place.

And only pausing at the door,
　　Her sad eyes met the troubled gaze
　　Of one who, in her better days,

Had been her warm and steady friend,
　　Ere yet her mother's doom had made
　　Even Esek Harden half afraid.

He felt that mute appeal of tears,
　　And, starting, with an angry frown
　　Hushed all the wicked murmurs down.

"Good neighbors mine," he sternly said,
    "This passes harmless mirth or jest;
    I brook no insult to my guest.

"She is indeed her mother's child;
    But God's sweet pity ministers
    Unto no whiter soul than hers.

"Let Goody Martin rest in peace;
    I never knew her harm a fly,
    And witch or not, God knows,—not I.

"I know who swore her life away;
    And, as God lives, I'd not condemn
    An Indian dog on word of them."

The broadest lands in all the town,
    The skill to guide, the power to awe,
    Were Harden's; and his word was law.

None dared withstand him to his face,
    But one sly maiden spake aside:
    "The little witch is evil-eyed!

"Her mother only killed a cow,
    Or witched a churn or dairy-pan;
    But she, forsooth, must charm a man!"

Poor Mabel, in her lonely home,
    Sat by the window's narrow pane,
    White in the moonlight's silver rain.

The river, on its pebbled rim,
    Made music such as childhood knew;
    The door-yard tree was whispered through

By voices such as childhood's ear
   Had heard in moonlights long ago;
   And through the willow-boughs below

She saw the rippled waters shine;
   Beyond, in waves of shade and light
   The hills rolled off into the night.

Sweet sounds and pictures mocking so
   The sadness of her human lot,
   She saw and heard, but heeded not.

She strove to drown her sense of wrong,
   And, in her old and simple way,
   To teach her bitter heart to pray.

Poor child! the prayer, begun in faith,
   Grew to a low, despairing cry
   Of utter misery: "Let me die!

"Oh! take me from the scornful eyes
   And hide me where the cruel speech
   And mocking finger may not reach!

"I dare not breathe my mother's name:
   A daughter's right I dare not crave
   To weep above her unblest grave!

"Let me not live until my heart,
   With few to pity, and with none
   To love me, hardens into stone.

"O God! have mercy on thy child,
   Whose faith in thee grows weak and small,
   And take me ere I lose it all!"

A shadow on the moonlight fell,
  And murmuring wind and wave became
  A voice whose burden was her name.

Had then God heard her? Had he sent
  His angel down? In flesh and blood,
  Before her Esek Harden stood!

He laid his hand upon her arm:
  "Dear Mabel, this no more shall be;
  Who scoffs at you, must scoff at me.

"You know rough Esek Harden well;
  And if he seems no suitor gay,
  And if his hair is touched with gray,

"The maiden grown shall never find
  His heart less warm than when she smiled,
  Upon his knees, a little child!"

Her tears of grief were tears of joy,
  As, folded in his strong embrace,
  She looked in Esek Harden's face.

"O truest friend of all!" she said,
  "God bless you for your kindly thought,
  And make me worthy of my lot!"

He led her through his dewy fields,
  To where the swinging lanterns glowed,
  And through the doors the huskers showed.

"Good friends and neighbors!" Esek said,
  "I'm weary of this lonely life;
  In Mabel see my chosen wife!

"She greets you kindly, one and all;
   The past is past, and all offence
   Falls harmless from her innocence.

"Henceforth she stands no more alone;
   You know what Esek Harden is:—
   He brooks no wrong to him or his."

Now let the merriest tales be told,
   And let the sweetest songs be sung
   That ever made the old heart young!

For now the lost has found a home;
   And a lone hearth shall brighter burn,
   As all the household joys return!

O, pleasantly the harvest-moon,
   Between the shadow of the mows,
   Looked on them through the great elm-boughs!

On Mabel's curls of golden hair,
   On Esek's shaggy strength it fell;
   And the wind whispered, "It is well!"

23

SKIPPER IRESON'S RIDE [1]

John Greenleaf Whittier

Of all the rides since the birth of time,
Told in story or sung in rhyme,—
On Apuleius's Golden Ass, [2]
Or one-eyed Calendar's horse of brass, [3]
Witch astride of a human back,
Islam's prophet [4] on Al-Borák,— [5]
The strangest ride that ever was sped
Was Ireson's, out from Marblehead! [6]
   Old Floyd Ireson, for his hard heart,
   Tarred and feathered and carried in a cart
     By the women of Marblehead!

Body of turkey, head of owl,
Wings adroop like a rained-on fowl,
Feathered and ruffled in every part,
Skipper Ireson stood in the cart.

   1. "The story of 'Skipper Ireson' was told to Mr. Whittier by a schoolmate at the Academy, who came from Marblehead. He supposed it was a tradition of the last century,—was not aware that the poor man who was so harshly treated was a contemporary of his own; for the poet was nearly a year old when the Skipper took his ride."— Pickard, *Life and Letters of Whittier*.
   It is but justice to say that, according to Mr. Samuel Roads his *History and Tradition of Marblehead*, Ireson was probably not more to blame than his crew; and, possibly, not at all. He seems to have tried to stay by the sinking vessel, but his crew refused to obey. Fearing the wrath of the people of Marblehead, they threw all the blame upon Skipper Ireson. It is interesting to note that during the ride, Ireson maintained a dignified silence, and after he was released his only remark was, "I thank you for my ride, gentlemen, but you will live to regret it." And they did.
   2. Apuleius's Golden Ass. "The Golden Ass," a romance by Apuleius, a Roman philosopher of about the second century.
   3. Calendar's horse of brass. The reference is to a wonderful horse of brass in the *Arabian Nights*.
   4. Islam's prophet. Mohammed.
   5. Al-Borák. A wonderful animal with a human face, two wings, and a peacock's tail, on which Mohammed rode to the seventh heaven.
   6. Marblehead. Then a small fishing village a few miles north of Boston.

Scores of women, old and young,
Strong of muscle, and glib of tongue,
Pushed and pulled up the rocky lane,
Shouting and singing the shrill refrain:
 "Here's Flud Oirson, fur his horrd horrt,
 Torr'd an' futherr'd an' corr'd in a corrt
   By the women o' Morble'ead!"

Wrinkled scolds with hands on hips,
Girls in bloom of cheek and lips,
Wild-eyed, free-limbed, such as chase
Bacchus [7] round some antique vase,
Brief of skirt, with ankles bare,
Loose of kerchief and loose of hair,
With conch shells blowing and fish horns' twang,
Over and over the Mænads [8] sang:
 "Here's Flud Oirson, fur his horrd horrt,
 Torr'd an' futherr'd an' corr'd in a corrt
   By the women o' Morble'ead!"

Small pity for him!—He sailed away
From a leaking ship in Chaleur Bay,— [9]
Sailed away from a sinking wreck,
With his own town's people on her deck!
"Lay by! lay by!" they called to him.
Back he answered, "Sink or swim!
Brag of your catch of fish again!"
And off he sailed through the fog and rain!
 Old Floyd Ireson, for his hard heart,
 Tarred and feathered and carried in a cart
   By the women of Marblehead!

---

7. **Bacchus.** God of wine and revelry.
8. **Mænad.** A bacchante, a follower of Bacchus; hence an woman beside herself with frenzy or excitement.
9. **Chaleur Bay.** A bay in the Gulf of St. Lawrence near Quebec.

Fathoms deep in dark Chaleur
That wreck shall lie forevermore.
Mother and sister, wife and maid,
Looked from the rocks of Marblehead
Over the moaning and rainy sea,—
Looked for the coming that might not be!
What did the winds and the sea birds say
Of the cruel captain who sailed away?—
  Old Floyd Ireson, for his hard heart,
  Tarred and feathered and carried in a cart
    By the women of Marblehead.

Through the street, on either side,
Up flew windows, doors swung wide;
Sharp-tongued spinsters, old wives gray,
Treble lent the fish horn's bray.
Sea-worn grandsires, cripple-bound,
Hulks of old sailors run aground,
Shook head, and fist, and hat, and cane,
And cracked with curses the hoarse refrain:
  "Here's Flud Oirson, fur his horrd horrt,
  Torr'd an' futherr'd an' corr'd in a corrt
    By the women o' Morble'ead!"

Sweetly along the Salem road
Bloom of orchard and lilac showed.
Little the wicked skipper knew
Of the fields so green and the sky so blue.
Riding there in his sorry trim,
Like an Indian idol glum and grim,
Scarcely he seemed the sound to hear
Of voices shouting, far and near:
  "Here's Flud Oirson, fur his horrd horrt,
  Torr'd an' futherr'd an' corr'd in a corrt
    By the women o' Morble'ead!"

"Hear me, neighbors!" at last he cried,—
"What to me is this noisy ride?
What is the shame that clothes the skin
To the nameless horror that lives within?
Waking or sleeping, I see a wreck,
And hear a cry from a reeling deck!
Hate me and curse me,—I only dread
The hand of God and the face of the dead!"
 Said old Floyd Ireson, for his hard heart,
 Tarred and feathered and carried in a cart
  By the women of Marblehead!

Then the wife of the skipper lost at sea
Said, "God has touched him! why should we?"
Said an old wife mourning her only son,
"Cut the rogue's tether and let him run!"
So with soft relentings and rude excuse,
Half scorn, half pity, they cut him loose,
And gave him a cloak to hide him in,
And left him alone with his shame and sin.
 Poor Floyd Ireson, for his hard heart,
 Tarred and feathered and carried in a cart
  By the women of Marblehead!

24

BERNARDO DEL CARPIO [1]

FELICIA DOROTHEA HEMANS

The warrior bowed his crested head, and tamed his heart
of fire,
And sued the haughty king to free his long imprisoned
sire:
"I bring thee here my fortress-keys, I bring my captive
train,
I pledge thee faith, my liege, my lord! O, break my
father's chain!"

"Rise! rise! even now thy father comes, a ransomed man
this day!
Mount thy good horse; and thou and I will meet him on
his way."
Then lightly rose that loyal son, and bounded on his
steed,
And urged, as if with lance in rest, the charger's foamy
speed.

And, lo, from far, as on they pressed, there came a
glittering band,
With one that midst them stately rode, as a leader in
the land:
"Now haste, Bernardo, haste! for there, in very truth,
is he,
The father whom thy faithful heart hath yearned so long
to see."

1. This story is based upon fact. Bernardo del Carpio, after failing
by peaceful means to secure the release of his father, the Count
Saldana, declared war against King Alphonso of Asturias. The king
finally agreed to release his prisoner in exchange for the castle of
Carpio and the captives confined therein. When del Carpio pressed
forward to greet his father, he found a corpse on horseback.

His dark eye flashed, his proud breast heaved, his cheek's
hue came and went;
He reached that gray-haired chieftain's side, and there,
dismounting, bent;
A lowly knee to earth he bent, his father's hand he took,—
What was there in its touch that all his fiery spirit shook?

That hand was cold,—a frozen thing,—it dropped from
his like lead!
He looked up to the face above,—the face was of the dead!
A plume waved o'er the noble brow,—the brow was fixed
and white;
He met, at last, his father's eyes,—but in them was no
sight!

Up from the ground he sprang and gazed; but who could
paint that gaze?
They hushed their very hearts that saw its horror and
amaze:
They might have chained him, as before that stony form
he stood;
For the power was stricken from his arm, and from his
lip the blood.

"Father!" at length, he murmured low, and wept like
childhood then:
Talk not of grief till thou hast seen the tears of warlike
men!
He thought on all his glorious hopes, and all his young
renown;
He flung his falchion [2] from his side, and in the dust sat
down.

2. **Falchion.** A broad bladed, slightly curved sword.

Then covering with his steel-gloved hands his darkly
    mournful brow,—

"No more, there is no more," he said, "to lift the sword
    for now;

My king is false,—my hope betrayed! My father,—O
    the worth,

The glory, and the loveliness are passed away from earth!

"I thought to stand where banners waved, my sire, beside
    thee, yet;

I would that there our kindred blood on Spain's free soil
    had met!

Thou wouldst have known my spirit, then; for thee my
    fields were won;

And thou hast perished in thy chains, as though thou
    hadst no son!"

Then, starting from the ground once more, he seized the
    monarch's rein,

Amidst the pale and wildered looks of all the courtier
    train;

And with a fierce, o'ermastering grasp, the rearing war-
    horse led,

And sternly set them face to face,—the king before the
    dead:

"Came I not forth, upon thy pledge, my father's hand
    to kiss?

Be still, and gaze thou on, false king! and tell me what
    is this?

The voice, the glance, the heart I sought,—give answer,
    where are they?

If thou wouldst clear thy perjured soul, send life through
    this cold clay;

"Into these glassy eyes put light;—be still! keep down
thine ire!

Bid these white lips a blessing speak,—this earth is not
my sire:

Give me back him for whom I strove,—for whom my
blood was shed.

Thou canst not?—and a king!—his dust be mountains on
thy head!"

He loosed the steed,—his slack hand fell; upon the silent
face

He cast one long, deep, troubled look, then turned from
that sad place.

His hope was crushed, his after fate untold in martial
strain:

His banner led the spears no more amidst the hills of
Spain.

25

THE BARON'S LAST BANQUET

Albert Gorton Greene

O'er a low couch the setting sun had thrown its latest ray,

Where in his last strong agony a dying warrior lay,

The stern old Baron Rudiger, whose frame had ne'er been
bent

By wasting pain, till time and toil its iron strength had
spent.

"They come around me here, and say my days of life are
o'er,

That I shall mount my noble steed and lead my band no
more;

They come, and to my beard they dare to tell me now,
    that I,
Their own liege lord and master born,—that I, ha! ha!
    must die.

"And what is death? I've dared him oft before the
    Paynim [1] spear,—
Think ye he's entered at my gate, has come to seek me
    here?
I've met him, faced him, scorned him, when the fight was
    raging hot,—
I'll try his might—I'll brave his power; defy, and fear him
    not.

"Ho! sound the tocsin [2] from my tower, and fire the cul-
    verin,— [3]
Bid each retainer arm with speed,—call every vassal in,
Up with my banner on the wall,—the banquet board
    prepare;
Throw wide the portal of my hall, and bring my armor
    there!"

An hundred hands were busy then—the banquet forth was
    spread—
And rung the heavy oaken floor with many a martial tread,
While from the rich, dark tracery along the vaulted wall,
Lights gleamed on harness, plume, and spear, o'er the
    proud old Gothic hall.

Fast hurrying through the outer gate the mailed retainers
    poured,
On through the portal's frowning arch, and thronged
    around the board.

1. **Paynim.** Pagan, especially Mohammedan.
2. **Tocsin.** Alarm bell.
3. **Culverin.** A long cannon.

While at its head, within his dark, carved oaken chair of
  state,
Armed cap-a-pie, stern Rudiger, with girded falchion,[4]
  sate.

"Fill every beaker up, my men, pour forth the cheering
  wine;
There's life and strength in every drop,—thanksgiving
  to the vine!
Are ye all there, my vassals true?—mine eyes are waxing
  dim;
Fill round, my tried and fearless ones, each goblet to the
  brim.

"You're there, but yet I see ye not. Draw forth each
  trusty sword
And let me hear your faithful steel clash once around
  my board;
I hear it faintly:—Louder yet!—What clogs my heavy
  breath?
Up all, and shout for Rudiger, 'Defiance unto Death!'"

Bowl rang to bowl—steel clanged to steel—and rose a
  deafening cry
That made the torches flare around, and shook the flags
  on high:—
"Ho! cravens, do ye fear him?—Slaves, traitors! have ye
  flown?
Ho! cowards, have ye left me to meet him here alone!

"But I defy him:—let him come!" Down rang the massy
  cup,
While from its sheath the ready blade came flashing half-
  way up;

4. Falchion. A sword

And with the black and heavy plumes scarce trembling on
  his head,
There in his dark, carved oaken chair Old Rudiger sat,
  dead.

26

SPANISH WATERS

JOHN MASEFIELD

Spanish waters, Spanish waters, you are ringing in my
  ears,
Like a slow sweet piece of music from the gray forgotten years;
Telling tales, and beating tunes, and bringing weary
  thoughts to me
Of the sandy beach at Muertos,[1] where I would that I
  could be.

There's a surf breaks on Los Muertos, and it never stops
  to roar,
And it's there we came to anchor, and it's there we went
  ashore,
Where the blue lagoon is silent amid snags of rotting
  trees,
Dropping like the clothes of corpses cast up by the seas.

We anchored at Los Muertos when the dipping sun was
  red,
We left her half-a-mile to sea, to west of Nigger Head;
And before the mist was on the Cay,[2] before the day
  was done,
We were all ashore on Muertos with the gold that we
  had won.

1. **Muertos.** Islands off the southern coast of Cuba.
2. **Cay.** Bay.

We bore it through the marshes in a half-score battered
    chests,
Sinking, in the sucking quagmires to the sunburn on our
    breasts,
Heaving over tree-trunks, gasping, damning at the flies
    and heat,
Longing for a long drink, out of silver, in the ship's cool
    lazareet.[3]

The moon came white and ghostly as we laid the treasure
    down,
There was gear there'd make a beggarman as rich as
    Lima Town,[4]
Copper charms and silver trinkets from the chests of
    Spanish crews,
Gold doubloons and double moydores, louis d'ors and
    ortagues,[5]

Clumsy yellow-metal earrings from the Indians of Brazil,
Uncut emeralds out of Rio, bezoar [6] stones from Guaya-
    quil,
Silver, in the crude and fashioned, pots of old Arica
    bronze,
Jewels from the bones of Incas [7] desecrated by the Dons.[8]

We smoothed the place with mattocks, and we took and
    blazed the tree,
Which marks yon where the gear is hid that none will
    ever see,

3. **Lazareet.** A store-room near a vessel's stern.
4. **Lima Town.** Lima, capital of Peru, from which the Spaniards
got a great amount of gold.
5. **Doubloons, moydores, louis d'ors, portagues.** Gold coins worth
from about $5 to $22.50.
6. **Bezoar.** A stone, to drive out poison.
7. **Incas.** Indians of South America.
8. **Dons.** Spaniards.

And we laid aboard the ship again, and south away we
    steers,
Through the loud surf of Los Muertos which is beating
    in my ears.

I'm the last alive that knows it. All the rest have gone
    their ways
Killed, or died, or come to anchor in the old Mulatas Cays,
And I go singing, fiddling, old and starved and in despair,
And I know where all that gold is hid, if I were only
    there.

It's not the way to end it all. I'm old and nearly blind,
And an old man's past's a strange thing, for it never
    leaves his mind.
And I see in dreams, awhiles, the beach, the sun's disc
    dipping red,
And the tall ship, under topsails, swaying in past Nigger
    Head.

I'd be glad to step ashore there. Glad to take a pick
    and go
To the lone blazed coco-palm tree in the place no others
    know,
And lift the gold and silver that has mouldered there
    for years
By the loud surf of Los Muertos which is beating in my
    ears.

27

"HOW THEY BROUGHT THE GOOD NEWS FROM GHENT TO AIX" [1]

Robert Browning

I sprang to the stirrup, and Joris, and he;
I galloped, Dirck galloped, we galloped all three;
"Good speed!" cried the watch, as the gatebolts undrew;
"Speed!" echoed the wall to us galloping through;
Behind shut the postern, the lights sank to rest
And into the midnight we galloped abreast.

Not a word to each other; we kept the great pace
Neck by neck, stride by stride, never changing our place;
I turned in my saddle and made its girths tight,
Then shortened each stirrup, and set the pique right,
Rebuckled the cheek-strap, chained slacker the bit,
Nor galloped less steadily Roland a whit.

'Twas moonset at starting; but while we drew near
Lokeren, the cocks crew and twilight dawned clear;
At Boom, a great yellow star came out to see;
At Düffeld, 'twas morning as plain as could be;
And from Mecheln church-steeple we heard the half-
    chime,
So, Joris broke silence with, "Yet there is time!"

At Aershot, up leaped of a sudden the sun,
And against him the cattle stood black every one,
To stare thro' the mist at us galloping past,

---

1. "There is no sort of historical foundation about 'Good News from Ghent.' I wrote it under the bulwark of a vessel off the African coast, after I had been at sea long enough to appreciate even the fancy of a gallop on the back of a certain good horse 'York,' then in my stable at home."—Browning.

And I saw my stout galloper Roland at last,
With resolute shoulders, each butting away
The haze, as some bluff river headland its spray:

And his low head and crest, just one sharp ear bent back
For my voice, and the other pricked out on his track;
And one eye's black intelligence,—ever that glance
O'er its white edge at me, his own master, askance!
And the thick heavy spume-flakes which aye and anon
His fierce lips shook upwards in galloping on.

By Hasselt, Dirck groaned; and cried Joris, "Stay spur!
Your Roos galloped bravely, the fault's not in her,
We'll remember at Aix"—for one heard the quick wheeze
Of her chest, saw the stretched neck and staggering knees,
And sunk tail, and horrible heave of the flank,
As down on her haunches she shuddered and sank.

So, we were left galloping, Joris and I,
Past Looz and past Tongres, no cloud in the sky;
The broad sun above laughed a pitiless laugh,
'Neath our feet broke the brittle bright stubble like chaff:
Till over by Dalhem a dome-spire sprang white,
And "Gallop," gasped Joris, "for Aix is in sight!"

"How they'll greet us!"—and all in a moment his roan
Rolled neck and croup over, lay dead as a stone;
And there was my Roland to bear the whole weight
Of the news which alone could save Aix from her fate,
With his nostrils like pits full of blood to the brim,
And with circles of red for his eye-sockets' rim.

Then I cast loose my buffcoat, each holster let fall,
Shook off both my jack-boots, let go belt and all,
Stood up in the stirrup, leaned, patted his ear,
Called my Roland his pet-name, my horse without peer;

Clapped my hands, laughed and sang, any noise, bad or
    good,
Till at length into Aix Roland galloped and stood.

And all I remember is—friends flocking round
As I sat with his head 'twixt my knees on the ground;
And no voice but was praising this Roland of mine,
As I poured down his throat our last measure of wine,
Which (the burgesses voted by common consent)
Was no more than his due who brought good news from
    Ghent.[2]

28

PAUL REVERE'S RIDE [1]

Henry Wadsworth Longfellow

Listen, my children, and you shall hear
Of the midnight ride of Paul Revere,
On the eighteenth of April, in Seventy-five;
Hardly a man is now alive
Who remembers that famous day and year.

He said to his friend, "If the British march
By land or sea from the town tonight,
Hang a lantern aloft in the belfry arch
Of the North Church tower as a signal light,—
One, if by land, and two, if by sea;
And I on the opposite shore will be,

2. From Ghent, Belgium, to Aix, Prussia, is ninety miles.

1. Paul Revere was one of a group of men who formed a secret organization just before the breaking out of the Revolutionary War to watch the movements of the British officials. When the British planned to capture some military supplies stored at Concord, about twenty miles northwest of Boston, the plan was discovered and Paul Revere gave the alarm to the colonists all along the road from Boston to Lexington. A little way out of Lexington he was captured by a British patrol. The alarm had been given, however, and the colonists were ready.

Ready to ride and spread the alarm
Through every Middlesex village and farm,
For the country-folk to be up and to arm."

Then he said, "Good night!" and with muffled **oar**
Silently rowed to the Charlestown shore,
Just as the moon rose over the bay,
Where swinging wide at her moorings lay
The Somerset, British man-of-war;
A phantom ship, with each mast and spar
Across the moon like a prison bar,
And a huge black hulk, that was magnified
By its own reflection in the tide.

Meanwhile, his friend, through alley and street,
Wanders and watches with eager ears,
Till in the silence around him he hears
The muster of men at the barrack door,
The sound of arms, and the tramp of feet,
And the measured tread of the grenadiers,
Marching down to their boats on the shore.

Then he climbed to the tower of the church,
Up the wooden stairs, with stealthy tread,
To the belfry-chamber overhead,
And startled the pigeons from their perch
On the somber rafters that round him made
Masses and moving shapes of shade,—
Up the trembling ladder, steep and tall,
To the highest window in the wall,
Where he paused to listen and look down
A moment on the roofs of the town,
And the moonlight flowing over all.

Beneath, in the churchyard, lay the dead,
In their night-encampment on the hill,

Wrapped in silence so deep and still
That he could hear, like a sentinel's tread,
The watchful night-wind, as it went
Creeping along from tent to tent,
And seeming to whisper, "All is well!"
A moment only he feels the spell
Of the place and the hour, and the secret dread
Of the lonely belfry and the dead;
For suddenly all his thoughts are bent
On a shadowy something far away,
Where the river widens to meet the bay,—
A line of black that bends and floats
On the rising tide, like a bridge of boats.

Meanwhile, impatient to mount and ride,
Booted and spurred, with a heavy stride
On the opposite shore walked Paul Revere.
Now he patted his horse's side,
Now gazed at the landscape far and near,
Then, impetuous, stamped the earth,
And turned and tightened his saddle-girth;
But mostly he watched with eager search
The belfry-tower of the Old North Church,
As it rose above the graves on the hill,
Lonely and spectral and somber and still.
And lo! as he looks, on the belfry's height
A glimmer, and then a gleam of light!
He springs to the saddle, the bridle he turns,
But lingers and gazes, till full on his sight
A second lamp in the belfry burns!

A hurry of hoofs in a village street,
A shape in the moonlight, a bulk in the dark,
And beneath, from the pebbles, in passing, a spark
Struck out by a steed flying fearless and fleet;
That was all! And yet, through the gloom and the light,

The fate of a nation was riding that night;
And the spark struck out by that steed, in his flight,
Kindled the land into flame with its heat.
He has left the village and mounted the steep,
And beneath him, tranquil and broad and deep,
Is the Mystic, meeting the ocean tides;
And under the alders, that skirt its edge,
Now soft on the sand, now loud on the ledge,
Is heard the tramp of his steed as he rides.

It was twelve by the village clock
When he crossed the bridge into Medford town.
He heard the crowing of the cock,
And the barking of the farmer's dog,
And felt the damp of the river fog,
That rises after the sun goes down.

It was one by the village clock,
When he galloped into Lexington.
He saw the gilded weathercock
Swim in the moonlight as he passed,
And the meeting-house windows, blank and bare,
Gaze at him with a spectral glare,
As if they already stood aghast
At the bloody work they would look upon.

It was two by the village clock,
When he came to the bridge in Concord town.
He heard the bleating of the flock,
And the twitter of birds among the trees,
And felt the breath of the morning breeze
Blowing over the meadows brown.
And one was safe and asleep in his bed
Who at the bridge would be first to fall,
Who that day would be lying dead,
Pierced by a British musket-ball.

You know the rest. In the books you have read,
How the British Regulars fired and fled,—
How the farmers gave them ball for ball,
From behind each fence and farm-yard wall,
Chasing the red-coats down the lane,
Then crossing the fields to emerge again
Under the trees at the turn of the road,
And only pausing to fire and load.

So through the night rode Paul Revere;
And so through the night went his cry of alarm
To every Middlesex village and farm,—
A cry of defiance and not of fear,
A voice in the darkness, a knock at the door,
And a word that shall echo forevermore!
For, borne on the night-wind of the Past,
Through all our history, to the last,
In the hour of darkness and peril and need,
The people will waken and listen to hear
The hurrying hoof-beats of that steed,
And the midnight message of Paul Revere.

29

THE BALLAD OF EAST AND WEST

RUDYARD KIPLING

*Oh East is East, and West is West, and never the twain
    shall meet,*
*Till Earth and Sky stand presently at God's great Judg-
    ment Seat;*
*But there is neither East nor West, Border, nor Breed,
    nor Birth,*
*When two strong men stand face to face, tho' they come
    from the ends of the earth!*

Kamal is out with twenty men to raise the Border side,
And he has lifted the Colonel's mare that is the Colonel's
    pride:
He has lifted her out of the stable-door between the dawn
    and the day,
And turned the calkins [1] upon her feet, and ridden her far
    away.
Then up and spoke the Colonel's son that led a troop of
    the Guides:
"Is there never a man of all my men can say where
    Kamal hides?"
Then up and spoke Mahommed Khan, the son of the
    Ressaldar, [2]
"If ye know the track of the morning-mist, ye know where
    his pickets are.
"At dusk he harries the Abazai—at dawn he is into
    Bonair,
"But he must go by Fort Bukloh to his own place to fare,
"So if ye gallop to Fort Bukloh as fast as a bird can fly,
"By the favor of God ye may cut him off, ere he win to
    the Tongue of Jagai,
"But if he be passed the Tongue of Jagai, right swiftly
    turn ye then,
"For the length and the breadth of that grisly plain is
    sown with Kamal's men.
"There is rock to the left, and rock to the right, and low,
    lean thorn between,
"And ye may hear a breech bolt snick where never a man
    is seen."
The Colonel's son has taken a horse, and a raw rough
    dun was he,
With the mouth of a bell and the heart of Hell, and the
    head of the gallows-tree.

---

1. **Calkins.** Calks; spurs on a horse's shoe to prevent slipping.
2. **Ressaldar.** A commander of a risala, a troop of native Indian
irregular horse.

The Colonel's son to the Fort has won, they bid him
    stay to eat—

Who rides at the tail of a Border thief, he sits not long
    at his meat.

He's up and away from Fort Bukloh as fast as he can fly,

Till he was aware of his father's mare in the gut of the
    Tongue of Jagai,

Till he was aware of his father's mare with Kamal upon
    her back,

And when he could spy the white of her eye, he made
    the pistol crack.

He has fired once, he has fired twice, but the whistling
    ball went wide.

"Ye shoot like a soldier," Kamal said. "Show now if ye
    can ride."

It's up and over the Tongue of Jagai, as blown dust-devils
    go,

The dun he fled like a stag of ten, but the mare like a
    barren doe.

The dun he leaned against the bit and slugged his head
    above,

But the red mare played with the snaffle-bars,[3] as a maiden
    plays with a glove.

There was rock to the left and rock to the right, and low
    lean thorn between,

And thrice he heard a breech-bolt snick tho' never a man
    was seen.

They have ridden the low moon out of the sky, their
    hoofs drum up the dawn,

The dun he went like a wounded bull, but the mare like
    a new-roused fawn.

The dun he fell at a water-course—in a woful heap fell he,

And Kamal has turned the red mare back, and pulled the
    rider free.

3. **Snaffle-bars.** Bridle bit.

He has knocked the pistol out of his hand—small room
    was there to strive,

" 'Twas only by favor of mine," quoth he, "ye rode so long
    alive:

"There was not a rock for twenty miles, there was not a
    clump of tree,

"But covered a man of my own men with his rifle cocked
    on his knee.

"If I had raised my bridle-hand, as I have held it low,

"The little jackals that flee so fast, were feasting all in a
    row:

"If I had bowed my head on my breast, as I have held
    it high,

"The kite that whistles above us now were gorged till
    she could not fly."

Lightly answered the Colonel's son: "Do good to bird
    and beast,

"But count who come for the broken meats before thou
    makest a feast.

"If there should follow a thousand swords to carry my
    bones away,

"Belike the price of a jackal's meal were more than a
    thief could pay.

"They will feed their horse on the standing crop, their
    men on the garnered grain,

"The thatch of the byres [4] will serve their fires when all
    the cattle are slain.

"But if thou thinkest the price be fair,—thy brethren
    wait to sup,

"The hound is kin to the jackal-spawn,—howl, dog, and
    call them up!

"And if thou thinkest the price be high, in steer and gear
    and stack,

"Give me my father's mare again, and I'll fight my own
    way back!"

4. **Byres.** Cow stables.

Kamal has gripped him by the hand and set him upon
  his feet.

"No talk shall be of dogs," said he, "when wolf and gray
  wolf meet.

"May I eat dirt if thou hast hurt of me in deed or breath;

"What dam of lances brought thee forth to jest at the
  dawn with Death?"

Lightly answered the Colonel's son: "I hold by the blood
  of my clan:

"Take up the mare for my father's gift—by God, she has
  carried a man!"

The red mare ran to the Colonel's son, and nuzzled against
  his breast;

"We be two strong men," said Kamal then, "but she
  loveth the younger best.

"So she shall go with a lifter's dower, my turquoise-
  studded rein,

"My broidered saddle and saddle-cloth, and silver stirrups
  twain."

The Colonel's son a pistol drew and held it muzzle-end,

"Ye have taken the one from a foe," said he; "will ye
  take the mate from a friend?"

"A gift for a gift," said Kamal straight; "a limb for the
  risk of a limb.

"Thy father has sent his son to me, I'll send my son to
  him!"

With that he whistled his only son, that dropped from a
  mountain-crest—

He trod the ling [5] like a buck in spring, and he looked
  like a lance in rest.

"Now here is thy master," Kamal said, "who leads a troop
  of the Guides,

"And thou must ride at his left side as shield on
  shoulder rides.

5. **Ling.** Heath or heather.

"Till Death or I cut loose the tie, at camp and board
    and bed,

"Thy life is his—thy fate is to guard him with thy head.

"So thou must eat the White Queen's meat, and all her
    foes are thine,

"And thou must harry thy father's hold for the peace
    of the Border-line,

"And thou must make a trooper tough and hack thy
    way to power—

"Belike they will raise thee to Ressaldar when I am
    hanged in Peshawur."

They have looked each other between the eyes, and there
    they have found no fault,

They have taken the Oath of the Brother-in-Blood on
    leavened bread and salt;

They have taken the Oath of the Brother-in-Blood on fire
    and fresh-cut sod,

On the hilt and the haft of the Khyber [6] knife, and the
    Wondrous Names of God.

The Colonel's son he rides the mare and Kamal's boy
    the dun,

And two have come back to Fort Bukloh where there
    went forth but one.

And when they drew to the Quarter-Guard, full twenty
    swords flew clear—

There was not a man but carried his feud with the blood
    of the mountaineer.

"Ha' done! ha' done!" said the Colonel's son, "Put up
    the steel at your sides!

"Last night ye had struck at a Border thief—tonight 'tis
    a man of the Guides!"

6. **Khyber.** Khaibar; a native state in the Punjab, India.

Oh East is East and West is West, and never the twain
    shall meet,
Till Earth and Sky stand presently at God's great Judg-
    ment Seat;
But there is neither East nor West, Border, nor Breed,
    nor Birth,
When two strong men stand face to face, tho' they come
    from the ends of the earth.

30

JOHN GILPIN

WILLIAM COWPER

John Gilpin was a citizen
    Of credit and renown,
A trainband captain eke was he
    Of famous London town.

John Gilpin's spouse said to her dear,
    "Though wedded we have been
These twice ten tedious years, yet we
    No holiday have seen.

"Tomorrow is our wedding-day,
    And we will then repair
Unto the Bell at Edmonton,
    All in a chaise and pair.

"My sister, and my sister's child,
    Myself, and children three,
Will fill the chaise; so you must ride
    On horseback after we."

He soon replied—"I do admire
　　Of womankind but one,
And you are she, my dearest dear,
　　Therefore it shall be done.

"I am a linendraper bold,
　　As all the world doth know,
And my good friend the calender [1]
　　Will lend his horse to go."

Quoth Mrs. Gilpin,—"That's well said;
　　And for that wine is dear,
We will be furnished with our own,
　　Which is both bright and clear."

John Gilpin kissed his loving wife;
　　O'erjoyed was he to find,
That, though on pleasure she was bent,
　　She had a frugal mind.

The morning came, the chaise was brought,
　　But yet was not allowed
To drive up to the door, lest all
　　Should say that she was proud.

So three doors off the chaise was stayed,
　　Where they did all get in;
Six precious souls, and all agog
　　To dash through thick and thin.

Smack went the whip, round went the wheels,
　　Were never folk so glad,
The stones did rattle underneath,
　　As if Cheapside [2] were mad.

---

1. **Calender.** One who runs a calender, a machine to press cloth between rollers to glaze it.
2. **Cheapside.** One of the principal streets of London.

John Gilpin at his horse's side
  Seized fast the flowing mane,
And up he got, in haste to ride,
  But soon came down again;

For saddletree scarce reached had he,
  His journey to begin,
When, turning round his head, he saw
  Three customers come in.

So down he came; for loss of time,
  Although it grieved him sore,
Yet loss of pence, full well he knew,
  Would trouble him much more.

'T was long before the customers
  Were suited to their mind,
When Betty screaming came down stairs,
  "The wine is left behind!"

"Good lack!" quoth he, "yet bring it me
  My leathern belt likewise,
In which I bear my trusty sword
  When I do exercise."

Now Mistress Gilpin (careful soul!)
  Had two stone bottles found,
To hold the liquor that she loved,
  And keep it safe and sound.

Each bottle had a curling ear,
  Through which the belt he drew,
And hung a bottle on each side
  To make his balance true.

Then over all, that he might be
  Equipped from top to toe,
His long red cloak, well brushed and neat,
  He manfully did throw.

Now see him mounted once again
  Upon his nimble steed,
Full slowly pacing o'er the stones,
  With caution and good heed.

But finding soon a smoother road
  Beneath his well-shod feet,
The snorting beast began to trot,
  Which galled him in his seat.

So "Fair and softly," John he cried,
  But John he cried in vain;
That trot became a gallop soon,
  In spite of curb and rein.

So stooping down, as needs he must
  Who cannot sit upright,
He grasped the mane with both his hands
  And eke with all his might.

His horse, who never in that sort
  Had handled been before,
What thing upon his back had got
  Did wonder more and more.

Away went Gilpin, neck or nought;
  Away went hat and wig;
He little dreamt, when he set out,
  Of running such a rig.

The wind did blow, the cloak did fly,
  Like streamer long and gay,
Till, loop and button failing both,
  At last it flew away.

Then might all people well discern
  The bottles he had slung;
A bottle swinging at each side,
  As hath been said or sung.

The dogs did bark, the children screamed,
  Up flew the windows all;
And every soul cried out, "Well done!"
  As loud as he could bawl.

Away went Gilpin—who but he?
  His fame soon spread around;
"He carries weight!" "He rides a race!"
  "'T is for a thousand pound!"

And still as fast as he drew near,
  'T was wonderful to view,
How in a trice the turnpike men
  Their gates wide open threw.

And now, as he went bowing down
  His reeking head full low,
The bottles twain behind his back
  Were shattered at a blow.

Down ran the wine into the road,
  Most piteous to be seen,
Which made his horse's flanks to smoke
  As they had basted been.

But still he seemed to carry weight,
　With leathern girdle braced;
For all might see the bottle necks
　Still dangling at his waist.

Thus all through merry Islington,
　These gambols he did play,
Until he came unto the Wash
　Of Edmonton so gay;

And there he threw the Wash about,
　On both sides of the way,
Just like unto a trundling mop,
　Or a wild goose at play.

At Edmonton, his loving wife
　From the balcony spied
Her tender husband, wondering much
　To see how he did ride.

"Stop, stop, John Gilpin!—Here's the house!"
　They all at once did cry;
"The dinner waits, and we are tired."—
　Said Gilpin—"So am I!"

But yet his horse was not a whit
　Inclined to tarry there;
For why?—his owner had a house
　Full ten miles off, at Ware.

So like an arrow swift he flew
　Shot by an archer strong;
So did he fly—which brings me to
　The middle of my song.

Away went Gilpin, out of breath,
    And sore against his will,
Till, at his friend the calender's,
    His horse at last stood still.

The calender, amazed to see
    His neighbor in such trim,
Laid down his pipe, flew to the gate,
    And thus accosted him:—

"What news? what news? your tidings tell;
    Tell me you must and shall—
Say why bareheaded you are come,
    Or why you come at all?"

Now Gilpin had a pleasant wit,
    And loved a timely joke;
And thus unto the calender,
    In merry guise, he spoke:—

"I came because your horse would come;
    And, if I well forebode,
My hat and wig will soon be here,—
    They are upon the road."

The calender, right glad to find
    His friend in merry pin,[3]
Returned him not a single word,
    But to the house went in;

When straight he came with hat and wig;
    A wig that flowed behind,
A hat not much the worse for wear,
    Each comely in its kind.

3. **Pin.** Humor, mood.

He held them up, and in his turn,
    Thus showed his ready wit:
"My head is twice as big as yours,
    They therefore needs must fit.

"But let me scrape the dirt away
    That hangs upon your face;
And stop and eat, for well you may
    Be in a hungry case."

Said John,—"It is my wedding day,
    And all the world would stare,
If wife should dine at Edmonton,
    And I should dine at Ware."

So turning to his horse, he said,
    "I am in haste to dine;
'T was for your pleasure you came here,
    You shall go back for mine."

Ah! luckless speech, and bootless boast,
    For which he paid full dear;
For while he spake, a braying ass
    Did sing most loud and clear;

Whereat his horse did snort, as he
    Had heard a lion roar,
And galloped off with all his might,
    As he had done before.

Away went Gilpin, and away
    Went Gilpin's hat and wig;
He lost them sooner than at first,
    For why?—they were too big.

Now Mistress Gilpin, when she saw
   Her husband posting down
Into the country far away,
   She pulled out half-a-crown;

And thus unto the youth she said,
   That drove them to the Bell,
"This shall be yours, when you bring back
   My husband safe and well."

The youth did ride, and soon did meet
   John coming back amain;
Whom in a trice he tried to stop
   By catching at his rein;

But not performing what he meant,
   And gladly would have done,
The frighted steed he frighted more
   And made him faster run.

Away went Gilpin, and away
   Went postboy at his heels,
The postboy's horse right glad to miss
   The lumbering of the wheels.

Six gentlemen upon the road,
   Thus seeing Gilpin fly,
With postboy scampering in the rear,
   They raised the hue and cry:—

"Stop thief! stop thief!—a highwayman!"
   Not one of them was mute;
And all and each that passed that way
   Did join in the pursuit.

And now the turnpike-gates again
  Flew open in short space;
The toll-men thinking as before,
  That Gilpin rode a race.

And so he did, and won it too,
  For he got first to town,
Nor stopped till where he had got up
  He did again get down.

Now let us sing, Long live the King,
  And Gilpin, long live he;
And when he next doth ride abroad,
  May I be there to see!

31

TAM O' SHANTER [1]

ROBERT BURNS

When chapman [2] billies [3] leave the street,
And droughty neebors, neebors meet;
As market days are wearing late,
And folk begin to tak the gate; [4]
While we sit bousin' [5] at the nappy, [6]
An' getting fou [7] and unco [8] happy,

---

1. In an edition of selected poems from Burns, Hudson says: "The original of Tam O'Shanter was an individual named Douglas Graham, a Carrick farmer. The man was, in sober truth, the 'bletherin,' blusterin' blellum' that the poet has described, and his wife was as veritably a lady who most anxiously discouraged drinking in her husband."

2. **Chapman.** A peddler.
3. **Billie.** A companion.
4. **Gate.** Road.
5. **Bousin'.** Drinking.

6. **Nappy.** Ale.
7. **Fou.** Full, drunk.
8. **Unco.** Very.

We think na on the lang Scots miles,[9]
The mosses,[10] waters, slaps,[11] and styles,
That lie between us and our hame,
Whare sits our sulky, sullen dame.
Gathering her brows like gathering storm,
Nursing her wrath to keep it warm.

This truth fand [12] honest Tam o' Shanter,
As he frae Ayr ae night did canter:
(Auld Ayr, wham ne'er a town surpasses,
For honest men and bonie lasses).

O Tam! had'st thou but been sae wise,
As ta'en thy ain wife Kate's advice!
She tauld thee weel thou wast a skellum; [13]
A blethering,[14] blustering, drunken blellum; [15]
That frae November till October,
Ae market-day thou wasna sober;
That ilka [16] melder [17] wi' the Miller,
Thou sat as lang as thou had siller;
That ev'ry naig was ca'd [18] a shoe on
The smith and thee gat roarin fou on;
That at the Lord's house, ev'n on Sunday,
Thou drank wi' Kirkton Jean till Monday;
She prophesied that late or soon,
Thou wad be found deep drown'd in Doon,
Or catch'd wi' warlocks [19] in the mirk,[20]
By Alloway's auld haunted kirk.

Ah, gentle dames! it gars [21] me greet,[22]
To think how mony counsels sweet,
How mony lengthen'd sage advices,
The husband frae the wife despises!

But to our tale:—Ae market night,
Tam had got planted unco right,
Fast by an ingle,[23] bleezing finely,
Wi' reaming [24] swats,[25] that drank divinely;
And at his elbow, Souter [26] Johnie,
His ancient, trusty, drouthy crony:
Tam lo'ed him like a very brither;
They had been fou for weeks thegither.
The night drave on wi' sangs an' clatter;
And aye the ale was growing better:
The Landlady and Tam grew gracious,
Wi' favors secret, sweet, and precious:
The Souter tauld his queerest stories;
The Landlord's laugh was ready chorus:
The storm without might rair [27] and rustle,
Tam did na mind the storm a whistle.

Care, mad to see a man sae happy,
E'en drown'd himsel amang the nappy.
As bees flee hame wi' lades o' treasure,
The minutes wing'd their way wi' pleasure:
Kings may be blest, but Tam was glorious,
O'er a' the ills o' life victorious!

But pleasures are like poppies spread,
You seize the flow'r, its bloom is shed;
Or like the snow falls in the river,
A moment white—then melts forever;

21. **Gars.** Makes.
22. **Greet.** Weep.
23. **Ingle.** Fireplace.
24. **Reaming.** Brimful, frothing.

25. **Swats.** New ale.
26. **Souter.** Shoemaker.
27. **Rair.** Roar.

Or like the Borealis race,
That flit ere you can point their place;
Or like the Rainbow's lovely form,
Evanishing amid the storm.—
Nae man can tether Time or Tide;
The hour approaches Tam maun [28] ride:
That hour, o' night's black arch the key-stane,
That dreary hour he mounts his beast in;
And sic a night he taks the road in,
As ne'er poor sinner was abroad in.

The wind blew as 't wad blawn its last;
The rattling showers rose on the blast;
The speedy gleams the darkness swallow'd;
Loud, deep, and lang the thunder bellow'd:
That night, a child might understand,
The Deil had business on his hand.

Weel-mounted on his gray mare Meg,
A better never lifted leg,
Tam skelpit [29] on thro' dub [30] and mire,
Despising wind, and rain, and fire;
Whiles holding fast his gude blue bonnet,
Whiles crooning o'er some auld Scots sonnet,
Whiles glow'rin round wi' prudent cares,
Lest bogles [31] catch him unawares;
Kirk-Alloway was drawing nigh,
Where ghaists and houlets [32] nightly cry.

By this time he was cross the ford,
Whare in the snaw the chapman smoor'd; [33]
And past the birks [34] and meikle [35] stane,
Whare drunken Charlie brak's neck-bane;

28.	**Maun.** Must.	32.	**Houlets.** Owls.
29.	**Skelpit.** Rode hard.	33.	**Smoor'd.** Smothered.
30.	**Dub.** Puddle.	34.	**Birks.** Birches.
31.	**Bogles.** Goblins.	35.	**Meikle.** Great.

And thro' the whins,[36] and by the cairn,[37]
Where hunters fand the murder'd bairn;
And near the thorn, aboon the well,
Whare Mungo's mither hang'd hersel'.
Before him Doon pours all his floods;
The doubling storm roars thro' the woods,
The lightnings flash from pole to pole,
Near and more near the thunders roll,
When, glimmering thro' the groaning trees,
Kirk-Alloway seem'd in a bleeze,
Thro' ilka bore [38] the beams were glancing,
And loud resounded mirth and dancing.

Inspiring bold John Barleycorn!
What dangers thou canst make us scorn!
Wi' tippenny,[39] we fear nae evil;
Wi' usquebae,[40] we'll face the devil!
The swats sae ream'd in Tammie's noddle,
Fair play, he car'd na deils a boddle,[41]
But Maggie stood, right sair astonish'd,
Till, by the heel and hand admonish'd,
She ventur'd forward on the light;
And, wow! Tam saw an unco [42] sight!

Warlocks and witches in a dance:
Nae cotillion, brent new frae France,
But hornpipes, jigs, strathspeys, and reels,
Put life and mettle in their heels.
At winnock-bunker [43] in the east,
There sat auld Nick, in shape o' beast;

36. **Whin.** Furze, gorse.
37. **Cairn.** Heap of loose stones.
38. **Bore.** Hole in the wall.
39. **Tippenny.** Two-penny ale.
40. **Usquabae.** Whisky.

41. **Boddle.** Copper coin of small value.
42. **Unco.** Strange.
43. **Winnock-bunker.** Window seat.

A towzie tyke,[44] black, grim, and large,
To gie them music was his charge;
He screw'd the pipes and gart [45] them skirl,[46]
Till roof and rafters a' did dirl.[47]
Coffins stood round, like open presses,
That shaw'd the dead in their last dresses;
And (by some devilish cantraip [48] sleight)
Each in its cauld hand held a light.
By which heroic Tam was able
To note upon the haly table,
A murderer's banes, in gibbet-airns; [49]
Twa span-lang, wee, unchristened bairns;
A thief, new-cutted frae a rape,
Wi' his last gasp his gab [50] did gape;
Five tomahawks, wi' blude red-rusted;
Five scimitars, wi' murder crusted;
A garter with a babe had strangled,
A knife, a father's throat had mangled,
Whom his ain son of life bereft,
The gray-hairs yet stack [51] to the heft; [52]
Wi' mair of horrible and awfu',
Which even to name wad be unlawfu'.

As Tammie glowr'd amaz'd, and curious,
The mirth and fun grew fast and furious;
The Piper loud and louder blew,
The dancers quick and quicker flew;
They reel'd, they set, they cross'd, they cleekit, [53]
Till ilka carlin [54] swat and reekit,[55]

44. **Tyke.** Dog.   50. **Gab.** Mouth.
45. **Gart.** Made.   51. **Stack.** Stuck.
46. **Skirl.** Shriek.   52. **Heft.** Handle.
47. **Dirl.** Ring, tremble.   53. **Cleekit.** Joined hands.
48. **Cantraip.** Spell, charm.   54. **Carlin.** Old woman.
49. **Airns.** Irons.   55. **Reekit.** Smoked.

And coost [56] her duddies [57] to the wark,[58]
And linket [59] at it in her sark ! [60]

Now Tam, O Tam ! had thae [61] been queans,[62]
A' plump and strapping in their teens !
Their sarks, instead o' creeshie flannen,[63]
Been snaw-white seventeen-hunder linen !—
Thir breeks [64] o' mine, my only pair,
That ance were plush, o' guid blue hair,
I wad hae gi'en them off my hurdies,[65]
For ae blink o' the bonie burdies ! [66]
But wither'd beldams, auld and droll,
Rigwoodie [67] hags wad [68] spean [69] a foal,
Louping [70] an' flinging on a crummock,[71]
I wonder didna turn thy stomach.

But Tam kend what was what fu' brawlie: [72]
There was ae winsome wench and waulie [73]
That night enlisted in the core,[74]
Lang after kend on Carrick shore;
(For mony a beast to dead she shot,
And perish'd mony a bonie boat,
And shook baith meikle corn and bear,[75]
And kept the country-side in fear);
Her cutty sark,[76] o' Paisley harn,[77]
That while a lassie she had worn,

56. **Coost.** Cast.
57. **Duddies.** Ragged garments.
58. **Wark.** Work.
59. **Linket.** Tripped.
60. **Sarks.** Shirts.
61. **Thae.** Those.
62. **Queans.** Young women.
63. **Creeshie flannen.** Greasy flannel.
64. **Thir breeks.** These breeches.
65. **Hurdies.** Loins, hips.
66. **Burdies.** Maidens.
67. **Rigwoodie.** Wizened; gallows-worthy.
68. **Wad.** Would.
69. **Spean.** Wean.
70. **Louping.** Leaping.
71. **Crummock.** A staff with crooked head.
72. **Brawlie.** Very well.
73. **Waulie.** Large, lusty.
74. **Core.** Party; company
75. **Bear.** Barley.
76. **Cutty Sark.** Short skirt.
77. **Harn.** A coarse linen.

In longitude tho' sorely scanty,
It was her best, and she was vauntie.[78]
Ah! little kend thy reverend grannie,
That sark she coft [79] for her wee Nannie,
Wi' twa pund Scots [80] ('twas a' her riches),
Wad ever grac'd a dance o' witches!

But here my Muse her wing maun cower,[81]
Sic flights are far beyond her power;
To sing how Nannie lap and flang,[82]
(A souple jade [83] she was and strang),
And how Tam stood, like ane bewitch'd,
And thought his very een enrich'd:
Even Satan glowr'd [84] and fidg'd fu' fain,[85]
And hotch'd [86] and blew wi' might and main:
Till first ae caper, syne [87] anither,
Tam tint [88] his reason a' thegither,
And roars out, "Weel done, Cutty-sark!"
And in an instant all was dark:
And scarcely had he Maggie rallied,
When out the hellish legion sallied.

As bees bizz out wi' angry fyke,[89]
When plundering herds assail their byke;[90]
As open pussie's [91] mortal foes,
When, pop! she starts before their nose;
As eager runs the market-crowd,
When "Catch the thief!" resounds aloud;
So Maggie runs, the witches follow,
Wi' mony an eldritch [92] skreich and hollow.

78. **Vauntie.** Proud; overjoyed.
79. **Coft.** Bought.
80. **Twa pund Scots.** About eighty cents.
81. **Cower.** Let down.
82. **Lap and flang.** Leaped and kicked.
83. **Jade.** A giddy young girl.
84. **Glowr'd.** Stared.
85. **Fain.** Glad.
86. **Hotched.** Fidgeted.
87. **Syne.** Then.
88. **Tint.** Lost.
89. **Fyke.** Fuss.
90. **Byke.** Hive.
91. **Pussie.** Hare.
92. **Eldrich.** Frightful.

Ah, Tam! ah, Tam! thou'll thy fairin! [93]
In hell they'll roast thee like a herrin!
In vain thy Kate awaits thy comin!
Kate soon will be a woefu' woman!
Now, do thy speedy-utmost, Meg,
And win the key-stane o' the brig;
There, at them thou thy tail may toss,
A running stream they dare na cross!
But ere the key-stane she could make,
The fient [94] a tail she had to shake!
For Nannie, far before the rest,
Hard upon noble Maggie prest,
And flew at Tam wi' furious ettle; [95]
But little wist she Maggie's mettle!
Ae spring brought off her master hale,
But left behind her ain gray tail:
The carlin [96] claught [97] her by the rump,
And left poor Maggie scarce a stump.

Now, wha this tale o' truth shall read,
Ilk man, and mother's son, take heed:
Whene'er to Drink you are inclin'd,
Or Cutty-sarks run in your mind,
Think! ye may buy the joys o'er dear;
Remember Tam o' Shanter's mare.

---

93. **Fairin.** Reward.
94. **Fient.** Devil.
95. **Ettle.** Effort.

96. **Carlin.** Witch.
97. **Claught.** Clutched.

32

JOCK OF HAZELDEAN

Sir Walter Scott

"Why weep ye by the tide, ladie?
 Why weep ye by the tide?
I'll wed ye to my youngest son,
 And ye sall be his bride:
And ye sall be his bride, ladie,
 Sae comely to be seen"—
But aye she loot the tears down fa'
 For Jock of Hazeldean.

"Now let this wilfu' grief be done,
 And dry that cheek so pale;
Young Frank is chief of Errington
 And lord of Langley-dale;
His step is first in peaceful ha',[1]
 His sword in battle keen"—
But aye she loot the tears down fa'
 For Jock of Hazeldean.

"A chain of gold ye sall not lack,
 Nor braid to bind your hair;
Nor mettled hound, nor managed [2] hawk,
 Nor palfrey fresh and fair;
And you, the foremost of them a',
 Shall ride our forest-queen"—
But aye she loot the tears down fa'
 For Jock of Hazeldean.

1. **Ha'.** Manor-house.
2. **Managed.** Trained.

The kirk was deck'd at morning-tide,
    The tapers glimmered fair;
The priest and bridegroom wait the bride,
    And dame and knight are there:
They sought her baith by bower and ha'; [3]
    The ladie was not seen!
She's o'er the border and awa'
    Wi' Jock of Hazeldean.

33

THE GLOVE AND THE LIONS [1]

Leigh Hunt

King Francis [2] was a hearty king, and loved a royal sport,
And one day as his lions fought, sat looking on the court;
The nobles filled the benches, with the ladies by their side,
And 'mongst them sat the Count de Lorge, with one for
    whom he sighed.
And truly 't was a gallant thing to see that crowning show,
Valor and love; and a king above; and the royal beasts
    below.

Ramped and roared the lions, with horrid laughing jaws;
They bit, they glared, gave blows like bears, a wind went
    with their paws;
With wallowing might and stifled roar they rolled on one
    another,
Till all the pit with sand and mane, was in a thunderous
    smother;

3. **Bower and ha'.** Inner or private room and large room; that is, they sought everywhere.

1. It will be noted that this poem and the following are based upon the same incident. The German poet Schiller also wrote a poem upon this subject. It will be interesting to compare methods of handling in the two poems given.

2. **King Francis.** Francis I of France, 1494-1547.

The bloody foam above the bars came whizzing through
    the air,
Said Francis then, "Faith, gentlemen, we're better here
    than there."

De Lorge's love o'erheard the King, a beauteous lively
    dame,
With smiling lips and sharp bright eyes, which always
    seemed the same;
She thought, the Count, my lover is brave as brave can be;
He surely would do wondrous things to show his love of
    me;
"King, ladies, lovers, all look on; the occasion is divine;
I'll drop my glove, to prove his love; great glory will be
    mine."

She dropped her glove, to prove his love, then looked at
    him and smiled;
He bowed, and in a moment leaped among the lions wild:
The leap was quick, return was quick, he has regained
    his place,
Then threw the glove, but not with love, right in the
    lady's face.
"By heaven!" said Francis, "rightly done!" and he rose
    from where he sat:
"No love," quoth he, "but vanity, sets love a task like
    that."

34

THE GLOVE

ROBERT BROWNING

(Peter Ronsard [1] *Loquitur* [2]*)*

"Heigho!" yawned one day King Francis,
"Distance all value enhances!
When a man's busy, why leisure
Strikes him as wonderful pleasure:
'Faith, and at leisure once is he?
Straightway he wants to be busy.
Here we've got peace; and aghast I'm
Caught thinking war the true pastime.
Is there a reason in meter?
Give us your speech, master Peter!"
I who, if mortal dare say so,
Ne'er am at loss with my Naso,[3]
"Sire," I replied, "joys prove cloudlets:
Men are the merest Ixions"— [4]
Here the King whistled aloud, "Let's
—Heigho—go look at our lions!"
Such are the sorrowful chances
If you talk fine to King Francis.

And so, to the courtyard proceeding,
Our company, Francis was leading,
Increased by new followers tenfold
Before he arrived at the penfold;

1. **Peter Ronsard.** A French poet (1524-1585).
2. **Loquitur.** Speaks.
3. **Naso.** The Latin poet Ovid.
4. **Ixion.** Ixion was tormented in Tartarus by being forever turned
on a wheel. The poet means that men can scarcely hope to be happy.

Lords, ladies, like clouds which bedizen
At sunset the western horizon.
And Sir De Lorge pressed 'mid the foremost
With the dame he professed to adore most.
Oh, what a face! One by fits eyed
Her, and the horrible pitside;
For the penfold surrounded a hollow
Which led where the eye scarce dared follow,
And shelved to the chamber secluded
Where Bluebeard, the great lion, brooded.
The King hailed his keeper, an Arab
As glossy and black as a scarab,[5]
And bade him make sport and at once stir
Up and out of his den the old monster.
They opened a hole in the wire-work
Across it, and dropped there a firework,
And fled: one's heart's beating redoubled;
A pause, while the pit's mouth was troubled,
The blackness and silence so utter,
By the firework's slow sparkling and sputter;
Then earth in a sudden contortion
Gave out to our gaze her abortion.
Such a brute! Were I friend Clement Marot[6]
(Whose experience of nature's but narrow,
And whose faculties move in no small mist
When he versifies David the Psalmist)
I should study that brute to describe you
Illum Juda Leonem de Tribu.[7]
One's whole blood grew curdling and creepy
To see the black mane, vast and heapy,
The tail in the air stiff and straining,
The wide eyes, nor waxing nor waning,
As over the barrier which bounded

5. **Scarab.** A beetle.
6. **Clement Marot.** A court poet, 1496-1544.
7. **Illum Juda Leonem de Tribu.** The lion of the tribe of Judah.

His platform, and us who surrounded
The barrier, they reached and they rested
On space that might stand him in best stead:
For who knew, he thought, what the amazement,
The eruption of clatter and blaze meant,
And if, in this minute of wonder,
No outlet, 'mid lightning and thunder,
Lay broad, and, his shackles all shivered,
The lion at last was delivered?
Ay, that was the open sky o'erhead!
And you saw by the flash on his forehead,
By the hope in those eyes wide and steady,
He was leagues in the desert already,
Driving the flocks up the mountain,
Or catlike couched hard by the fountain
To waylay the date-gathering negress:
So guarded he entrance or egress.
"How he stands!" quoth the King: "we may well swear
(No novice, we've won our spurs elsewhere
And so can afford the confession),
We exercise wholesome discretion
In keeping aloof from his threshold;
Once hold you, those jaws want no fresh hold,
Their first would too pleasantly purloin
The visitor's brisket or sirloin:
But who's he would prove so foolhardy?
Not the best man of Marignan, pardie!"

The sentence no sooner was uttered,
Than over the rails a glove fluttered,
Fell close to the lion, and rested:
The dame 't was, who flung it and jested
With life so, De Lorge had been wooing
For months past; he sat there pursuing
His suit, weighing out with nonchalance
Fine speeches like gold from a balance.

Sound the trumpet, no true knight's a tarrier!
De Lorge made one leap at the barrier,
Walked straight to the glove,—while the lion
Ne'er moved, kept his far-reaching eye on
The palm-tree-edged desert-spring's sapphire,
And the musky oiled skin of the Kaffir,—
Picked it up, and as calmly retreated,
Leaped back where the lady was seated,
And full in the face of its owner
Flung the glove.

"Your heart's queen, you dethrone her?
So should I!"—cried the King—"'t was mere vanity,
Not love, set that task to humanity!"
Lords and ladies alike turned with loathing
From such a proved wolf in sheep's clothing.

Not so, I; for I caught an expression
In her brow's undisturbed self-possession
Amid the Court's scoffing and merriment,—
As if from no pleasing experiment
She rose, yet of pain not much heedful
So long as the process was needful,—
As if she had tried, in a crucible,
To what "speeches like gold" were reducible,
And, finding the finest prove copper,
Felt the smoke in her face was but proper;
To know what she had *not* to trust to,
Was worth all the ashes and dust too.
She went out 'mid hooting and laughter;
Clement Marot stayed; I followed after,
And asked, as a grace, what it all meant?
If she wished not the rash deed's recallment?
"For I"—so I spoke—"am a poet:
Human nature—behoves that I know it!"

She told me, "Too long had I heard
Of the deed proved alone by the word:
For my love—what De Lorge would not dare!
With my scorn—what De Lorge could compare!
And the endless descriptions of death
He would brave when my lip formed a breath,
I must reckon as braved, or, of course,
Doubt his word—and moreover, perforce,
For such gifts as no lady could spurn,
Must offer my love in return.
When I looked on your lion, it brought
All the dangers at once to my thought,
Encountered by all sorts of men,
Before he was lodged in his den,—
From the poor slave whose club or bare hands
Dug the trap, set the snare on the sands,
With no King and no Court to applaud,
By no shame, should he shrink, overawed,
Yet to capture the creature made shift,
That his rude boys might laugh at the gift,
—To the page who last leaped o'er the fence
Of the pit, on no greater pretense
Than to get back the bonnet he dropped,
Lest his pay for a week should be stopped.
So, wiser I judged it to make
One trial what 'death for my sake'
Really meant, while the power was yet mine,
Than to wait until time should define
Such a phrase not so simply as I,
Who took it to mean 'just to die.'
The blow a glove gives is but weak:
Does the mark yet discolor my cheek?
But when the heart suffers a blow,
Will the pain pass so soon, do you know?"

I looked, as away she was sweeping,
And saw a youth eagerly keeping
As close as he dared to the doorway.
No doubt that a noble should more weigh
His life than befits a plebeian;
And yet, had our brute been Nemean [8]
(I judge by a certain calm fervor
The youth stepped with, forward to serve her)
—He'd have scarce thought you did him the worst turn
If you whispered, "Friend, what you'd get, first earn!"
And when, shortly after, she carried
Her shame from the Court, and they married,
To that marriage some happiness, mauger
The voice of the Court, I dared augur.

For De Lorge, he made women with men vie,
Those in wonder and praise, these in envy;
And in short stood so plain a head taller
That he wooed and won . . . how do you call her?
The beauty, that rose in the sequel
To the King's love, who loved her a week well.
And 't was noticed he never would honor
De Lorge (who looked daggers upon her)
With the easy commission of stretching
His legs in the service, and fetching
His wife, from her chamber, those straying
Sad gloves she was always mislaying,
While the King took the closet to chat in,—
But of course this adventure came pat in.
And never the King told the story,
How bringing a glove brought such glory,
But the wife smiled—"His nerves are grown firmer:
Mine he brings now and utters no murmur."

8. **Nemean.** The Nemean lion was slain by Hercules.

Venienti occurrite morbo! [9]
With which moral I drop my theorbo.[10]

35

THE COURTIN'

JAMES RUSSELL LOWELL

God makes sech nights, all white an' still
    Fur 'z you can look or listen,
Moonshine an' snow on field an' hill,
    All silence an' all glisten.

Zekle crep' up quite unbeknown
    An' peeked in thru the winder,
An' there sot Huldy all alone,
    'ith no one nigh to hender.

A fireplace filled the room's one side
    With half a cord o' wood in—
There warn't no stoves (tell comfort died)
    To bake ye to a puddin'.

The wa'nut logs shot sparkles out
    Towards the pootiest, bless her,
An' leetle flames danced all about
    The chiny on the dresser.

Agin the chimbley crook-necks [1] hung,
    An' in amongst 'em rusted
The ole queen's-arm thet gran'ther Young
    Fetched back f'om Concord busted.

---

9. **Venienti occurrite morbo.** Meet the coming disease.
10. **Theorbo.** A musical instrument like a large lute.
1. **Crooknecks.** Squashes.

The very room, coz she was in,
　　Seemed warm f'om floor to ceilin',
An' she looked full ez rosy agin
　　Ez the apples she was peelin'.

'Twas kin' o' kingdom-come to look
　　On sech a blessed cretur;
A dogrose blushin' to a brook
　　Ain't modester nor sweeter.

He was six foot o' man, A 1,
　　Clear grit an' human natur';
None couldn't quicker pitch a ton
　　Nor dror a furrer straighter.

He'd sparked it with full twenty gals,
　　He'd squired 'em, danced 'em, druv **'em,**
Fust this one, an' then thet, by spells—
　　All is, he couldn't love 'em.

But long o' her his veins 'ould run
　　All crinkly like curled maple;
The side she breshed fell full o' sun
　　Ez a south slope in Ap'il.

She thought no v'ice hed sech a swing
　　Ez hisn in the choir;
My! when he made Ole Hunderd ring
　　She *knowed* the Lord was nigher.

An' she'd blush scarlit, right in prayer,
　　When her new meetin'-bunnet
Felt somehow thru' its crown a pair
　　O' blue eyes sot upun it.

Thet night, I tell ye, she looked *some!*
　　She seemed to 've gut a new soul,
For she felt sartin-sure he'd come,
　　Down to her very shoe-sole.

She heered a foot, an' knowed it tu,
　　A-raspin' on the scraper,—
All ways to once her feelin's flew
　　Like sparks in burnt-up paper.

He kin' o' l'itered on the mat,
　　Some doubtfle o' the sekle;
His heart kep' goin' pity-pat,
　　But hern went pity Zekle.

An' yit she gin her cheer a jerk
　　Ez though she wished him furder,
An' on her apples kep' to work,
　　Parin' away like murder.

"You want to see my Pa, I s'pose?"
　　"Wal . . . no . . . I come dasignin'"—
"To see my Ma? She's sprinklin' clo'es
　　Agin tomorrer's i'nin'."

To say why gals act so or so,
　　Or don't, 'ould be presumin';
Mebby to mean *yes* an' say *no*
　　Comes nateral to women.

He stood a spell on one foot fust,
　　Then stood a spell on t'other,
An' on which one he felt the wust
　　He couldn't ha' told ye nuther.

Says he, "I'd better call agin";
   Says she, "Think likely, Mister";
Thet last word pricked him like a pin,
   An' . . . Wal, he up an' kist her.

When Ma bimeby upon 'em slips,
   Huldy sot pale ez ashes,
All kin' o' smily roun' the lips
   An' teary roun' the lashes.

For she was jes' the quiet kind
   Whose naturs never vary,
Like streams that keep a summer mind
   Snowhid in Jenoory.

The blood clost roun' her heart felt glued
   Too tight for all expressin',
Tell mother see how metters stood,
   An' gin 'em both her blessin'.

Then her red come back like the tide
   Down to the Bay o' Fundy,
An' all I know is they was cried [2]
   In meetin' come nex' Sunday.

---

2. **They was cried.** The engagement was announced in accordance with the custom generally referred to as "the crying of the bans."

36

THE PIED PIPER OF HAMELIN; [1]

A CHILD'S STORY

ROBERT BROWNING

I

Hamelin Town's in Brunswick, [2]
  By famous Hanover city;
The river Weser, deep and wide,
Washes its wall on the southern side;
A pleasanter spot you never spied;
  But, when begins my ditty,
Almost five hundred years ago,
To see the townsfolk suffer so
  From vermin, was a pity.

II

Rats!
They fought the dogs and killed the cats,
  And bit the babies in the cradles,
And ate the cheese out of the vats,
  And licked the soup from the cooks' own ladles,
Split open the kegs of salted sprats,
Made nests inside men's Sunday hats,
And even spoiled the women's chats
      By drowning their speaking
      With shrieking and squeaking
In fifty different sharps and flats.

---

1. "Mr. Browning wrote this poem to amuse little Willie Macready, the son of the famous actor. The story told in the poem is one of a class of legends dealing with the subject of cheating magicians of a promised reward for services rendered."—Berdoe, *Browning Encyclopedia*.

2. **Brunswick.** A province in Germany.

III

At last the people in a body
  To the Town Hall came flocking:
" 'Tis clear," cried they, "our Mayor's a noddy;
And as for our Corporation [3]—shocking
To think we buy gowns lined with ermine
For dolts that can't or won't determine
What's best to rid us of our vermin!
You hope, because you're old and obese,
To find in the furry civic robe ease?
Rouse up, sirs! Give your brains a racking
To find the remedy we're lacking,
Or, sure as fate, we'll send you packing!"
At this the Mayor and Corporation
Quaked with a mighty consternation.

IV

An hour they sat in council,
  At length the Mayor broke silence:
"For a guilder I'd my ermine gown sell,
  I wish I were a mile hence!
It's easy to bid one rack one's brain—
I'm sure my poor head aches again,
I've scratched it so, and all in vain.
Oh for a trap, a trap, a trap!"
Just as he said this, what should hap
At the chamber door but a gentle tap?
"Bless us," cried the Mayor, "what's that?"
(With the Corporation as he sat,
Looking little though wondrous fat;
Nor brighter was his eye, nor moister
Than a too-long-opened oyster,

3. **Corporation.** The governing body.

Save when at noon his paunch grew mutinous
For a plate of turtle green and glutinous)
"Only a scraping of shoes on the mat?
Anything like the sound of a rat
Makes my heart go pit-a-pat!"

v

"Come in!"—the Mayor cried, looking bigger:
And in did come the strangest figure!
His queer long coat from heel to head
Was half of yellow and half of red,
And he himself was tall and thin,
With sharp blue eyes, each like a pin,
And light loose hair, yet swarthy skin,
No tuft on cheek nor beard on chin,
But lips where smiles went out and in;
There was no guessing his kith and kin:
And nobody could enough admire
The tall man and his quaint attire.
Quoth one: "It's as my great-grandsire,
Starting up at the Trump of Doom's tone,
Had walked this way from his painted tombstone!"

VI

He advanced to the council-table:
And, "Please your honors," said he, "I'm able,
By means of a secret charm, to draw
    All creatures living beneath the sun
    That creep or swim or fly or run,
After me so as you never saw!
And I chiefly use my charm
On creatures that do people harm,
The mole and toad and newt and viper;
And people call me the Pied Piper."

(And here they noticed round his neck
   A scarf of red and yellow stripe,
To match with his coat of the self-same cheque;
   And at the scarf's end hung a pipe;
And his fingers, they noticed, were ever straying
As if impatient to be playing
Upon this pipe, as low it dangled
Over his vesture so old-fangled.)
"Yet," said he, "poor piper as I am,
In Tartary I freed the Cham,[4]
   Last June, from his huge swarms of gnats;
I eased in Asia the Nizam [5]
   Of a monstrous brood of vampire-bats:
And as for what your brain bewilders,
   If I can rid your town of rats
Will you give me a thousand guilders?" [6]
"One? fifty thousand!"—was the exclamation
Of the astonished Mayor and Corporation.

VII

Into the street the Piper stept,
   Smiling first a little smile,
As if he knew what magic slept
   In his quiet pipe the while;
Then, like a musical adept,
To blow the pipe his lips he wrinkled,
And green and blue his sharp eyes twinkled,
Like a candle-flame where salt is sprinkled;
And ere three shrill notes the pipe uttered,
You heard as if an army muttered;
And the muttering grew to a grumbling;
And the grumbling grew to a mighty rumbling;

4. **Cham.** Khan, ruler.
5. **Nizam.** Title of the native ruler of a division of India.
6. **Guilder.** A Dutch coin worth about forty cents.

And out of the houses the rats came tumbling.
Great rats, small rats, lean rats, brawny rats,
Brown rats, black rats, gray rats, tawny rats,
Grave old plodders, gay young friskers,
   Fathers, mothers, uncles, cousins,
Cocking tails and pricking whiskers,
   Families by tens and dozens,
Brothers, sisters, husbands, wives—
Followed the Piper for their lives.
From street to street he piped advancing,
And step for step they followed dancing,
Until they came to the river Weser,
   Wherein all plunged and perished!
—Save one who, stout as Julius Cæsar,[7]
Swam across and lived to carry
   (As he, the manuscript he cherished)
To Rat-land home his commentary:
Which was, "At the first shrill notes of the pipe,
I heard a sound as of scraping tripe,
And putting apples, wondrous ripe,
Into a cider-press's gripe:
And a moving away of pickle-tub-boards,
And a leaving ajar of conserve-cupboards,
And a drawing the corks of train-oil-flasks,
And a breaking the hoops of butter-casks:
And it seemed as if a voice
   (Sweeter far than by harp or by psaltery
Is breathed) called out, 'Oh rats, rejoice!
   The world is grown to one vast drysaltery!
So munch on, crunch on, take your nuncheon,[8]
Breakfast, supper, dinner, luncheon!'
And just as a bulky sugar-puncheon,

---

   7. **Julius Caesar.** At the siege of Alexandria in 48 B. C. the ship
in which Caesar was sailing was captured, and Caesar had to swim
for his life. It is said he swam with one hand, and with the other
held his commentaries up out of the water for safe keeping.

   8. **Nuncheon.** Luncheon.

All ready staved, like a great sun shone
Glorious scarce an inch before me,
Just as methought it said, 'Come, bore me!'
—I found the Weser rolling o'er me."

VIII

You should have heard the Hamelin people
Ringing the bells till they rocked the steeple.
"Go," cried the Mayor, "and get long poles,
Poke out the nests and block up the holes!
Consult with carpenters and builders,
And leave in our town not even a trace
Of the rats!"—when suddenly, up the face
Of the Piper perked in the market-place,
With a, "First, if you please, my thousand guilders!"

IX

A thousand guilders! The Mayor looked blue;
So did the Corporation too.
For council dinners made rare havoc
With Claret, Moselle, Vin-de-Grace, Hock;
And half the money would replenish
Their cellar's biggest butt with Rhenish.
To pay this sum to a wandering fellow
With a gipsy coat of red and yellow!
"Beside," quoth the Mayor with a knowing wink,
"Our business was done at the river's brink;
We saw with our eyes the vermin sink,
And what's dead can't come to life, I think.
So, friend, we're not the folks to shrink
From the duty of giving you something for drink,
And a matter of money to put in your poke;
But as for the guilders, what we spoke
Of them, as you very well know, was in joke.

Beside, our losses have made us thrifty.
A thousand guilders! Come, take fifty!"

X

The Piper's face fell, and he cried,
"No trifling! I can't wait, beside!
I've promised to visit by dinner time
Bagdad, and accept the prime
Of the Head-Cook's pottage, all he's rich in,
For having left, in the Caliph's kitchen,
Of a nest of scorpions no survivor:
With him I proved no bargain-driver,
With you, don't think I'll bate a stiver!
And folks who put me in a passion
May find me pipe after another fashion."

XI

"How?" cried the Mayor, "d'ye think I brook
Being worse treated than a Cook?
Insulted by a lazy ribald
With idle pipe and vesture piebald?
You threaten us, fellow? Do your worst,
Blow your pipe there till you burst!"

XII

Once more he stept into the street
    And to his lips again
Laid his long pipe of smooth straight cane;
    And ere he blew three notes (such sweet
Soft notes as yet musician's cunning
    Never gave the enraptured air)
There was a rustling that seemed like a bustling
Of merry crowds justling at pitching and hustling;

Small feet were pattering, wooden shoes clattering,
Little hands clapping and little tongues chattering,
And, like fowls in a farm-yard when barley is scattering,
Out came the children running.
All the little boys and girls,
With rosy cheeks and flaxen curls,
And sparkling eyes and teeth like pearls,
Tripping and skipping, ran merrily after
The wonderful music with shouting and laughter.

XIII

The Mayor was dumb, and the Council stood
As if they were changed into blocks of wood,
Unable to move a step, or cry
To the children merrily skipping by,
—Could only follow with the eye
That joyous crowd at the Piper's back.
But how the Mayor was on the rack,
And the wretched Council's bosoms beat,
As the Piper turned from the High Street
To where the Weser rolled its waters
Right in the way of their sons and daughters!
However, he turned from South to West,
And to Koppelberg Hill his steps addressed,
And after him the children pressed;
Great was the joy in every breast.
"He never can cross that mighty top!
He's forced to let the piping drop,
And we shall see our children stop!"
When, lo, as they reached the mountain-side,
A wondrous portal opened wide,
As if a cavern was suddenly hollowed;
And the Piper advanced and the children followed,
And when all were in to the very last,
The door in the mountain-side shut fast.

Did I say all? No! One was lame,
   And could not dance the whole of the way;
And in after years, if you would blame
   His sadness, he was used to say,—
"It's dull in our town since my playmates left!
I can't forget that I'm bereft
Of all the pleasant sights they see,
Which the Piper also promised me.
For he led us, he said, to a joyous land,
Joining the town and just at hand,
Where waters gushed and fruit-trees grew
And flowers put forth a fairer hue,
And everything was strange and new;
The sparrows were brighter than peacocks here,
And their dogs outran our fallow deer,
And honey-bees had lost their stings,
And horses were born with eagles' wings:
And just as I became assured
My lame foot would be speedily cured,
The music stopped and I stood still,
And found myself outside the hill,
Left alone against my will,
To go now limping as before,
And never hear of that country more!"

XIV

Alas, alas for Hamelin!
   There came into many a burgher's pate
A text which says that heaven's gate
Opes to the rich at as easy rate
As the needle's eye takes a camel in!
The Mayor sent East, West, North, and South,
To offer the Piper, by word of mouth,
   Wherever it was men's lot to find him,

Silver and gold to his heart's content,
If he'd only return the way he went,
  And bring the children behind him.
But when they saw 'twas a lost endeavor,
And Piper and dancers were gone forever,
They made a decree that lawyers never
  Should think their records dated duly
If, after the day of the month and year,
These words did not as well appear,
"And so long after what happened here
  On the Twenty-second of July,
Thirteen hundred and seventy-six:"
And the better in memory to fix
The place of the children's last retreat,
They called it, the Pied Piper's Street—
Where any one playing on pipe or tabor
Was sure for the future to lose his labor.
Nor suffered they hostelry or tavern
  To shock with mirth a street so solemn;
But opposite the place of the cavern
  They wrote the story on a column,
And on the great church-window painted
The same, to make the world acquainted
How their children were stolen away,
And there it stands to this very day.
And I must not omit to say
That in Transylvania [9] there's a tribe
Of alien people who ascribe
The outlandish ways and dress
On which their neighbors lay such stress,
To their fathers and mothers having risen
Out of some subterraneous prison
Into which they were trepanned [10]
Long time ago in a mighty band

9. **Transylvania.** A province in East Hungary.
10. **Trepanned.** Ensnared.

Out of Hamelin town in Brunswick land,
But how or why, they don't understand.

xv

So, Willy, let me and you be wipers
Of scores out with all men—especially pipers!
And, whether they pipe us free fróm rats or fróm mice,
If we've promised them aught, let us keep our promise!

37

THE WELL OF ST. KEYNE

ROBERT SOUTHEY

A well there is in the West country,
  And a clearer one never was seen;
There is not a wife in the West country
  But has heard of the well of St. Keyne.

An oak and an elm tree stand beside,
  And behind does an ash-tree grow,
And a willow from the bank above
  Droops to the water below.

A traveler came to the well of St. Keyne;
  Pleasant it was to his eye,
For from cock-crow he had been traveling,
  And there was not a cloud in the sky.

He drank of the water so cool and clear,
  For thirsty and hot was he,
And he sat down upon the bank,
  Under the willow tree.

There came a man from the neighboring town
  At the well to fill his pail,
On the well-side he rested it,
  And bade the stranger hail.

"Now art thou a bachelor, stranger?" quoth he,
  "For an if thou hast a wife,
The happiest draught thou hast drank this day
  That ever thou didst in thy life.

"Or has your good woman, if one you have,
  In Cornwall ever been?
For an if she have, I'll venture my life
  She has drank of the well of St. Keyne."

"I have left a good woman who never was here,"
  The stranger he made reply;
"But that my draught should be better for that,
  I pray you answer me why."

"St. Keyne," quoth the countryman, "many a time
  Drank of this crystal well,
And before the angel summoned her
  She laid on the water a spell.

"If the husband of this gifted well
  Shall drink before his wife,
A happy man thenceforth is he,
  For he shall be master for life.

"But if the wife should drink of it first,
  Heaven help the husband then!"
The stranger stooped to the well of St. Keyne,
  And drank of the waters again.

"You drank of the well I warrant, betimes?"
   He to the countryman said.
But the countryman smiled as the stranger spake,
   And sheepishly shook his head.

"I hastened, as soon as the wedding was done,
   And left my wife in the porch.
But i' faith, she had been wiser than me,
   For she took a bottle to church."

38

THE DEACON'S MASTERPIECE

Or, The Wonderful "One-Hoss Shay"

Oliver Wendell Holmes

A LOGICAL STORY

Have you heard of the wonderful one-hoss shay,
That was built in such a logical way
It ran a hundred years to a day,
And then, of a sudden, it—ah, but stay,
I'll tell you what happened without delay,
Scaring the parson into fits,
Frightening people out of their wits,—
Have you ever heard of that, I say?

Seventeen hundred and fifty-five,
Georgius Secundus was then alive,—
Snuffy old drone [1] from the German hive;
That was the year when Lisbon-town
Saw the earth open and gulp her down,

---

1. **Snuffy old drone from the German hive.** George II, King of England, belonged to the House of Hanover, Germany.

And Braddock's army was done so brown,
Left without a scalp to its crown.
It was on the terrible Earthquake-day
That the Deacon finished the one-hoss shay.

Now in building of chaises, I tell you what,
There is always *somewhere* a weakest spot,—
In hub, tire, felloe, in spring or thill,
In panel, or crossbar, or floor, or sill,
In screw, bolt, thoroughbrace,—lurking still,
Find it somewhere you must and will,—
Above or below, within or without,—
And that's the reason, beyond a doubt,
That a chaise *breaks down,* but doesn't *wear out.*

But the Deacon swore, (as Deacons do,
With an "I dew vum," or an "I tell *yeou,*")
He would build one shay to beat the taown
'N' the keounty 'n' all the kentry raoun';
It should be so built that it couldn't break daown;
"Fur," said the Deacon, "t's mighty plain
That the weakes' place mus' stan' the strain;
'N' the way t' fix it, uz I maintain,
      Is only jist
T' make that place uz strong uz the rest."

So the Deacon inquired of the village folk
Where he could find the strongest oak,
That couldn't be split nor bent nor broke,—
That was for spokes and floor and sills;
He sent for lancewood to make the thills;
The crossbars were ash, from the straightest trees,
The panels of white-wood, that cuts like cheese,
But lasts like iron for things like these;
The hubs of logs from the "Settler's ellum,"—
Last of its timber,—they couldn't sell 'em,

Never an axe had seen their chips,
And the wedges flew from between their lips,
Their blunt ends frizzled like celery-tips;
Step and prop-iron, bolt and screw,
Spring, tire, axle, and linchpin too,
Steel of the finest, bright and blue;
Throughbrace bison-skin, thick and wide;
Boot, top, dasher, from tough old hide
Found in the pit when the tanner died.
That was the way he "put her through."—
"There!" said the Deacon, "naow she'll dew!"

Do! I tell you, I rather guess
She was a wonder, and nothing less!
Colts grew horses, beards turned gray,
Deacon and deaconess dropped away,
Children and grandchildren—where were they?
But there stood the stout old one-hoss shay
As fresh as on Lisbon-earthquake-day!

EIGHTEEN HUNDRED;—it came and found
The Deacon's masterpiece strong and sound.
Eighteen hundred increased by ten;—
"Hahnsum kerridge" they called it then.
Eighteen hundred and twenty came;—
Running as usual; much the same.
Thirty and forty at last arrive,
And then came fifty, and FIFTY-FIVE.

Little of all we value here
Wakes on the morn of its hundredth year
Without both feeling and looking queer.
In fact, there's nothing that keeps its youth,
So far as I know, but a tree and truth.
(This is a moral that runs at large;
Take it.—You're welcome.—No extra charge.)

FIRST OF NOVEMBER,—the Earthquake-day
There are traces of age in the one-hoss shay,
A general flavor of mild decay,
But nothing local, as one may say.
There couldn't be,—for the Deacon's art
Had made it so like in every part
That there wasn't a chance for one to start.
For the wheels were just as strong as the thills.
And the floor was just as strong as the sills
And the panels just as strong as the floor,
And the whipple-tree neither less nor more,
And the back-crossbar as strong as the fore,
And spring and axle and hub *encore.*
And yet, *as a whole,* it is past a doubt,
In another hour it will be *worn out!*

First of November, 'Fifty-five!
This morning the parson takes a drive.
Now, small boys, get out of the way!
Here comes the wonderful one-hoss shay,
Drawn by a rat-tailed, ewe-necked bay.
"Huddup!" said the parson.—Off went they.
The parson was working his Sunday's text,—
Had got to *fifthly,* and stopped perplexed
At what the—Moses—was coming next.
All at once the horse stood still,
Close by the meet'n'-house on the hill.
—First a shiver, and then a thrill,
Then something decidedly like a spill,—
And the parson was sitting upon a rock,
At half past nine by the meet'n'-house clock,—
Just the hour of the Earthquake shock!
—What do you think the parson found,
When he got up and stared around?
The poor old chaise in a heap or mound,
As if it had been to the mill and ground!

You see, of course, if you're not a dunce,
How it went to pieces all at once,—
All at once, and nothing first,—
Just as bubbles do when they burst.

End of the wonderful one-hoss shay.
Logic is logic.   That's all I say.

39

HOW THE OLD HORSE WON THE BET

OLIVER WENDELL HOLMES

'T was on the famous trotting-ground,
The betting men were gathered round
From far and near; the "cracks" were there
Whose deeds the sporting prints declare:
The swift g. m.,[1] Old Hiram's nag,
The fleet s. h.,[2] Dan Pfeiffer's brag,
With these a third—and who is he
That stands beside his fast b. g.[3]?
Budd Doble, whose catarrhal name
So fills the nasal trump of fame.
There too stood many a noted steed
Of Messenger and Morgan breed;
Green horses also, not a few;
Unknown as yet what they could do:
And all the hacks that know so well
The scourgings of the Sunday swell.

1. G. m.   Gray mare.
2. S. h.   Sorrel horse.
3. B. g.   Bay gelding.

Blue are the skies of opening day;
The bordering turf is green with May;
The sunshine's golden gleam is thrown
On sorrel, chestnut, bay, and roan;
The horses paw and prance and neigh,
Fillies and colts like kittens play,
And dance and toss their rippled manes
Shining and soft as silken skeins;
Wagons and gigs are ranged about,
And fashion flaunts her gay turn-out;
Here stands—each youthful Jehu's [4] dream—
The jointed tandem, ticklish team!
And there in ampler breadth expand
The splendors of the four-in-hand;
On faultless ties and glossy tiles
The lovely bonnets beam their smiles;
(The style's the man, so books avow;
The style's the woman, anyhow);
From flounces frothed with creamy lace
Peeps out the pug-dog's smutty face,
Or spaniel rolls his liquid eye,
Or stares the wiry pet of Skye,—
O woman,[5] in your hours of ease
So shy with us, so free with these!

"Come on! I'll bet you two to one
I'll make him do it!" "Will you? Done!"

What was it who was bound to do?
I did not hear and can't tell you,—
Pray listen till my story's through.

---

4. **Jehu.** A king of Israel of whom it was said, "He driveth
furiously."

5. **O woman,** etc. Adapted from lines in Scott's *Marmion,*
     "O woman! in our hours of ease,
         Uncertain, coy, and hard to please."

Scarce noticed, back behind the rest,
By cart and wagon rudely prest,
The parson's lean and bony bay
Stood harnessed in his one-horse shay—
Lent to his sexton for the day
(A funeral—so the sexton said;
His mother's uncle's wife was dead).

Like Lazarus [6] bid to Dives' feast,
So looked the poor forlorn old beast;
His coat was rough, his tail was bare,
The gray was sprinkled in his hair;
Sportsmen and jockeys knew him not,
And yet they say he once could trot
Among the fleetest of the town,
Till something cracked and broke him down,—
The steed's the statesman's, common lot!
"And are we then so soon forgot?"
Ah me! I doubt if one of you
Has ever heard the name "Old Blue,"
Whose fame through all this region rung
In those old days when I was young!

"Bring forth the horse!" Alas! he showed
Not like the one Mazeppa rode; [7]
Scant-maned, sharp-backed, and shaky-kneed,
The wreck of what was once a steed,
Lips thin, eyes hollow, stiff in joints;
Yet not without his knowing points.
The sexton laughing in his sleeve,
As if 't were all a make-believe,
Led forth the horse, and as he laughed
Unhitched the breeching from a shaft,

6. Lazarus. A poor beggar who lay at the gate of the rich man,
Dives. See *Luke* XVI: 20-26.
7. The one Mazeppa rode. A spirited horse in Byron's *Mazeppa.*

Unclasped the rusty belt beneath,
Drew forth the snaffle from his teeth,
Slipped off his head-stall, set him free
From strap and rein,—a sight to see!

So worn, so lean in every limb,
It can't be they are saddling him!
It is! his back the pig-skin strides
And flaps his lank, rheumatic sides;
With look of mingled scorn and mirth
They buckle round the saddle-girth;
With horsy wink and saucy toss
A youngster throws his leg across,
And so, his rider on his back,
They lead him, limping, to the track,
Far up behind the starting-point,
To limber out each stiffened joint.

As through the jeering crowd he past,
One pitying look Old Hiram cast;
"Go it, ye cripple, while ye can!"
Cried out unsentimental Dan;
"A Fast-Day dinner for the crows!"
Budd Doble's scoffing shout arose.

Slowly, as when the walking-beam
First feels the gathering head of steam,
With warning cough and threatening wheeze
The stiff old charger crooks his knees;
At first with cautious step sedate,
As if he dragged a coach of state;
He's not a colt; he knows full well
That time is weight and sure to tell;
No horse so sturdy but he fears
The handicap of twenty years.

As through the throng on either hand
The old horse nears the judges' stand,
Beneath his jockey's feather-weight
He warms a little to his gait,
And now and then a step is tried
That hints of something like a stride.

"Go!"—Through his ear the summons stung
As if a battle-trump had rung;
The slumbering instincts long unstirred
Start at the old familiar word;
It thrills like flame through every limb,—
What mean his twenty years to him?
The savage blow his rider dealt
Fell on his hollow flanks unfelt;
The spur that pricked his staring hide
Unheeded tore his bleeding side;
Alike to him are spur and rein,—
He steps a five-year-old again!

Before the quarter pole was past,
Old Hiram said, "He's going fast."
Long ere the quarter was a half,
The chuckling crowd had ceased to laugh;
Tighter his frightened jockey clung
As in a mighty stride he swung,
The gravel flying in his track,
His neck stretched out, his ears laid back,
His tail extended all the while
Behind him like a rat-tail file!
Off went a shoe,—away it spun,
Shot like a bullet from a gun;
The quaking jockey shapes a prayer
From scraps of oaths he used to swear;
He drops his whip, he drops his rein,
He clutches fiercely for a mane:

He'll lose his hold—he sways and reels—
He'll slide beneath those trampling heels!
The knees of many a horseman quake,
The flowers on many a bonnet shake,
And shouts arise from left and right,
"Stick on! Stick on!" "Hould tight! Hould tight!"
"Cling round his neck and don't let go—
That pace can't hold—there! steady! whoa!"
But like the sable steed that bore
The spectral lover of Lenore,[8]
His nostrils snorting foam and fire,
No stretch his bony limbs can tire;
And now the stand he rushes by,
And "Stop him!—stop him!" is the cry.
Stand back! he's only just begun—
He's having out three heats in one!

"Don't rush in front! he'll smash your brains;
But follow up and grab the reins!"
Old Hiram spoke. Dan Pfeiffer heard,
And sprang impatient at the word;
Budd Doble started on his bay,
Old Hiram followed on his gray,
And off they spring, and round they go,
The fast ones doing "all they know."
Look! twice they follow at his heels,
As round the circling course he wheels,
And whirls with him that clinging boy
Like Hector round the walls of Troy;[9]
Still on, and on, the third time round!
They're tailing off! they're losing ground!

---

8. **Lover of Lenore.** After his death the lover of Lenore appeared on a black horse and carried Lenore to the graveyard where their marriage was celebrated amid a crew of howling goblins.

9. **Like Hector.** After being slain by Achilles, Hector was dragged three times around the walls of Troy.

Budd Doble's nag begins to fail!
Dan Pfeiffer's sorrel whisks his tail!
And see! in spite of whip and shout,
Old Hiram's mare is giving out!
Now for the finish! at the turn,
The old horse—all the rest astern—
Comes swinging in, with easy trot;
By Jove! he's distanced all the lot!

That trot no mortal could explain;
Some said, "Old Dutchman come again!"
Some took his time,—at least they tried,
But what it was could none decide;
One said he could n't understand
What happened to his second hand;
One said 2:10; *that* could n't be—
More like two twenty-two or -three;
Old Hiram settled it at last;
"The time was two—too dee-vel-ish fast!"

The parson's horse had won the bet;
It cost him something of a sweat;
Back in the one-horse shay he went;
The parson wondered what it meant,
And murmured, with a mild surprise
And pleasant twinkle of the eyes,
"That funeral must have been a trick,
Or corpses drive at double-quick;
I should n't wonder, I declare,
If brother—Jehu—made the prayer!"

And this is all I have to say
About that tough old trotting bay.
Huddup! Huddup! G'lang! Good day!

Moral for which this tale is told:
A horse *can* trot, for all he's old.

40

THE BALLAD OF THE OYSTERMAN

Oliver Wendell Holmes

It was a tall young oysterman lived by the riverside,
His shop was just upon the bank, his boat was on the tide;
The daughter of a fisherman, that was so straight and slim,
Lived over on the other bank, right opposite to him.

It was the pensive oysterman that saw a lovely maid,
Upon a moonlight evening, a-sitting in the shade;
He saw her wave a handkerchief, as much as if to say,
"I'm wide awake, young oysterman, and all the folks away."

Then up arose the oysterman, and to himself said he,
"I guess I'll leave the skiff at home, for fear that folks should see;
I read it in the story book, that, for to kiss his dear,
Leander swam the Hellespont [1]—and I will swim this here."

And he has leaped into the waves, and crossed the shining stream,
And he has clambered up the bank, all in the moonlight gleam;
Oh, there are kisses sweet as dew, and words as soft as rain—
But they have heard her father's steps, and in he leaps again!

---

1. **Leander.** To see Hero, Leander nightly swam the Hellespont, but was finally drowned. In her grief Hero then drowned herself.

Out spoke the ancient fisherman: "Oh, what was that,
    my daughter?"
" 'Twas nothing but a pebble, sir, I threw into the water."
"And what is that, pray tell me, love, that paddles off so
    fast?"
"It's nothing but a porpoise, sir, that's been a-swimming
    past."

Out spoke the ancient fisherman: "Now bring me my
    harpoon!
I'll get into my fishing boat, and fix the fellow soon."
Down fell the pretty innocent, as falls a snow-white lamb;
Her hair drooped round her pallid cheeks, like seaweed
    on a clam.

Alas for those two loving ones! she waked not from her
    swound,
And he was taken with the cramp, and in the waves was
    drowned;
But Fate has metamorphosed them, in pity of their woe,
And now they keep an oyster shop for mermaids down
    below.

41

THE YARN OF THE NANCY BELL

William Schwenck Gilbert

'Twas on the shores that round our coast
    From Deal to Ramsgate [1] span,
That I found alone on a piece of stone
    An elderly naval man.

1. **Deal, Ramsgate.** Seaport towns in Kent County, England.

His hair was weedy, his beard was long,
   And weedy and long was he;
And I heard this wight on the shore recite,
   In a singular minor key:—

"Oh, I am a cook, and a captain bold,
   And the mate of the Nancy brig,
And a bo'sun tight, and a midshipmite,
   And the crew of the captain's gig."

And he shook his fists and he tore his hair,
   Till I really felt afraid,
For I couldn't help thinking the man had been drinking,
   And so I simply said:—

"O elderly man, it's little I know
   Of the duties of men of the sea,
And I'll eat my hand if I understand
   However you can be

"At once a cook, and a captain bold,
   And the mate of the Nancy brig,
And a bo'sun tight, and a midshipmite,
   And the crew of the captain's gig."

And he gave a hitch to his trousers, which
   Is a trick all seamen larn,
And having got rid of a thumping quid,
   He spun his painful yarn:—

"'Twas in the good ship Nancy Bell
   That we sailed to the Indian Sea,
And there on a reef we come to grief,
   Which has often occurred to me.

"And pretty nigh all the crew was drowned
   (There was seventy-seven o' soul),
And only ten of the Nancy's men
   Said 'Here!' to the muster-roll.

"There was me and the cook and the captain bold,
   And the mate of the Nancy brig,
And the bo'sun tight, and a midshipmite,
   And the crew of the captain's gig.

"For a month we'd neither wittles nor drink,
   Till a-hungry we did feel;
So we drawed a lot, and accordin', shot
   The captain for our meal.

"The next lot fell to the Nancy's mate,
   And a delicate dish he made;
Then our appetite with the midshipmite
   We seven survivors stayed.

"And then we murdered the bo'sun tight,
   And he much resembled pig;
Then we wittled free, did the cook and me,
   On the crew of the captain's gig.

"Then only the cook and me was left,
   And the delicate question, 'Which
Of us two goes to the kettle?' arose,
   And we argued it out as sich.

"For I loved that cook as a brother, I did,
   And the cook he worshiped me;
But we'd both be blowed if we'd either be stowed
   In the other chap's hold, you see.

"'I'll be eat if you dines off me,' says Tom;
    'Yes, that,' says I, 'you'll be:
I'm boiled if I die, my friend,' quoth I;
    And 'Exactly so,' quoth he.

"Says he, 'Dear James, to murder me
    Were a foolish thing to do,
For don't you see that you can't cook *me,*
    While I can—and will—cook *you?'*

"So he boils the water, and takes the salt
    And the pepper in portions true
(Which he never forgot), and some chopped shalot,
    And some sage and parsley too.

"'Come here,' says he, with a proper pride,
    Which his smiling features tell;
''Twill soothing be if I let you see
    How extremely nice you'll smell.'

"And he stirred it round and round and round,
    And he sniffed at the foaming froth;
When I ups with his heels, and smothers his squeals
    In the scum of the boiling broth.

"'And I eat that cook in a week or less,
    And—as I eating be
The last of his chops, why, I almost drops,
    For a wessel in sight I see!

.   .   .   .

"And I never larf, and I never smile,
    And I never lark nor play,
But sit and croak, and a single joke
    I have—which is to say:—

" 'Oh, I am a cook, and a captain bold,
  And the mate of the Nancy brig,
And a bo'sun tight, and a midshipmite,
  And the crew of the captain's gig!'"

42

THE EVE OF ST. JOHN [1]

SIR WALTER SCOTT

The Baron of Smaylh'ome rose with day,
  He spurred his courser on,
Without stop or stay, down the rocky way,
  That leads to Brotherstone.

He went not with the bold Buccleuch,
  His banner broad to rear;
He went not 'gainst the English yew,[2]
  To lift the Scottish spear.

Yet his plate-jack [3] was braced, and his helmet was laced,
  And his vaunt-brace [4] of proof he wore;
At his sadle-gerthe was a good steel sperthe,[5]
  Full ten pound weight and more.

The Baron returned in three days' space,
  And his looks were sad and sour;
And weary was his courser's pace,
  As he reached his rocky tower.

1. Smaylho'me Tower, the scene of this ballad, is situated on the northern boundary of Roxburghshire, among a cluster of wild rocks. The catastrophe of the tale is founded upon an old tradition.
2. **Yew.** English bows were made from the yew tree.
3. **Plate-jack.** Coat-armor.
4. **Vaunt-brace.** Armor for the body.
5. **Sperthe.** A battle-ax.

He came not from where Ancram Moor [6]
  Ran red with English blood;
Where the Douglas true, and the bold Buccleuch,
  'Gainst keen Lord Evers stood.

Yet was his helmet hacked and hewed,
  His acton [7] pierced and tore,
His axe and his dagger with blood imbued—
  But it was not English gore.

Hè lighted at the Chappellage,
  He held him close and still;
And he whistled thrice for his little foot-page,
  His name was English Will.

"Come thou hither, my little foot-page,
  Come hither to my knee;
Though thou art young, and tender of age,
  I think thou art true to me.

"Come, tell me all that thou hast seen,
  And look thou tell me true!
Since I from Smaylho'me tower have been,
  What did my lady do?"—

"My lady, each night, sought the lonely light
  That burns on the wild Watchfold;
For, from height to height, the beacons bright
  Of the English foemen told.

"The bittern clamored from the moss,
  The wind blew loud and shrill;
Yet the craggy pathway she did cross,
  To the eiry Beacon Hill.

6. **Ancram Moor.** A battle in Roxburghshire in which the Scotch defeated the English, 1545.
7. **Acton.** A quilted tunic worn under armor to prevent chafing.

"I watched her steps, and silent came
  Where she sat her on a stone;
No watchman stood by the dreary flame;
  It burned all alone.

'The second night I kept her in sight,
  Till to the fire she came,
And, by Mary's might! an armèd Knight
  Stood by the lonely flame.

"And many a word that warlike lord
  Did speak to my lady there;
But the rain fell fast, and loud blew the blast,
  And I heard not what they were.

"The third night there the sky was fair,
  And the mountain-blast was still,
As again I watched the secret pair,
  On the lonesome Beacon Hill.

"And I heard her name the midnight hour,
  And name this holy eve;
And say, 'Come this night to thy lady's bower;
  Ask no bold Baron's leave.

"'He lifts his spear with the bold Buccleuch;
  His lady is all alone;
The door she'll undo to her knight so true,
  On the eve of good St. John.'—

"'I cannot come; I must not come;
  I dare not come to thee;
On the eve of St. John I must wander alone;
  In thy bower I may not be.'—

" 'Now, out on thee, faint-hearted knight!
  Thou shouldst not say me nay;
For the eve is sweet, and when lovers meet,
  Is worth the whole summer's day.

" 'And I'll chain the blood-hound, and the warder shall
      not sound,
  And rushes shall be strewed on the stair;
So, by the black rood-stone,[8] and by holy St. John,
  I conjure thee, my love, to be there!'

" 'Though the blood-hound be mute, and the rush beneath
      my foot,
  And the warder his bugle should not blow,
Yet there sleepeth a priest in the chamber to the east,
  And my footstep he would know.'

" 'O fear not the priest, who sleepeth to the east;
  For to Dryburgh the way he has ta'en;
And there to say mass, till three days do pass,
  For the soul of a knight that is slain.'—

"He turned him around, and grimly he frowned;
  Then he laughed right scornfully—
'He who says the mass-rite for the soul of that knight,
  May as well say mass for me:

" 'At the lone midnight hour, when bad spirits have power,
  In thy chamber will I be.'—
With that he was gone, and my lady left alone,
  And no more did I see."—

8. **Black-rood stone.** The black-rood of Melrose was a crucifix of black marble, and of superior sanctity.

Then changed, I trow, was that bold Baron's brow,
  From the dark to the blood-red high;
"Now tell me the mien of the knight thou last seen,
  For, by Mary, he shall die!"—

"His arms shone full bright, in the beacon's red light;
  His plume it was scarlet and blue;
On his shield was a hound, in a silver leash bound,
  And his crest was a branch of the yew."—

"Thou liest, thou liest, thou little foot-page,
  Loud dost thou lie to me!
For that knight is cold, and low laid in the mold,
  All under the Eildon-tree."

"Yet hear but my word, my noble lord!
  For I heard her name his name;
And that lady bright, she called the knight,
  Sir Richard of Coldinghame."

The bold Baron's brow then changed, I trow,
  From high blood-red to pale—
"The grave is deep and dark—and the corpse is stiff and
      stark—
  So I may not trust thy tale.

"Where fair Tweed flows round holy Melrose,
  And Eildon slopes to the plain,
Full three nights ago, by some secret foe,
  That gay gallant was slain.

"The varying light deceived thy sight,
  And the wild winds drowned the name;
For the Dryburgh bells ring, and the white monks do sing,
  For Sir Richard of Coldinghame!"

He passed the court-gate, and he oped the tower grate,
  And he mounted the narrow stair
To the bartizan-seat,[9] where, with maids that on her
    wait,
  He found his lady fair.

That lady sat in mournful mood;
  Looked over hill and vale;
Over Tweed's fair flood, and Mertoun's wood,
  And all down Teviotdale.

"Now hail, now hail, thou lady bright!"—
  "Now hail, thou Baron true!
What news, what news from Ancram fight?
  What news from the bold Buccleuch?"

"The Ancram Moor is red with gore,
  For many a Southron fell;
And Buccleuch has charged us, evermore
  To watch our beacons well."

The lady blushed red, but nothing she said;
  Nor added the Baron a word;
Then she stepped down the stair to her chamber fair,
  And so did her moody lord.

In sleep the lady mourned, and the Baron tossed and
    turned,
  And oft to himself he said—
"The worms around him creep, and his bloody grave is
    deep,
  It cannot give up the dead!"

9. **Bartizan-seat.** A seat on the bartizan, a part of the castle
wall used for defense or a look-out.

It was near the ringing of matin-bell,
  The night was well-nigh done,
When a heavy sleep on that Baron fell,
  On the eve of good St. John.

The lady looked through the chamber fair
  By the light of a dying flame;
And she was aware of a knight stood there—
  Sir Richard of Coldinghame!

"Alas! away, away!" she cried,
  "For the holy Virgin's sake!"—
"Lady, I know who sleeps by thy side;
  But, lady, he will not awake.

"By Eildon-tree, for long nights three,
  In bloody grave have I lain;
The mass and the death-prayer are said for me,
  But lady, they are said in vain.

"By the Baron's brand, near Tweed's fair strand,
  Most foully slain I fell;
And my restless sprite on the beacon's height
  For a space is doomed to dwell.

"At our trysting-place, for a certain space
  I must wander to and fro;
But I had not had power to come to thy bower,
  Hadst thou not conjured me so."—

Love mastered fear—her brow she crossed;
  "How, Richard, hast thou sped? [10]
And art thou saved, or art thou lost?"—
  The Vision shook his head!

10. **Sped.** Prospered.

"Who spilleth life, shall forfeit life,
  So bid thy lord believe;
That lawless love is guilt above,
  This awful sign receive."

He laid his left palm on an oaken beam;
  His right upon her hand;
The lady shrunk, and fainting sunk,
  For it scorched like a fiery brand.

The sable score, of fingers four,
  Remains on that board impressed;
And for evermore that lady wore
  A covering on her wrist. [11]

There is a Nun in Dryburgh bower,
  Ne'er looks upon the sun:
There is a Monk in Melrose tower,
  He speaketh word to none.

That Nun, who ne'er beholds the day,
  That Monk, who speaks to none—
That Nun was Smaylho'me's Lady gay,
  That Monk the bold Baron.

11. **On her wrist.** There is an old tradition that the bodies of certain spirits and devils are scorchingly hot, so that they leave upon anything they touch an impression as of red-hot iron.

43

ARNOLD VON WINKELRIED [1]

JAMES MONTGOMERY

"Make way for Liberty!"—he cried:
Made way for Liberty, and died!

In arms the Austrian phalanx stood,
A living wall, a human wood!
A wall, where every conscious stone
Seemed to its kindred thousands grown;
A rampart all assaults to bear,
Till time to dust their frame should wear;
A wood, like that enchanted grove
In which with fiends Rinaldo [2] strove,
Where every silent tree possessed
A spirit prisoned in its breast,
Which the first stroke of coming strife
Would startle into hideous life;
So dense, so still, the Austrians stood,
A living wall, a human wood!
Impregnable their front appears,
All horrent with projected spears,
Whose polished points before them shine,
From flank to flank, one brilliant line,
Bright as the breakers' splendors run
Along the billows to the sun.

1. This poem is based upon the achievement of Arnold von Winkelried at the battle of Sempach, in which the Swiss insurgents in the fourteenth century secured the freedom of their country from Austria.
2. Rinaldo. A hero of many early romances, French and Italian.

Opposed to these, a hovering band
Contended for their native land:
Peasants, whose new-found strength had broke
From manly necks the ignoble yoke,
And forged their fetters into swords,
On equal terms to fight their lords,
And what insurgent rage had gained
In many a mortal fray maintained;
Marshalled once more at Freedom's call,
They came to conquer or to fall,
Where he who conquered, he who fell,
Was deemed a dead, or living Tell![3]
Such virtue had that patriot breathed,
So to the soil his soul bequeathed,
That wheresoe'er his arrows flew,
Heroes in his own likeness grew,
And warriors sprang from every sod
Which his awakening footsteps trod.

And now the work of life and death
Hung on the passing of a breath;
The fire of conflict burnt within,
The battle trembled to begin;
Yet, while the Austrians held their ground,
Point for attack was nowhere found,
Where'er the impatient Switzers gazed,
The unbroken line of lances blazed;
That line 't were suicide to meet,
And perish at their tyrants' feet,—
How could they rest within their graves,
And leave their homes the homes of slaves?
Would they not feel their children tread
With clanging chains above their head?

8. Tell. William Tell, a famous Swiss legendary patriot.

It must not be: this day, this hour,
Annihilates the oppressor's power;
All Switzerland is in the field,
She will not fly, she cannot yield,—
She must not fall; her better fate
Here gives her an immortal date.
Few were the number she could boast;
But every freeman was a host,
And felt as though himself were he
On whose sole arm hung victory.

It did depend on *one* indeed;
Behold him,—Arnold Winkelried!
There sounds not to the trump of fame
The echo of a nobler name.
Unmarked he stood amid the throng,
In rumination deep and long,
Till you might see, with sudden grace,
The very thought come o'er his face,
And by the motion of his form
Anticipate the bursting storm,
And by the uplifting of his brow
Tell where the bolt would strike, and how.

But 't was no sooner thought than done,
The field was in a moment won:—

"Make way for Liberty!" he cried,
Then ran, with arms extended wide,
As if his dearest friend to clasp;
Ten spears he swept within his grasp.

"Make way for Liberty!" he cried;
Their keen points met from side to side;
He bowed amongst them like a tree,
And thus made way for Liberty.

Swift to the breach his comrades fly;
"Make way for Liberty!" they cry,
And through the Austrian phalanx dart,
As rushed the spears through Arnold's heart;
While, instantaneous as his fall,
Rout, ruin, panic, scattered all;
An earthquake could not overthrow
A city with a surer blow.

Thus Switzerland again was free;
Thus death made way for Liberty!

44

THE DEFENSE OF THE ALAMO [1]

Joaquin Miller

Santa Anna came storming, as a storm might come;
There was rumble of cannon; there was rattle of blade;
There was cavalry, infantry, bugle and drum—
Full seven proud thousand in pomp and parade,
The chivalry, flower of all Mexico;
And a gaunt two hundred in the Alamo!

1. At the beginning of the war for the independence of Texas, Santa Anna, the president of Mexico, attacked the Alamo, a fortified convent, held by about a hundred and fifty men under William Travis. February 24, 1836, Travis sent out a letter "to the people of Texas and all Americans in the World," as follows:

"Fellow citizens and compatriots—I am besieged by a thousand or more of the Mexicans under Santa Anna. The enemy has demanded a surrender at discretion, otherwise, the garrison are to be put to the sword, if the fort is taken. I call on you in the name of Liberty, of Patriotism, and everything dear to American character, to come to our aid with all despatch. The enemy is receiving reinforcements daily and will no doubt increase to three or four thousand in four or five days. If this call is neglected, I am determined to sustain myself as long as possible and die like a soldier who never forgets what is due to his own honor and that of his country, Victory or Death!"

The little garrison at the Alamo held the Mexicans in check until other Texan forces were organized. When, however, Houston hurried forward to relieve the besieged, he received word that Santa Anna had captured the Alamo and that every man who defended its walls had died at his post.

And thirty lay sick, and some were shot through;
For the siege had been bitter, and bloody and long.
"Surrender, or die!"—"Men, what will you do?"
And Travis, great Travis, drew sword, quick and strong
Drew a line at his feet . . . Will you come? Will
    you go?
I die with my wounded, in the Alamo."

Then Bowie [2] gasped, "Guide me over that line!"
Then Crockett,[3] one hand to the sick, one hand to his gun
Crossed with him; then never a word or a sign,
Till all, sick or well, all, all, save but one,
One man. Then a woman stopped praying and slow
Across, to die with the heroes of the Alamo.

Then that one coward fled, in the night, in that night
When all men silently prayed and thought
Of home; of tomorrow; of God and the right,
Till dawn; then Travis sent his single last cannon-shot,
In answer to insolent Mexico,
From the old bell-tower of the Alamo.

Then came Santa Anna; a crescent of flame!
Then the red escalade;[4] then the fight hand to hand;
Such an unequal fight as never had name
Since the Persian hordes [5] butchered that doomed Spartan
    band.
All day—all day and all night, and the morning, so slow,
Through the battle smoke mantling the Alamo.

2. **Bowie.** A Georgian after whom the bowie knife is named; active in the movement for the independence of Texas.

3. **Crockett.** A famous frontiersman and hunter.

4. **Escalade.** An attack on a fortified place, in which an attempt is made to pass the walls, ramparts, etc., by means of ladders or by scaling.

5. **Persian Hordes . . . Spartan band:** At the battle of Thermopylae, 480 B. C., three hundred Spartans under Leonidas, with about six thousand allies, withstood for two days the attack of an immense army of Persians under Xerxes. At last the Persians succeeded in getting into the rear of the Spartans. Most of the allies sought safety in retreat, but the Spartans stood their ground and were slain to a man.

Then silence! Such silence! Two thousand lay dead
In a crescent outside! And within? Not a breath
Save the gasp of a woman, with gory, gashed head,
All alone, with her dead there, waiting for death;
And she but a nurse. Yet when shall we know
Another like this of the Alamo?

Shout "Victory, victory, victory ho!"
I say, 'tis not always with the hosts that win:
I say that the victory, high or low,
Is given the hero who grapples with sin,
Or legion or single; just asking to know
When duty fronts death in his Alamo.

45

THE BATTLE FLAG AT SHENANDOAH

Joaquin Miller

The tented field wore a wrinkled frown,
And the emptied church from the hill looked down
On the emptied road and the emptied town,
That summer Sunday morning.

And here was the blue, and there was the gray;
And a wide green valley rolled away
Between where the battling armies lay,
That sacred Sunday morning.

And Custer sat, with impatient will,
His restless horse, 'mid his troopers still,
As he watched with glass from the oak-set hill,
That silent Sunday morning.

Then fast he began to chafe and to fret;
"There's a battle flag on a bayonet
Too close to my own true soldiers set
For peace this Sunday morning!"

"Ride over, some one," he haughtily said,
"And bring it to me! Why, in bars blood red
And in stars I will stain it, and overhead
Will flaunt it this Sunday morning!"

Then a West-born lad, pale-faced and slim,
Rode out, and touching his cap to him,
Swept down, swept swift as Spring swallows swim,
That anxious Sunday morning.

On, on through the valley! up, up anywhere!
That pale-faced lad like a bird through the air
Kept on till he climbed to the banner there
That bravest Sunday morning!

And he caught up the flag, and around his waist
He wound it tight, and he turned in haste,
And swift his perilous route retraced
That daring Sunday morning.

All honor and praise to the trusty steed!
Ah! boy, and banner, and all, God speed!
God's pity for you in your hour of need
This deadly Sunday morning.

O deadly shot! and O shower of lead!
O iron rain on the brave, bare head!
Why, even the leaves from the tree fall dead
This dreadful Sunday morning!

But he gains the oaks! Men cheer in their might!
Brave Custer is laughing in his delight!
Why, he is embracing the boy outright
This glorious Sunday morning!

But, soft! Not a word has the pale boy said.
He unwinds the flag. It is starred, striped, red
With his heart's best blood; and he falls down dead,
In God's still Sunday morning.

So wrap this flag to his soldier's breast;
Into stars and stripes it is stained and blest;
And under the oaks let him rest and rest
Till God's great Sunday morning.

46

THE SONG OF THE CAMP

BAYARD TAYLOR

"Give us a song!" the soldiers cried,
    The outer trenches guarding,
When the heated guns of the camps allied
    Grew weary of bombarding.

The dark Redan,[1] in silent scoff,
    Lay grim and threatening, under;
And the tawny mound of the Malakoff [2]
    No longer belched its thunder.

1. **Redan.** A fortification. The story has to do with the **Crimean** War between England with her allies and Russia, 1854-1856.
2. **Malakoff.** A Russian tower in Sebastopol, Crimea.

There was a pause. A guardsman said:
"We storm the forts tomorrow;
Sing while we may, another day
Will bring enough of sorrow."

They lay along the battery's side,
Below the smoking cannon:
Brave hearts, from Severn and from Clyde,
And from the banks of Shannon.[3]

They sang of love, and not of fame;
Forgot was Britain's glory:
Each heart recalled a different name,
But all sang "Annie Lawrie."

Voice after voice caught up the song,
Until its tender passion
Rose like an anthem, rich and strong,—
Their battle-eve confession.

Dear girl, her name he dared not speak,
But, as the song grew louder,
Something upon the soldier's cheek
Washed off the stains of powder.

Beyond the darkening ocean burned
The bloody sunset's embers,
While the Crimean valleys learned
How English love remembers.

And once again a fire of hell
Rained on the Russian quarters,
With scream of shot, and burst of shell,
And bellowing of the mortars!

3. Severn, Clyde, Shannon. Rivers in England, Scotland, and
Ireland.

And Irish Nora's eyes are dim
  For a singer, dumb and gory;
And English Mary mourns for him
  Who sang of "Annie Lawrie."

Sleep, soldiers! still in honored rest
  Your truth and valor wearing:
The bravest are the tenderest,—
  The loving are the daring.

47

MARCO BOZZARIS [1]

FITZ-GREENE HALLECK

At midnight, in his guarded tent,
  The Turk was dreaming of the hour
When Greece, her knee in suppliance bent,
  Should tremble at his power:
In dreams, through camp and court, he bore
The trophies of a conqueror;
  In dreams his song of triumph heard;
Then wore his monarch's signet ring:
Then pressed that monarch's throne—a king;
As wild his thoughts, and gay of wing,
  As Eden's garden bird.

At midnight, in the forest shades,
  Bozzaris ranged his Suliote [2] band,
True as the steel of their tried blades,
  Heroes in heart and hand.

1. **Marco Bozzaris.** A Greek patriot (1790-1823), killed in the War of Independence against Turkey.
2. **Suliote.** Grecian troops from Souli.

There had the Persian's thousands stood,
There had the glad earth drunk their blood
  On old Platæa's [3] day;
And now there breathed that haunted air
The sons of sires who conquered there,
With arm to strike and soul to dare,
  As quick, as far as they.

An hour passed on—the Turk awoke;
  That bright dream was his last;
He woke—to hear his sentries shriek,
"To arms! they come! the Greek! the Greek!"
He woke—to die midst flame, and smoke,
And shout, and groan, and saber stroke,
  And death shots falling thick and fast
As lightnings from the mountain cloud;
And heard, with voice as trumpet loud,
  Bozzaris cheer his band:
"Strike—till the last armed foe expires;
Strike—for your altars and your fires;
Strike—for the green graves of your sires;
  God—and your native land!"

They fought—like brave men, long and well;
  They piled that ground with Moslem slain,
They conquered—but Bozzaris fell,
  Bleeding at every vein.
His few surviving comrades saw
His smile when rang their proud hurrah,
  And the red field was won;
Then saw in death his eyelids close
Calmly, as to a night's repose,
  Like flowers at set of sun.

3. **Plataea.** At the battle of Plataea the Greeks won a great victory
over the Persians, 479 B. C.

Come to the bridal-chamber, Death!
 Come to the mother's, when she feels,
For the first time, her first-born's breath;
 Come when the blessed seals
That close the pestilence are broke,
And crowded cities wail its stroke;
Come in consumption's ghastly form,
The earthquake shock, the ocean storm;
Come when the heart beats high and warm
 With banquet song, and dance, and wine;
And thou art terrible—the tear,
The groan, the knell, the pall, the bier,
And all we know, or dream, or fear
 Of agony, are thine.

But to the hero, when his sword
 Has won the battle for the free,
Thy voice sounds like a prophet's word;
And in its hollow tones are heard
 The thanks of millions yet to be.
Come, when his task of fame is wrought—
Come, with her laurel leaf, blood-bought—
 Come in her crowning hour—and then
Thy sunken eye's unearthly light
To him is welcome as the sight
 Of sky and stars to prisoned men;
Thy grasp is welcome as the hand
Of brother in a foreign land;
Thy summons welcome as the cry
That told the Indian isles were nigh
 To the world-seeking Genoese,[4]
When the land wind, from woods of palm,
And orange groves, and fields of balm,
 Blew o'er the Haytian seas.

4. **Genoese. Columbus.**

7

Bozzaris! with the storied brave
   Greece nurtured in her glory's time,
Rest thee—there is no prouder grave,
   Even in her own proud clime.
She wore no funeral weeds for thee,
   Nor bade the dark hearse wave its plume
Like torn branch from death's leafless tree
In sorrow's pomp and pageantry,
   The heartless luxury of the tomb;
But she remembers thee as one
Long loved and for a season gone;
For thee her poet's lyre is wreathed,
Her marble wrought, her music breathed;
For thee she rings the birthday bells;
Of thee her babe's first lisping tells;
For thine her evening prayer is said
At palace couch and cottage bed;
Her soldier, closing with the foe,
Gives for thy sake a deadlier blow;
His plighted maiden, when she fears
For him the joy of her young years,
Thinks of thy fate, and checks her tears;
   And she, the mother of thy boys,
Though in her eye and faded cheek
Is read the grief she will not speak,
   The memory of her buried joys,
And even she who gave thee birth,
Will, by their pilgrim-circled hearth,
   Talk of thy doom without a sigh;
For thou art Freedom's now, and Fame's:
One of the few, the immortal names,
   That were not born to die.

48

LITTLE GIFFEN [1]

Francis Orray Ticknor

Out of the focal [2] and foremost fire,
Out of the hospital walls as dire;
Smitten of grape-shot and gangrene,
(Eighteenth battle, and *he* sixteen!)
Specter! such as you seldom see,
Little Giffen, of Tennessee!

"Take him and welcome!" the surgeons said;
Little the doctor can help the dead!
So we took him; and brought him where
The balm was sweet in the summer air;
And we laid him down on a wholesome bed,—
Utter Lazarus,[3] heel to head!

And we watched the war with abated breath,—
Skeleton Boy against skeleton Death.
Months of torture, how many such?
Weary weeks of the stick and crutch;
And still a glint of the steel-blue eye
Told of a spirit that wouldn't die,

And didn't. Nay, more! in death's despite
The crippled skeleton "learned to write."
"Dear mother," at first, of course; and then
"Dear captain," inquiring about the men.
Captain's answer: "Of eighty-and-five,
Giffen and I are left alive."

1. This story of a young private in the Confederate army is taken
from real life.
2. Focal fire. The point upon which the firing was concentrated.
3. Lazarus. A man covered with sores.

Word of gloom from the war, one day;
Johnston [4] pressed at the front, they say.
Little Giffen was up and away;
A tear—his first—as he bade good-bye,
Dimmed the glint of his steel-blue eye.
"I'll write, if spared!"   There was news of the fight;
But none of Giffen.—He did not write.

I sometimes fancy that, were I king
Of the princely Knights of the Golden Ring, [5]
With the song of the minstrel in mine ear,
And the tender legend that trembles here,
I'd give the best on his bended knee,
The whitest soul of my chivalry,
For "Little Giffen," of Tennessee.

49

MUSIC IN CAMP

John Randolph Thompson

Two armies covered hill and plain,
  Where Rappahannock's waters
Ran deeply crimsoned with the stain
  Of battle's recent slaughters.

The summer clouds lay pitched like tents
  In meads of heavenly azure;
And each dread gun of the elements
  Slept in its hid embrasure.

4. **Johnston.** General Joseph E. Johnston, a Confederate leader.
5. **Knights of the Golden Ring.** King Arthur's knights of the Round Table.

The breeze so softly blew it made
   No forest leaf to quiver,
And the smoke of the random cannonade
   Rolled slowly from the river.

And now, where circling hills looked down
   With cannon grimly planted,
O'er listless camp and silent town
   The golden sunset slanted.

When on the fervid air there came
   A strain—now rich, now tender;
The music seemed itself aflame
   With day's departing splendor.

A Federal band, which, eve and morn,
   Played measures brave and nimble,
Had just struck up, with flute and horn
   And lively clash of cymbal.

Down flocked the soldiers to the banks,
   Till, margined by its pebbles,
One wooded shore was blue with "Yanks,"
   And one was gray with "Rebels."

Then all was still, and then the band,
   With movement light and tricksy,
Made stream and forest, hill and strand,
   Reverberate with "Dixie."

The conscious stream with burnished glow
   Went proudly o'er its pebbles,
But thrilled throughout its deepest flow
   With yelling of the Rebels.

Again a pause, and then again
  The trumpets pealed sonorous,
And "Yankee Doodle" was the strain
  To which the shore gave chorus.

The laughing ripple shoreward flew,
  To kiss the shining pebbles;
Loud shrieked the swarming Boys in Blue
  Defiance to the Rebels.

And yet once more the bugles sang
  Above the stormy riot;
No shout upon the evening rang—
  There reigned a holy quiet.

The sad, slow stream its noiseless flood
  Poured o'er the glistening pebbles;
All silent now the Yankees stood,
  And silent stood the Rebels.

No unresponsive soul had heard
  That plaintive note's appealing,
So deeply "Home, Sweet Home" had stirred
  The hidden founts of feeling.

Or Blue or Gray, the soldier sees,
  As by the wand of fairy,
The cottage 'neath the live-oak trees,
  The cabin by the prairie.

Or cold or warm, his native skies
  Bend in their beauty o'er him;
Seen through the tear-mist in his eyes,
  His loved ones stand before him.

As fades the iris after rain
  In April's tearful weather,
The vision vanished, as the strain
  And daylight died together.

But memory, waked by music's art,
  Expressed in simplest numbers,
Subdued the sternest Yankee's heart,
  Made light the Rebel's slumbers.

And fair the form of music shines,
  That bright celestial creature,
Who still, mid war's embattled lines,
  Gave this one touch of Nature.

50

AGINCOURT [1]

Michael Drayton

Fair stood the wind for France,
When we our sails advance;
Nor now to prove our chance
    Longer will tarry;
But putting to the main,
At Caux, the mouth of Seine,
With all his martial train
    Landed King Harry.

1. At the battle of Agincourt, France, in 1415, Henry V of England won against great odds a notable victory over the French. At Crecy in 1346, and at Poitiers in 1356 similar victories were won.

And taking many a fort,
Furnished in warlike sort,
Marcheth toward Agincourt
    In happy hour;
Skirmishing, day by day,
With those that stopped his way,
Where the French general lay
    With all his power.

Which, in his height of pride,
King Henry to deride,
His ransom to provide
    To the King sending;
Which he neglects the while,
As from a nation vile,
Yet with an angry smile,
    Their fall portending.

And turning to his men,
Quoth our brave Henry then:
"Though they to one be ten
    Be not amazèd!
Yet have we well begun:
Battles so bravely won
Have ever to the sun
    By Fame been raisèd!

"And for myself," quoth he,
"This my full rest [2] shall be:
England ne'er mourn for me,
    Nor more esteem me!
Victor I will remain,
Or on this earth lie slain;
Never shall She sustain
    Loss to redeem me!

---

2. **Rest.** Resolution.

"Poitiers and Cressy tell,
When most their pride did **swell**,
Under our swords they **fell**.
  No less our skill is,
Than when our Grandsire **great**,
Claiming the regal seat,
By many a warlike feat
  Lopped the French lilies."

The Duke of York so dread
The eager vanward led;
With the main, Henry sped
  Amongst his henchmen:
Exeter had the rear,
A braver man not there!
O Lord, how hot they were
  On the false Frenchmen!

They now to fight are gone:
Armor on armor shone;
Drum now to drum did groan:
  To hear was wonder;
That, with the cries they **make**,
The very earth did shake;
Trumpet to trumpet spake;
  Thunder to thunder.

Well it thine age became,
O noble Erpingham,
Which didst the signal aim
  To our hid forces!
When, from a meadow by,
Like a storm suddenly,
The English archery
  Stuck the French horses.

With Spanish yew so strong;
Arrows a cloth-yard long,
That like to serpents stung,
        Piercing the weather.
None from his fellow starts;
But, playing manly parts,
And like true English hearts,
        Stuck close together.

When down their bows they threw,
And forth their bilboes [3] drew,
And on the French they flew:
        Not one was tardy.
Arms were from shoulders sent,
Scalps to the teeth were rent,
Down the French peasants went:
        Our men were hardy.

This while our noble King,
His broad sword brandishing,
Down the French host did ding,
        As to o'erwhelm it;
And many a deep wound lent;
His arms with blood besprent,
And many a cruel dent
        Bruised his helmet.

Gloucester, that duke so good,
Next of the royal blood,
For famous England stood
        With his brave brother;
Clarence, in steel so bright,
Though but a maiden knight,
Yet in that furious fight
        Scarce such another!

3. **Bilboes.** Swords made in Bilboa, Spain.

Warwick in blood did wade,
Oxford, the foe invade,
And cruel slaughter made,
   Still as they ran up.
Suffolk his axe did ply;
Beaumont and Willoughby
Bare them right doughtily;
   Ferrers and Fanhope.

Upon Saint Crispin's Day [4]
Fought was this noble Fray;
Which Fame did not delay
   To England to carry.
O when shall English men
With such acts fill a pen?
Or England breed again
   Such a King Harry?

51

THE BATTLE OF BLENHEIM [1]

ROBERT SOUTHEY

I

It was a summer evening,
   Old Kaspar's work was done,
And he before his cottage door
   Was sitting in the sun,
And by him sported on the green
His little grandchild Wilhelmine.

---

4. **Crispin's Day.** October 25.

1. In the war of the Spanish Succession, the English under Marlborough, assisted by Prince Eugene, of Savoy, won a celebrated victory over the French and Bavarians at Blenheim, August 13, 1704. Point is added to the poem when one remembers that when peace was made, the original aim of the war was practically forgotten.

II

She saw her brother Peterkin
　　Roll something large and round,
Which he beside the rivulet
　　In playing there had found;
He came to ask what he had found,
That was so large, and smooth, and round.

III

Old Kaspar took it from the boy,
　　Who stood expectant by;
And then the old man shook his head,
　　And with a natural sigh,
" 'Tis some poor fellow's skull," said he,
"Who fell in the great victory.

IV

"I find them in the garden,
　　For there's many hereabout;
And often when I go to plow,
　　The plowshare turns them out!
For many thousand men," said he,
"Were slain in that great victory."

V

"Now tell us what 't was all about,"
　　Young Peterkin, he cries;
And little Wilhelmine looks up
　　With wonder-waiting eyes;
"Now tell us all about the war,
And what they fought each other for."

VI

"It was the English," Kaspar cried,
  "Who put the French to rout;
But what they fought each other for,
  I could not well make out;
But every body said," quoth he,
"That 'twas a famous victory.

VII

"My father lived at Blenheim then,
  Yon little stream hard by;
They burnt his dwelling to the ground,
  And he was forced to fly;
So with his wife and child he fled,
Nor had he where to rest his head.

VIII

"With fire and sword the country round
  Was wasted far and wide,
And many a childing mother then
  And new-born baby died;
But things like that, you know, must be
At every famous victory.

IX

"They say it was a shocking sight
  After the field was won;
For many thousand bodies here
  Lay rotting in the sun;
But things like that, you know, must be
After a famous victory.

X

"Great praise the Duke of Marlboro' won,
  And our good Prince Eugene."
"Why, 'twas a very wicked thing!"
  Said little Wilhelmine.
"Nay . . nay . . my little girl," quoth he,
"It was a famous victory.

XI

"And everybody praised the Duke
  Who this great fight did win."
"But what good came of it at last?"
  Quoth little Peterkin.
"Why, that I cannot tell," said he,
"But 'twas a famous victory."

52

INCIDENT OF THE FRENCH CAMP [1]

ROBERT BROWNING

You know, we French stormed Ratisbon:
  A mile or so away,
On a little mound, Napoleon
  Stood on our storming-day;
With neck out-thrust, you fancy how,
  Legs wide, arms locked behind,
As if to balance the prone brow
  Oppressive with its mind.

1. The French under Napoleon overcame the Austrians at Ratisbon,
Bavaria, in 1809. The story of the poem is true; but the hero was
a man, not a boy.

Just as perhaps he mused, "My plans
   That soar, to earth may fall,
Let once my army-leader Lannes
   Waver at yonder wall,"—
Out 'twixt the battery-smokes there flew
   A rider, bound on bound
Full-galloping; nor bridle drew
   Until he reached the mound.

Then off there flung in smiling joy,
   And held himself erect
By just his horse's mane, a boy:
   You hardly could suspect—
(So tight he kept his lips compressed,
   Scarce any blood came through,)
You looked twice e'er you saw his breast
   Was all but shot in two.

"Well," cried he, "Emperor, by God's grace
   We've got you Ratisbon!
The Marshal's in the market-place,
   And you'll be there anon
To see your flag-bird flap his vans
   Where I, to heart's desire,
Perched him!" The chief's eye flashed; his plans
   Soared up again like fire.

The chief's eye flashed; but presently
   Softened itself, as sheathes
A film the mother-eagle's eye
   When her bruised eaglet breathes;
"You're wounded!" "Nay," his soldier's **pride**
   Touched to the quick, he said:
"I'm killed, Sire!" And his chief beside,
   Smiling the boy fell dead.

53

THE CHARGE OF THE LIGHT BRIGADE[1]

ALFRED TENNYSON

Half a league, half a league,
Half a league onward,
All in the valley of Death,
   Rode the six hundred.
"Forward, the Light Brigade!
Charge for the guns!" he said:
Into the valley of Death
   Rode the six hundred.

"Forward, the Light Brigade!"
Was there a man dismayed?
Not though the soldiers knew
   Some one had blundered:
Theirs not to make reply,
Theirs not to reason why,
Theirs but to do and die;—
Into the valley of Death
   Rode the six hundred.

Cannon to right of them,
Cannon to left of them,
Cannon in front of them
   Volleyed and thundered;
Stormed at with shot and shell,
Boldly they rode and well;
Into the jaws of Death,
Into the mouth of Hell
   Rode the six hundred.

1. The charge described in this poem took place in 1854 at the battle of Balaclava in the Crimean War. Because the soldiers were fond of the poem, Tennyson sent to those at Sebastopol a thousand copies.

Flashed all their sabers bare,
Flashed as they turned in air,
Sabering the gunners there,
Charging an army, while
   All the world wondered:
Plunged in the battery smoke,
Right through the line they broke;
Cossack and Russian
Reeled from the saber stroke
   Shattered and sundered.
Then they rode back, but not—
   Not the six hundred.

Cannon to right of them,
Cannon to left of them,
Cannon behind them
   Volleyed and thundered.
Stormed at with shot and shell,
While horse and hero fell,
They that had fought so well
Came through the jaws of Death,
Back from the mouth of Hell,
All that was left of them,
   Left of six hundred.

When can their glory fade?
O the wild charge they made!
   All the world wondered.
Honor the charge they made!
Honor the Light Brigade!
   Noble six hundred.

54

THE BATTLE OF NASEBY [1]

Thomas Babington Macaulay

*(By Obadiah Bind-their-kings-in-chains-and-their-nobles-
with-links-of-iron, Sergeant in Ireton's Regiment.)*

Oh! wherefore come ye forth, in triumph from the North,
  With your hands, and your feet, and your raiment all
    red?
And wherefore doth your rout send forth a joyous shout?
  And whence be the grapes of the wine-press which ye
    tread?

Oh evil was the root, and bitter was the fruit,
  And crimson was the juice of the vintage that we trod;
For we trampled on the throng of the haughty and the
    strong,
  Who sate in the high places, and slew the saints of God.

It was about the noon of a glorious day of June,
  That we saw their banners dance, and their cuirasses [2]
    shine,
And the Man of Blood [3] was there, with his long essenced
    hair,
  And Astley, and Sir Marmaduke, and Rupert of the
    Rhine.

1. The battle of Naseby, 1645, was the first important victory of
the Puritans under Cromwell over the Royalists under Charles I. Concerning it Cromwell afterwards wrote: "I can say this of Naseby, that
when I saw the enemy draw up and march in gallant order towards us,
and we a company of poor ignorant men, I could not, riding alone
about my business, but smile out to God in praises, in assurance of
victory, because God would by things that are not bring to naught
things that are. Of which I had great assurance; and God did it."
The story is represented as being told by a sergeant, whose name
indicates the zeal of the Puritans.

2. **Cuirasses.** Breastplates.

3. **Man of blood.** Charles I.

Like a servant of the Lord, with his Bible and his sword,
  The General [4] rode along us to form us to the fight,
When a murmuring sound broke out, and swelled into a
    shout
  Among the godless horsemen upon the tyrant's right.

And hark! like the roar of the billows on the shore,
  The cry of battle rises along their charging line!
For God! for the Cause! for the Church! for the Laws!
  For Charles, King of England, and Rupert of the Rhine!

The furious German comes, with his clarions and his
    drums,
  His bravoes of Alsatia,[5] and pages of Whitehall;[6]
They are bursting on our flanks. Grasp your pikes, close
    your ranks;
  For Rupert never comes but to conquer or to fail.

They are here! They rush on! We are broken! We are
    gone!
  Our left is borne before them like stubble on the blast.
O Lord, put forth thy might! O Lord, defend the right!
  Stand back to back, in God's name, and fight it to the
    last.

Stout Skippon hath a wound; the center hath given
    ground:
  Hark! hark!—What means the trampling of horsemen
    on our rear?
Whose banner do I see, boys? 'Tis he, thank God, 'tis he,
    boys.
  Bear up another minute; brave Oliver is here.

---

4. **General.** Cromwell.
5. **Alsatia.** A section of London frequented by law-breakers.
6. **Whitehall.** A famous palace in London.

Their heads all stooping low, their points all in a row,
    Like a whirlwind on the trees, like a deluge on the
        dykes,
Our cuirassiers have burst on the ranks of the Accurst,
    And at a shock have scattered the forest of his pikes.

Fast, fast, the gallants ride, in some safe nook to hide
    Their coward heads, predestined to rot on Temple Bar: [7]
And he—he turns, he flies:—shame on those cruel eyes
    That bore to look on torture, and dare not look on war!

Ho! comrades, scour the plain; and, ere ye strip the slain,
    First give another stab to make your search secure,
Then shake from sleeves and pockets their broad-pieces
        and lockets,
    The tokens of the wanton, the plunder of the poor.

Fools! your doublets shone with gold, and your hearts
        were gay and bold,
    When you kissed your lily hands to your lemans [8]
        today;
And tomorrow shall the fox, from her chambers in the
        rocks,
    Lead forth her tawny cubs to howl above the prey.

Where be your tongues that late mocked at heaven and
        hell and fate,
    And the fingers that once were so busy with your
        blades,
Your perfumed satin clothes, your catches and your oaths,
    Your stage-plays and your sonnets, your diamonds and
        your spades?

7. **Temple Bar.** A famous stone gateway in London, where heads
of traitors were often exposed as warnings.
    8. **Lemans.** Sweethearts.

Down, down, for ever down with the miter and the
crown,
  With the Belial [9] of the Court, and the Mammon of the
  Pope!
There is woe in Oxford Halls: there is wail in Durham's
Stalls: [10]
  The Jesuit smites his bosom: the Bishop rends his cope.

And She of the Seven Hills [11] shall mourn her children's
ills,
  And tremble when she thinks on the edge of England's
  sword;
And the Kings of earth in fear shall shudder when they
hear
  What the hand of God hath wrought for the Houses and
  the Word.

55

THE BURIAL OF SIR JOHN MOORE
AT CORUNNA[1]

CHARLES WOLFE

Not a drum was heard, not a funeral note,
  As his corpse to the rampart we hurried;
Not a soldier discharged his farewell shot
  O'er the grave where our hero we buried.

9. **Belial.** Devil, Prince of darkness.
10. **Durham's Stalls.** Seats in the choir of Durham Cathedral.
11. **She of the Seven Hills.** The Roman Catholic Church.
1. The British under Sir John Moore held back the French at
Corunna, Spain, in 1809, until the British army was enabled to
embark in safety; but their leader was killed.

We buried him darkly at dead of night,
  The sods with our bayonets turning;
By the struggling moonbeam's misty light
  And the lantern dimly burning.

No useless coffin enclosed his breast,
  Not in sheet or in shroud we wound him;
But he lay like a warrior taking his rest,
  With his martial cloak around him.

Few and short were the prayers we said,
  And we spoke not a word of sorrow;
But we steadfastly gazed on the face that was dead,
  And we bitterly thought of the morrow.

We thought, as we hollow'd his narrow bed
  And smoothed down his lonely pillow,
That the foe and the stranger would tread o'er his head,
  And we far away on the billow!

Lightly they'll talk of the spirit that's gone
  And o'er his cold ashes upbraid him,—
But little he'll reck, if they let him sleep on
  In the grave where a Briton has laid him.

But half of our heavy task was done
  When the clock struck the hour for retiring:
And we heard the distant and random gun
  That the foe was sullenly firing.

Slowly and sadly we laid him down,
  From the field of his fame fresh and gory;
We carved not a line, and we raised not a stone,
  But we left him alone with his glory.

56

THE SOLDIER'S DREAM

Thomas Campbell

Our bugles sang truce, for the night-cloud had lower'd
  And the sentinel stars set their watch in the sky;
And thousands had sunk on the ground overpower'd,
  The weary to sleep, and the wounded to die.

When reposing that night on my pallet of straw
  By the wolf-scaring faggot that guarded the slain,
At the dead of the night a sweet Vision I saw;
  And thrice ere the morning I dreamt it again.

Methought from the battlefield's dreadful array
  Far, far, I had roam'd on a desolate track:
'Twas Autumn,—and sunshine arose on the way
  To the home of my fathers, that welcomed me back.

I flew to the pleasant fields traversed so oft
  In life's morning march, when my bosom was young;
I heard my own mountain-goats bleating aloft,
  And knew the sweet strain that the corn-reapers sung.

Then pledged we the wine-cup, and fondly I swore
  From my home and my weeping friends never to part;
My little ones kiss'd me a thousand times o'er,
  And my wife sobb'd aloud in her fulness of heart.

"Stay—stay with us!—rest!—thou art weary and
      worn!"—
  And fain was their war-broken soldier to stay;—
But sorrow return'd with the dawning of morn,
  And the voice in my dreaming ear melted away.

57

DESTRUCTION OF SENNACHERIB [1]

Lord Byron

The Assyrian came down like the wolf on the fold,
And his cohorts were gleaming in purple and gold;
And the sheen of their spears was like stars on the sea,
When the blue wave rolls nightly on deep Galilee.

Like the leaves of the forest when Summer is green,
That host with their banners at sunset were seen:
Like the leaves of the forest when Autumn hath blown,
That host on the morrow lay withered and strown.

For the Angel of Death spread his wings on the blast,
And breathed in the face of the foe as he passed;
And the eyes of the sleepers waxed deadly and chill,
And their hearts but once heaved, and for ever grew still!

And there lay the steed with his nostril all wide,
But through it there rolled not the breath of his pride;
And the foam of his gasping lay white on the turf,
And cold as the spray of the rock-beating surf.

And there lay the rider distorted and pale,
With the dew on his brow and the rust on his mail:
And the tents were all silent, the banners alone,
The lances unlifted, the trumpet unblown.

1. Sennacherib, king of Assyria in the 7th century B. C., waged war against Hezekiah, king of Judah. The Assyrian army so greatly outnumbered the Jewish that the downfall of Judah seemed certain. Sennacherib, however, defied not only Hezekiah but also Hezekiah's God. "And it came to pass that night that the angel of the Lord went out and smote in the camp of the Assyrians an hundred and four score and five thousand; and when they arose early in the morning, behold they were all dead corpses." For the full account read II *Kings* 18 and 19.

And the widows of Ashur [2] are loud in their wail,
And the idols are broke in the temple of Baal; [3]
And the might of the Gentile, unsmote by the sword,
Hath melted like snow in the glance of the Lord!

58

THE REVENGE [1]

A BALLAD OF THE FLEET

ALFRED TENNYSON

I

At Flores in the Azores Sir Richard Grenville lay,
And a pinnace, like a flutter'd bird, came flying from far
away:
"Spanish ships of war at sea! we have sighted fifty-
three!"
Then sware Lord Thomas Howard: "'Fore God I am
no coward;
But I cannot meet them here, for my ships are out of gear,
And the half my men are sick. I must fly, but follow
quick.
We are six ships of the line; [2] can we fight with fifty-
three?"

2. **Ashur.** One of the principal cities of Assyria.
3. **Baal.** One of the principal gods of the Assyrians.
1. In the fall of 1591 a few English ships under Lord Howard
were sent to Flores in the Azores to intercept and capture some
Spanish ships laden with treasure. Many of the English soldiers
became sick; and when the Spanish treasure-ships appeared escorted
by fifty-three war vessels, Lord Howard thought discretion the better
part of valor and gave the signal for flight. Sir Richard Grenville,
in command of the *Revenge*, refused to leave his sick and wounded
ashore, and, by the time these were got on board, found his ship in
imminent danger. Scorning to run from the Spaniards, he tried to
escape through their line, but had the wind taken out of his sails
by the great *San Philip*. The fight of the one with the fifty-three
followed. An account of the fight of the *Revenge* was written by **Sir
Walter Raleigh** in 1591.
2. **Ships of the line.** Battle ships.

II

Then spake Sir Richard Grenville; "I know you are
  no coward;
You fly them for a moment to fight with them again.
But I've ninety men and more that are lying sick ashore.
I should count myself the coward if I left them, my Lord
  Howard,
To these Inquisition dogs and the devildoms of Spain."

III

So Lord Howard past away with five ships of war that
  day,
Till he melted like a cloud in the silent summer heaven;
But Sir Richard bore in hand all his sick men from the
  land
Very carefully and slow,
Men of Bideford in Devon,
And we laid them on the ballast down below;
For we brought them all aboard,
And they blest him in their pain, that they were not
  left to Spain,
To the thumbscrew and the stake, for the glory of the
  Lord.

IV

He had only a hundred seamen to work the ship and to
  fight,
And he sailed away from Flores till the Spaniard came
  in sight,
With his huge sea-castles heaving upon the weather bow.
"Shall we fight or shall we fly?
Good Sir Richard, tell us now,
For to fight is but to die!

There'll be little of us left by the time this sun be set."
And Sir Richard said again: "We be all good English
    men.
Let us bang these dogs of Seville, the children of the devil,
For I never turn'd my back upon Don or devil yet."

V

Sir Richard spoke and he laugh'd, and we roar'd a hurrah,
    and so
The little Revenge ran on sheer into the heart of the foe,
With her hundred fighters on deck, and her ninety sick
    below;
For half of their fleet to the right and half to the left
    were seen,
And the little Revenge ran on thro' the long sea-lane
    between.

VI

Thousands of their soldiers look'd down from their decks
    and laugh'd,
Thousands of their seamen made mock at the mad little
    craft
Running on and on, till delay'd
By their mountain-like San Philip that, of fifteen hundred
    tons.
And up-shadowing high above us with her yawning tiers
    of guns,
Took the breath from our sails, and we stay'd.

VII

And while now the great San Philip hung above us like
    a cloud
Whence the thunderbolt will fall
Long and loud,

Four galleons[3] drew away
From the Spanish fleet that day,
And two upon the larboard and two upon the starboard
lay,
And the battle-thunder broke from them all.

VIII

But anon the great San Philip, she bethought herself and
went
Having that within her womb that had left her ill content;
And the rest they came aboard us, and they fought us
hand to hand,
For a dozen times they came with their pikes and mus-
queteers,
And a dozen times we shook 'em off as a dog that shakes
his ears
When he leaps from the water to the land.

IX

And the sun went down, and the stars came out far over
the summer sea,
But never a moment ceased the fight of the one and the
fifty-three.
Ship after ship, the whole night long, their high built
galleons came,
Ship after ship, the whole night long, with her battle-
thunder and flame;
Ship after ship, the whole night long, drew back with her
dead and her shame.
For some were sunk and many were shatter'd, and so
could fight us no more—
God of battles, was ever a battle like this in the world
before?

3. **Galleons.** Sailing vessels of the 15th and following centuries,
often having three or four decks.

X

For he said "Fight on! fight on!"
Tho' his vessel was all but a wreck;
And it chanced that, when half of the short summer night
    was gone,
With a grisly wound to be drest he had left the deck,
But a bullet struck him that was dressing it suddenly dead,
And himself he was wounded again in the side and the
    head,
And he said "Fight on! fight on!"

XI

And the night went down, and the sun smiled out far over
    the summer sea,
And the Spanish fleet with broken sides lay round us all
    in a ring;
But they dared not touch us again, for they fear'd that
    we still could sting,
So they watch'd what the end would be.
And we had not fought them in vain,
But in perilous plight were we,
Seeing forty of our poor hundred were slain,
And half of the rest of us maim'd for life
In the crash of the cannonades and the desperate strife;
And the sick men down in the hold were most of them
    stark and cold,
And the pikes were all broken or bent, and the powder
    was all of it spent;
And the masts and the rigging were lying over the side;
But Sir Richard cried in his English pride,
"We have fought such a fight for a day and a night
As may never be fought again!
We have won great glory, my men!

And a day less or more
At sea or ashore,
We die—does it matter when?
Sink me the ship, Master Gunner—sink her, split her in
    twain!
Fall into the hands of God, not into the hands of Spain!"

XII

And the gunner said "Ay, ay," but the seamen made reply:
"We have children, we have wives,
And the Lord hath spared our lives.
We will make the Spaniard promise, if we yield, to let us
    go;
We shall live to fight again and to strike another blow."
And the lion there lay dying, and they yielded to the foe.

XIII

And the stately Spanish men to their flagship bore him
    then,
Where they laid him by the mast, old Sir Richard caught
    at last,
And they praised him to his face with their courtly foreign
    grace;
But he rose upon their decks, and he cried:
"I have fought for Queen and Faith like a valiant man
    and true;
I have only done my duty as a man is bound to do:
With a joyful spirit I Sir Richard Grenville die!"
And he fell upon their decks, and he died.

XIV

And they stared at the dead that had been so valiant and
　true,
And had holden the power and glory of Spain so cheap
That he dared her with one little ship and his English
　few;
Was he devil or man? He was devil for aught they knew,
But they sank his body with honor down into the deep,
And they mann'd the Revenge with a swarthier alien
　crew,
And away she sail'd with her loss and long'd for her own;
When a wind from the lands they had ruin'd awoke from
　sleep,
And the water began to heave and the weather to moan,
And or ever that evening ended a great gale blew,
And a wave like the wave that is raised by an earthquake
　grew,
Till it smote on their hulls and their sails and their masts
　and their flags,
And the whole sea plunged and fell on the shot-shatter'd
　navy of Spain,
And the little Revenge herself went down by the island
　crags
To be lost evermore in the main.

59

√HERVÉ RIEL [1]

Robert Browning

I

On the sea and at the Hogue, sixteen hundred ninety-two,
　　Did the English fight the French,—woe to France!
And, the thirty-first of May, helter-skelter through the
　　blue,
Like a crowd of frightened porpoises a shoal of sharks
　　pursue,
　　Came crowding ship on ship to St. Malo [2] on the Rance,
With the English fleet in view.

II

'Twas the squadron that escaped, with the victor in full
　　chase;
　　First and foremost of the drove, in his great ship, Dam-
　　freville;
　　　Close on him fled, great and small,
　　　Twenty-two good ships in all;
And they signalled to the place
"Help the winners of a race!
　　Give us guidance, give us harbor, take us quick—or,
　　　quicker still,
　　　Here's the English can and will!"

III

Then the pilots of the place put out brisk and leapt on
board;
  "Why, what hope or chance have ships like these to
    pass?" laughed they:
"Rocks to starboard, rocks to port, all the passage scarred
    and scored,
Shall the *Formidable* here with her twelve and eighty guns
  Think to make the river-mouth by the single narrow
    way,
Trust to enter where 'tis ticklish for a craft of twenty
    tons,
    And with fiow at full beside?
    Now, 'tis slackest ebb of tide.
  Reach the mooring? Rather say,
While rock stands or water runs,
  Not a ship will leave the bay!"

IV

Then was called a council straight.
Brief and bitter the debate:
"Here's the English at our heels; would you have them
    take in tow
All that's left us of the fleet, linked together stern and
    bow,
For a prize to Plymouth Sound?
Better run the ships aground!"
  (Ended Damfreville his speech.)
"Not a minute more to wait!
  Let the Captains all and each
  Shove ashore, then blow up, burn the vessels on the
    beach!
France must undergo her fate.
8

V

"Give the word!" But no such word
Was ever spoke or heard;
  For up stood, for out stepped, for in struck amid all
    these
—A Captain? A Lieutenant? A Mate—first, second,
    third?
  No such man of mark, and meet
  With his betters to compete!
  But a simple Breton sailor pressed by Tourville for
    the fleet,
A poor coasting-pilot he, Hervé Riel the Croisickese.

VI

And, "What mockery or malice have we here?" cries
    Hervé Riel:
  "Are you mad, you Malouins? Are you cowards, fools,
    or rogues?
Talk to me of rocks and shoals, me who took the sound-
    ings, tell
On my fingers every bank, every shallow, every swell
  'Twixt the offing here and Grève where the river dis-
    embogues?
Are you bought by English gold? Is it love the lying's
    for?
  Morn and eve, night and day,
  Have I piloted your bay,
Entered free and anchored fast at foot of Solidor.
  Burn the fleet and ruin France? That were worse than
    fifty Hogues!
  Sirs, they know I speak the truth! Sirs, believe me
    there's a way!

Only let me lead the line,
  Have the biggest ship to steer,
  Get this *Formidable* clear,
Make the others follow mine,
And I lead them, most and least, by a passage I know
      well,
  Right to Solidor past Grève,
    And there lay them safe and sound;
  And if one ship misbehave,
    —Keel so much as grate the ground,
Why, I've nothing but my life,—here's my head!" cries
      Hervé Riel.

VII

Not a minute more to wait.
"Steer us in, then, small and great!
  Take the helm, lead the line, save the squadron!" cried
      its chief.
Captains, give the sailor place!
  He is Admiral, in brief.
Still the north-wind, by God's grace!
See the noble fellow's face
As the big ship, with a bound,
Clears the entry like a hound,
Keeps the passage as its inch of way were the wide seas
      profound!
  See, safe through shoal and rock,
  How they follow in a flock,
Not a ship that misbehaves, not a keel that grates the
      ground,
  Not a spar that comes to grief!
The peril, see, is past,
All are harbored to the last,
And just as Hervé Riel hollas "Anchor!"—sure as fate
Up the English come—too late!

VIII

So, the storm subsides to calm:
  They see the green trees wave
  On the heights o'erlooking Grève.
Hearts that bled are stanched with balm.
"Just our rapture to enhance,
  Let the English rake the bay,
Gnash their teeth and glare askance
  As they cannonade away!
'Neath rampired Solidor pleasant riding on the Rance!"
How hope succeeds despair on each Captain's counte-
      nance!
Out burst all with one accord,
  "This is Paradise for Hell!
    Let France, let France's King
    Thank the man that did the thing!"
What a shout, and all one word,
  "Hervé Riel!"
As he stepped in front once more,
  Not a symptom of surprise
  In the frank blue Breton eyes,
Just the same man as before.

IX

Then said Damfreville, "My friend,
I must speak out at the end,
  Though I find the speaking hard.
Praise is deeper than the lips:
You have saved the King his ships,
  You must name your own reward.
'Faith, our sun was near eclipse!
Demand what'er you will,
France remains your debtor still.
Ask to heart's content and have! or my name's not
      Damfreville."

X

Then a beam of fun outbroke
On the bearded mouth that spoke,
As the honest heart laughed through
Those frank eyes of Breton blue:
"Since I needs must say my say,
  Since on board the duty's done,
  And from Malo Roads to Croisic Point, what is it but
    a run?—
Since 'tis ask and have, I may—
  Since the others go ashore—
Come! A good whole holiday!
  Leave to go and see my wife, whom I call the Belle
    Aurore!"
  That he asked and that he got,—nothing more.

XI

Name and deed alike are lost:
Not a pillar nor a post
  In his Croisic keeps alive the feat as it befell;
Not a head in white and black
On a single fishing smack,
In memory of the man but for whom had gone to wrack
  All that France saved from the fight whence England
    bore the bell.
Go to Paris: rank on rank
  Search the heroes flung pell-mell
On the Louvre, face and flank!
  You shall look long enough ere you come to Hervé Riel.
So, for better and for worse,
Hervé Riel, accept my verse!
In my verse, Hervé Riel, do thou once more
Save the squadron, honor France, love thy wife the Belle
    Aurore!

60

THE DEFENCE OF LUCKNOW [1]

ALFRED TENNYSON

I

Banner of England, not for a season, O banner of Britain, hast thou

Floated in conquering battle or flapt to the battle-cry!

Never with mightier glory than when we had rear'd thee on high

Flying at top of the roofs in the ghastly siege of Lucknow—

Shot thro' the staff or the halyard, but ever we raised thee anew,

And ever upon the topmost roof our banner of England blew.

II

Frail were the works that defended the hold that we held with our lives—

Women and children among us, God help them, our children and wives!

Hold it we might—and for fifteen days or for twenty at most.

"Never surrender, I charge you, but every man die at his post!"

Voice of the dead whom we loved, our Lawrence the best of the brave:

Cold were his brows when we kiss'd him—we laid him that night in his grave.

1. During the Sepoy rebellion in India, 1857, a small company of English soldiers, supported by a few native soldiers, were besieged at Lucknow by a greatly superior Indian force. After the death of Sir Henry Lawrence on July 4, Brigadier Inglis held the city for twelve weeks. It was then relieved by the arrival of General Havelock, September 25. The poem tells the story of the defense and the rescue.

"Every man die at his post!" and there hail'd on our
    houses and halls
Death from their rifle-bullets, and death from their
    cannon-balls,
Death in our innermost chamber, and death at our slight
    barricade,
Death while we stood with the musket, and death while
    we stoopt to the spade,
Death to the dying, and wounds to the wounded, for often
    there fell,
Striking the hospital wall, crashing thro' it, their shot and
    their shell,
Death—for their spies were among us, their marksmen
    were told of our best,
So that the brute bullet broke thro' the brain that could
    think for the rest;
Bullets would sing by our foreheads, and bullets would
    rain at our feet—
Fire from ten thousand at once of the rebels that girdled
    us round—
Death at the glimpse of a finger from over the breadth
    of a street,
Death from the heights of the mosque and the palace, and
    death in the ground!
Mine? yes, a mine! Countermine! down, down! and creep
    thro' the hole!
Keep the revolver in hand! you can hear him—the
    murderous mole!
Quiet, ah! quiet—wait till the point of the pickaxe be
    thro'!
Click with the pick, coming nearer and nearer again than
    before—
Now let it speak, and you fire, and the dark pioneer is
    no more;
And ever upon the topmost roof our banner of England
    blew!

III

Ay, but the foe sprung his mine many times, and it chanced on a day

Soon as the blast of that underground thunderclap echo'd away,

Dark thro' the smoke and the sulphur like so many fiends in their hell—

Cannon-shot, musket-shot, volley on volley, and yell upon yell—

Fiercely on all the defences our myriad enemy fell.

What have they done? where is it? Out yonder. Guard the Redan! [2]

Storm at the Water-gate; storm at the Bailey-gate! storm, and it ran

Surging and swaying all round us, as ocean on every side

Plunges and heaves at a bank that is daily devour'd by the tide—

So many thousands that if they be bold enough, who shall escape?

Kill or be kill'd, live or die, they shall know we are soldiers and men!

Ready! take aim at their leaders—their masses are gapp'd with our grape—

Backward they reel like the wave, like the wave flinging forward again,

Flying and foil'd at the last by the handful they could not subdue;

And ever upon the topmost roof our banner of England blew.

IV

Handful of men as we were, we were English in heart and in limb,

Strong with the strength of the race to command, to obey, to endure,

---

2. **Redan.** A kind of fortification.

Each of us fought as if hope for the garrison hung but
    on him;
Still—could we watch at all points? we were every day
    fewer and fewer.
There was a whisper among us, but only a whisper that
    past:
"Children and wives—if the tigers leap into the fold
    unawares—
Every man die at his post—and the foe may outlive us
    at last—
Better to fall by the hands that they love, than to fall into
    theirs!"
Roar upon roar in a moment two mines by the enemy
    sprung
Clove into perilous chasms our walls and our poor
    palisades.
Rifleman, true is your heart, but be sure that your hand
    be as true!
Sharp is the fire of assault, better aimed are your flank
    fusillades—
Twice do we hurl them to earth from the ladders to
    which they had clung,
Twice from the ditch where they shelter we drive them
    with hand-grenades;
And ever upon the topmost roof our banner of England
    blew.

V

Then on another wild morning another wild earthquake
    out-tore
Clean from our lines of defence ten or twelve good paces
    or more.
Rifleman, high on the roof, hidden there from the light
    of the sun—
One has leapt up on the breach, crying out: "Follow me,
    follow me!"—

Mark him—he falls! then another, and *him* too, and down
goes he.

Had they been bold enough then, who can tell but the
traitors had won?

Boardings and rafters and doors—an embrasure! make
way for the gun!

Now double-charge it with grape! It is charged and we
fire, and they run.

Praise to our Indian brothers, and let the dark face have
his due!

Thanks to the kindly dark faces who fought with us, faithful and few,

Fought with the bravest among us, and drove them, and
smote them, and slew,

That ever upon the topmost roof our banner in India blew.

VI

Men will forget what we suffer and not what we do.
We can fight!

But to be soldier all day and be sentinel all thro' the
night—

Ever the mine and assault, our sallies, their lying alarms,

Bugles and drums in the darkness, and shoutings and
soundings to arms,

Ever the labor of fifty that had to be done by five,

Ever the marvel among us that one should be left alive,

Ever the day with its traitorous death from the loopholes
around,

Ever the night with its coffinless corpse to be laid in the
ground,

Heat like the mouth of a hell, or a deluge of cataract
skies,

Stench of old offal decaying, and infinite torment of flies,

Thoughts of the breezes of May blowing over an English
field,

Cholera, scurvy, and fever, the wound that *would* not be
heal'd,

Lopping away of the limb by the pitiful pitiless knife,—

Torture and trouble in vain,—for it never could save us
a life.

Valor of delicate women who tended the hospital bed,

Horror of women in travail among the dying and dead,

Grief for our perishing children, and never a moment
for grief,

Toil and ineffable weariness, faltering hopes of relief,

Havelock baffled, or beaten, or butcher'd for all that we
knew—

Then day and night, day and night, coming down on the
still-shatter'd walls

Millions of musket-bullets, and thousands of cannon-
balls—

But ever upon the topmost roof our banner of England
blew.

VII

Hark cannonade, fusillade! is it true what was told by
the scout,

Outram and Havelock breaking their way through the fell
mutineers?

Surely the pibroch of Europe is ringing again in our ears!

All on a sudden the garrison utter a jubilant shout,

Havelock's glorious Highlanders answer with conquering
cheers,

Sick from the hospital echo them, women and children
come out,

Blessing the wholesome white faces of Havelock's good
fusileers,

Kissing the war-harden'd hand of the Highlander wet
with their tears!

Dance to the pibroch![3] saved! we are saved!—is it you?
   is it you?
Saved by the valor of Havelock, saved by the blessing
   of Heaven!
"Hold it for fifteen days!" we have held it for eighty-
   seven!
And ever aloft on the palace roof the old banner of
   England blew.

61

THE PIPES AT LUCKNOW[1]

JOHN GREENLEAF WHITTIER

Pipes of the misty moorlands,
   Voice of the glens and hills;
The droning of the torrents,
   The treble of the rills!
Not the braes[2] of broom and heather,
   Nor the mountains dark with rain,
Nor maiden bower, nor border tower,
   Have heard your sweetest strain!

Dear to the Lowland reaper,
   And plaided mountaineer,—
To the cottage and the castle
   The Scottish pipes are dear;—

3. **Pibroch.** A kind of music played on the bagpipes, usually martial.
1. In a letter to Lowell, Whittier says of this poem: "It is in
strict accordance with the facts of the rescue. In the distance the
beleaguered garrison heard the stern and vengeful slogan of the Mac-
Gregors; but when the troops of Havelock came in view of the English
flag still floating from the Residency, the pipers struck up the immortal air of Burns, 'Should Auld Acquaintance Be Forgot.'"—
Pickard, *Life and Letters of Whittier.* See the note on the preceding
poem.
2. **Braes.** Slopes, hillsides.

Sweet sounds the ancient pibroch [3]
O'er mountain, loch,[4] and glade;
But the sweetest of all music
The Pipes [5] at Lucknow played.

Day by day the Indian tiger
Louder yelled, and nearer crept;
Round and round the jungle-serpent
Near and nearer circles swept.
"Pray for rescue, wives and mothers,—
Pray today!" the soldier said;
"Tomorrow, death's between us
And the wrong and shame we dread."

Oh, they listened, looked, and waited,
Till their hope became despair;
And the sobs of low bewailing
Filled the pauses of their prayer.
Then up spake a Scottish maiden,
With her ear unto the ground:
"Dinna ye hear it?—dinna ye hear it?
The pipes o' Havelock sound!"

Hushed the wounded man his groaning;
Hushed the wife her little ones;
Alone they heard the drum-roll
And the roar of Sepoy [6] guns.
But to sounds of home and childhood
The Highland ear was true;—
As her mother's cradle-crooning
The mountain pipes she knew.

3. **Pibroch.** A kind of music played on the bagpipes, usually martial.
4. **Loch.** Lake or bay.
5. **Pipes.** Bagpipes.
6. **Sepoy.** A native Indian soldier employed by the English.

Like the march of soundless music
    Through the vision of the seer,
More of feeling than of hearing,
    Of the heart than of the ear,
She knew the droning pibroch,
    She knew the Campbell's call:
"Hark! hear ye no' MacGregor's,—
    The grandest o' them all!"

O, they listened, dumb and breathless,
    And they caught the sound at last;
Faint and far beyond the Goomtee [7]
    Rose and fell the piper's blast!
Then a burst of wild thanksgiving
    Mingled woman's voice and man's;
"God be praised!—the March of Havelock!
    The piping of the clans!"

Louder, nearer, fierce as vengeance,
    Sharp and shrill as swords at strife,
Came the wild MacGregor's clan-call,
    Stinging all the air to life.
But when the far-off dust-cloud
    To plaided legions grew,
Full tenderly and blithesomely
    The pipes of rescue blew!

Round the silver domes of Lucknow,
    Moslem mosque and Pagan shrine,
Breathed the air to Britons dearest,
    The air of Auld Lang Syne.
O'er the cruel roll of war-drums
    Rose that sweet and homelike strain;
And the tartan clove the turban,
    As the Goomtee cleaves the plain.

7. **Goomtee.** The river on which Lucknow is situated.

Dear to the corn-land reaper
 And plaided mountaineer,—
To the cottage and the castle
 The piper's song is dear.
Sweet sounds the Gaelic pibroch
 O'er mountain, glen, and glade;
But the sweetest of all music
 The Pipes at Lucknow played!

62

FIGHT [1]

THE TALE OF A GUNNER AT PLATTSBURGH, 1814

PERCY MACKAYE

I

Jock bit his mittens off and blew his thumbs;
He scraped the fresh sleet from the frozen sign:
Men Wanted—Volunteers. Like gusts of brine
 He whiffed deliriums
Of sound—the droning roar of rolling, rolling drums
And shrilling fifes, like needles in his spine,
And drank, blood-bright from sunrise and wild shore,
 The wine of war.

1. This poem is based upon the battle of Lake Champlain, near Plattsburg, N. Y., September 11, 1814. In this battle the Americans under Commodore MacDonough defeated the British squadron under Downie. At one time MacDonough was knocked senseless for a few moments by a falling boom. A short time after this he was struck forcibly in the face by the flying head of the first gunner, who was killed by a cannon ball. This poem was written in 1914, and read by the author at Plattsburg on the hundredth anniversary of the battle.

With ears and eyes he drank and dizzy brain
Till all the snow danced red. The little shacks
That lined the road of muffled hackmatacks [2]
   Were roofed with the red stain,
Which spread in reeling rings on icy-blue Champlain
And splotched the sky like daubs of sealing-wax,
That darkened when he winked, and when he stared
    Caught fire and flared.

Men Wanted—Volunteers! The village street,
Topped by the slouching store and slim flagpole,
Loomed grand as Rome to his expanding soul;
   Grandly the rhythmic beat
Of feet in file and flags and fifes and filing feet,
The roar of brass and unremitting roll
Of drums and drums bewitched his boyish mood—
    Till he hallooed.

His strident echo stung the lake's wild dawn
And startled him from dreams. Jock rammed his cap
And rubbed a numb ear with the furry flap,
   Then bolted like a faun,
Bounding though shin-deep sleigh-ruts in his shaggy
    brawn,
Blowing white frost-wreaths from red mouth agap
Till, in a gabled porch beyond the store,
    He burst the door;

"Mother!" he panted. "Hush! Your pa ain't up;
He's worser since this storm. What's struck ye so?"
"It's volunteers!" The old dame stammered
   "Oh!" and stopped, and stirred her sup
Of morning tea, and stared down in the trembling cup.
"They're musterin' on the common now." "I know,"
She nodded feebly; then with sharp surmise
    She raised her eyes:

2. **Hackmatacks.** Larch trees: tamaracks.

She raised her eyes, and poured their light on him
Who towered glowing there—bright lips apart,
Cap off, and brown hair tousled. With quick smart
   She felt the room turn dim
And seemed she heard, far off, a sound of cherubim
Soothing the sudden pain about her heart.
How many a lonely hour of after-woe
      She saw him so!

"Jock!" And once more the white lips murmured "Jock!"
Her fingers slipped; the spilling teacup fell
And shattered, tinkling—but broke not the spell.
   His heart began to knock,
Jangling the hollow rhythm of the ticking clock.
"Mother, it's fight, and men are wanted!" "Well,
Ah well, it's men may kill us women's joys,
      It's men—not boys!"

"I'm seventeen! I guess that seventeen—"
"My little Jock!" "Little! I'm six-foot one.
(Scorn twitched his lip.) You saw me, how I skun
   The town last Hallowe'en
At wrastlin'" (Now the mother shifted tack.)
   "But Jean?
You won't be leavin' *Jean?*" "I guess a gun
Won't rattle *her.*" He laughed, and turned his head.
      His face grew red.

"But if it does—a gal don't understand:
It's fight!" "Jock, boy, your pa can't last much more,
And who's to mind the stock—to milk and chore?"
   Jock frowned and gnawed his hand.
"Mother, it's *men* must mind the stock—our own born
      land,
And lick the invaders." Slowly in the door
Stubbed the old, worn-out man. "Woman, let be!
      It's liberty:

"It's struck him like fork-lightnin' in a pine.
I felt it, too, like that in seventy-six;
And now, if 'twa'nt for creepin' pains and cricks
   And this one leg o' mine,
I'd holler young Jerusalem like him, and jine
The fight; but fight don't come from burnt-out wicks;
It comes from fire." "Mebbe," she said, "it comes
    From fifes and drums."

"Dad, all the boys are down from the back hills.
The common's cacklin' like hell's cocks and hens;
There's swords and muskets stacked in the cow-pens
   And knapsacks in the mills;
They say at Isle aux Noix Redcoats are holding drills,
And we're to build a big fleet at Vergennes.
Dad, can't I go?" "I reckon you're a man:
    Of course you can.

"I'll do the chores to home, you do 'em *thar!*"
"Dad!"—"Lad!" The men gripped hands and gazed upon
The mother, when the door flew wide. There shone
   A young face like a star,
A gleam of bitter sweet 'gainst snowy islands far,
A freshness, like the scent of cinnamon,
Tingeing the air with ardor and bright sheen.
    Jock faltered: "Jean!"

"Jock, don't you hear the drums? I dreamed all night
I heard 'em, and they woke me in black dark.
Quick, ain't you comin'? Can't you hear 'em? Hark!
   The men-folks are to fight.
I wish I was a man!" Jock felt his throat clutch tight.
"Men-folks!" It lit his spirit like a spark
Flashing the pent gunpowder of his pride.
    "Come on!" he cried.

"Here—wait!" The old man stumped to the back wall
And handed down his musket. "You'll want this;
And mind what game you're after, and don't miss.
   Good-by: I guess that's all
For now. Come back and get your duds." Jock, looming
      tall
Beside his glowing sweetheart, stooped to kiss
The little shrunken mother. Tiptoe she rose
   And clutched him—close.

In both her twisted hands she held his head
Clutched in the wild remembrance of dim years—
A baby head, suckling, half dewed with tears;
   A tired boy abed
By candlelight; a laughing face beside the red
Log-fire; a shock of curls beneath her shears—
The bright hair falling. Ah, she tried to smother
   Her wild thoughts.—"Mother!"

"Mother!" he stuttered. "Baby Jock!" she moaned
And looked far in his eyes.—And he was gone.
The porch door banged. Out in the blood-bright dawn
   All that she once had owned—
Her heart's proud empire—passed, her life's dream sank
      unthroned.
With hands still reached, she stood there staring, wan.
"Hark, woman!" said the bowed old man. "What's toll-
      ing?"
   Drums—drums were rolling.

II

Shy wings flashed in the orchard, *glitter, glitter*;
Blue wings bloomed soft through blossom-colored **leaves**,
And *Phoebe! Phoebe!* whistled from gray eaves
   Through water-shine and twitter

And spurt of flamey green. All bane of earth and bitter
Took life and tasted sweet at the glad reprieves
Of spring, save only in an old dame's heart
    That grieved apart.

Crook-back and small, she poled the big wellsweep:
Creak went the pole; the bucket came up brimming,
On the bright water lay a cricket swimming
  Whose brown legs tried to leap
But, dragging, twitched and foundered in the circling deep.
The old dame gasped; her thin hand snatched him,
    skimming.
"Dear Lord, he's drowned," she mumbled with dry lips;
    "The ships! the ships!"

Gently she laid him in the sun and dried
The little dripping body. Suddenly
Rose-red gleamed through the budding apple tree
  And "Look! a letter!" cried
A laughing voice; "and lots of news for us inside!"
"How's that, Jean? News from Jock! Where—where is
    he?"
"Down in Vergennes—the ship yards." "Ships! Ah, no!
    It can't be so."

"He's going to fight with guns and be a tar.
See here: he's wrote himself. The post was late.
He couldn't write before. The ship is great!
  She's built, from keel to spar,
And called the *Saratoga;* and Jock's got a scar
Already—" "Scar?" the mother quavered. "Wait,"
Jean rippled, "let me read." "Quick, then, my dear,
    He'll want to hear—

"Jock's pa; I guess we'll find him in the yard.
He ain't scarce creepin' round these days, poor Dan!"
She gripped Jean's arm and stumbled as they ran,
   And stopped once, breathing hard.
Around them chimney-swallows skimmed the sheep-
    cropped sward
And yellow hornets hummed. The sick old man
Stirred at their steps, and muttered from deep muse:
   "Well, ma, what news?"

"From Jockie—there's a letter!" In his chair
The bowed form sat bolt upright. "What's he say?"
"He's wrote to Jean. I guess it's boys their way
   To think old folks don't care
For letters." "Girl, read out." Jean smoothed her wild-
    ing hair
And sat beside them. Out of the blue day
A golden robin called; across the road
   A heifer lowed;

And old ears listened while youth read: "'Friend Jean,
Vergennes: here's where we've played a Yankee trick.
I'm layin' in my bunk by Otter Crick
   And scribblin' you this mean
Scrawl for to tell the news—what-all I've heard and
    seen:
Jennie, we've built a ship, and built her slick—
A swan!—a seven hundred forty tonner,
   And I'm first gunner.

"'You ought to seen us launch her t'other day!
Tell dad we've christened her for a fight of hisn
He fought at Saratoga. Now just listen!
   She's twice as big, folks say,

As Perry's ship that took the prize at Put-in-Bay; [3]
Yet forty days ago, hull, masts, and mizzen,
The whole of her was growin', live and limber,
    In God's green timber.

"I helped to fell her main-mast back in March.
The woods was snowed knee-deep. She was a wonder:
A straight white pine. She fell like roarin' thunder
    And left a blue-sky arch
Above her, bustin' all to kindlin's a tall larch.—
Mebbe the scart jack-rabbits skun from under!
Us boys hoorayed, and me and every noodle
    Yelled Yankee Doodle!

"'My, how we haw'd and gee'd the big ox-sledges
Haulin' her long trunk through the hemlock dells,
A-bellerin' to the tinkle-tankle bells,
    And blunted our ax edges
Hackin' new roads of ice 'longside the rocky ledges.
We stalled her twice, but gave the oxen spells
And yanked her through at last on the home-clearin'—
    Lord, wa'n't we cheerin'!

"'Since then I've seen her born, as you might say:
Born out of fire and water and men's sweatin',
Blast-furnace rairin' and red anvils frettin'
    And sawmills, night and day,
Screech-owlin' like 'twas Satan's rumhouse run away
Smellin' of tar and pitch. But I'm forgettin'
The man that's primed her guns and paid her score:
    The Commodore.

    3. **Perry.** Captain Perry won a victory over the English in a
naval battle on Lake Erie at Put-in-Bay in 1813.

" 'Macdonough—he's her master, and she knows
His voice, like he was talkin' to his hound.
There ain't a man of her but ruther'd drown'd
   Than tread upon his toes;
And yet with his red cheeks and twinklin' eyes, a rose
Ain't friendler than his looks be. When he's round,
He makes you feel like you're a gentleman
      American.

" 'But I must tell you how we're hidin' here.
This Otter Crick is like a crook-neck jug,
And we're inside. The Redcoats want to plug
   The mouth, and cork our beer;
So last week Downie sailed his British lake fleet near
To fill our channel, but us boys had dug
Big shore intrenchments, and our batteries
      Stung 'em like bees

" 'Till they skedaddled whimperin' up the lake;
But while the shots was flyin', in the scrimmage,
I caught a ball that scotched my livin' image,—
   Now, Jean, for Sam Hill's sake,
Don't let-on this to mother, for, you know, she'd make
A deary-me-in' that would last a grim age.
'Tain't much, but when a feller goes to war
      What's he go for

" 'If 'taint to fight, and take his chances?' " Jean
Stopped and looked down. The mother did not speak.
"Go on," said the old man. Flush tinged her cheek.
   "Truly I didn't mean—
There ain't much more. He says: 'Goodbye now, little
      queen;
We're due to sail for Plattsburgh this day week.
Meantime I'm hopin' hard and takin' stock.
      Your obedient—Jock.' "

The girl's voice ceased in silence. *Glitter, glitter,*
The shy wings flashed through the blossom-colored leaves,
And *Phoebe! Phoebe!* whistled from gray eaves
   Through water-shine and twitter
And spurt of flamey green. But bane of thought is bitter.
The mother's heart spurned May's sweet make-believes,
For there, through falling masts and gaunt ships looming,
     Guns—guns were booming.

III

Plattsburgh—and windless beauty on the bay;
Autumnal morning and the sun at seven:
Southward a wedge of wild ducks in the heaven
   Dwindles, and far away
Dim mountains watch the lake, where lurking for their
     prey
Lie, with their muzzled thunders and pent levin,
The war-ships—Eagle, Preble, Saratoga,
    Ticonderoga.

And now a little wind from the northwest
Flutters the trembling blue with snowy flecks.
A gunner, on Macdonough's silent decks,
   Peers from his cannon's rest,
Staring beyond the low north headland. Crest on crest
Behind green spruce-tops, soft as wild-fowls' necks,
Glide the bright spars and masts and whitened wales
    Of bellying sails.

Rounding, the British lake-birds loom in view,
Ruffling their wings in silvery arrogance:
Chubb, Linnet, Finch, and lordly Confiance
   Leading with Downie's crew
The line. With long booms swung to starboard they
     heave to,

Whistling their flock of galleys who advance
Behind, then toward the Yankees, four abreast,
    Tack landward, west.
Landward the watching townsfolk strew the shore;
Mist-banks of human being blur the bluffs
And blacken the roofs, like swarms of roosting choughs.
    Waiting the cannon's roar
A nation holds its breath for knell of Nevermore
Or peal of life: this hour shall cast the sloughs
Of generations—and one old dame's joy:
    Her gunner boy.

One moment on the quarter-deck Jock kneels
Beside his Commodore and fighting squad.
Their heads are bowed, their prayers go up toward God—
    Toward God, to whom appeals
Still rise in pain and mangling wrath from blind ordeals
Of man, still boastful of his brother's blood.—
They stand from prayer. Swift comes and silently
    The enemy.

Macdonough holds his men, alert, devout:
"He that wavereth is like a wave of the sea
Driven with the wind. Behold the ships, that be
    So great, are turned about
Even with a little helm." Jock tightens the blue clout
Around his waist, and watches casually
Close-by a game-cock, in a coop, who stirs
    And spreads his spurs.

Now bristling near, the British war-birds swoop
Wings, and the Yankee Eagle screams in fire;
The English Linnet answers, aiming higher,
    And crash along Jock's poop
Her hurtling shot of iron crackles the game-cock's coop,
Where, lo! the ribald cock, like a town crier
Strutting a gunslide, flaps to the cheering crew—
    Yankee-doodle-doo!

Boys yell, and yapping laughter fills the roar:
"You bet we'll do 'em!" "You're a prophet, cocky!"
"Hooray, old rooster!" "Hip, hip, hip!" cries Jockie.
   Calmly the Commodore
Touches his cannon's fuse and fires a twenty-four.
Smoke belches black. "Huzza! That's blowed 'em pocky!"
And Downie's men, like pins before the bowling,
    Fall scatter-rolling.

Boom! flash the long guns, echoed by the galleys.
The Confiance, wind-baffled in the bay
With both her port-bow anchors torn away,
   Flutters, but proudly rallies
To broadside, while her gunboats range the water-alleys.
Then Downie grips Macdonough in the fray,
And double-shotted from his roaring flail
    Hurls the black hail.

The hail turns red, and drips in the hot gloom.
Jock snuffs the reek and spits it from his mouth
And grapples with great winds. The winds blow south,
   And scent of lilac bloom
Steals from his mother's porch in his still sleeping-room.
Lilacs! But now it stinks of blood and drouth!
He staggers up, and stares at blinding light:
    "God! This is fight!"

Fight! The sharp loathing retches in his loins;
He gulps the black air, like a drowner swimming,
Where little round suns in a dance go rimming
   The dark with golden coins;
Round him and round the splintering masts and jangled
     quoins
Reel, rattling, and overhead he hears the hymning—
Lonely and loud—of ululating [4] choirs
    Strangling with wires.

  4. **Ululating.** Wailing, howling mournfully.

Fight! But no more the roll of chanting drums,
The fifing flare, the flags, the magic spume
Filling his spirit with a wild perfume;
  Now noisome anguish numbs
His sense, that mocks and leers at monstrous vacuums.
Whang! splits the spanker near him, and the boom
Crushes Macdonough, in a jumbled wreck,
    Stunned on the deck.

No time to glance where wounded leaders lie,
Or think on fallen sparrows in the storm—
Only to fight! The prone commander's form
  Stirs, rises stumblingly,
And gropes where, under shrieking grape and musketry,
Men's bodies wamble like a mangled swarm
Of bees. He bends to sight his gun again,
    Bleeding, and then—

Oh, out of void and old oblivion
And reptile slime first rose Apollo's [5] head;
And God in likeness of Himself, 'tis said,
  Created such an one,
Now shaping Shakespeare's forehead, now Napoleon,
Various, by infinite invention bred,
In His own image molding beautiful
    The human skull.

Jock lifts his head; Macdonough sights his gun
To fire—but in his face a ball of flesh,
A whizzing clod, has hurled him in a mesh
  Of tangled rope and tun,[6]

5. **Apollo.** The sun-god.
6. **Tun.** Large cask.

While still about the deck the lubber clod is spun
And bouncing from the rail, lies in a plesh [7]
Of oozing blood, upstaring eyeless, red—
    A gunner's head.

*   *   *   *   *   *   *   *

Above the ships, enormous from the lake,
Rises a wraith [8]—a phantom dim and gory,
Lifting her wondrous limbs of smoke and glory;
    And little children quake
And lordly nations bow their foreheads for her sake,
And bards proclaim her in their fiery story;
And in her phantom breast, heartless, unheeding,
    Hearts—hearts are bleeding.

Macdonough lies with Downie in one land.
Victor and vanquished long ago were peers.
Held in the grip of peace an hundred years,
    England has laid her hand
In ours, and we have held—and still shall hold—the band
That makes us brothers of the hemispheres;
Yea, still shall keep the lasting brotherhood
    Of law and blood.

Yet one whose terror racked us long of yore
Still wreaks upon the world her lawless might:
Out of the deeps again the phantom Fight
    Looms on her wings of war,
Sowing in armèd camps and fields her venomed spore,
Embattling monarch's whim against man's right,
Trampling with iron hoofs the blooms of time
    Back in the slime.

7. **Plesh.** Plash; shallow pool.
8. **Wraith.** A personification of the spirit of Fight.

We, who from dreams of justice, dearly wrought,
First rose in the eyes of patient Washington,
And through the molten heart of Lincoln won
   To liberty forgot,
Now standing lone in peace, 'mid titans strange distraught,
Pray much for patience, more—God's will be done!—
For vision and for power nobly to see
   The world made free.

63

ARNOLD AT STILLWATER [1]

Thomas Dunn English

Ah, you mistake me, comrades, to think that my heart
   is steel!
Cased in a cold endurance, nor pleasure nor pain to feel;
Cold as I am in my manner, yet over these cheeks so
   seared
Teardrops have fallen in torrents, thrice since my chin
   grew beard.

Thrice since my chin was bearded I suffered the tears to
   fall;
Benedict Arnold, the traitor, he was the cause of them all!
Once, when he carried Stillwater, proud of his valor, I
   cried;
Then, with my rage at his treason—with pity when André
   died.

---

1. At the battle of Stillwater, better known as the battle of
Saratoga, October 7, 1777, the Americans under Gates defeated the
British under Burgoyne. Benedict Arnold, who later attempted, with
the aid of Major André of the British army, to betray West Point
into the hands of the British, played a conspicuous part in the battle.
The poem, even in detail, is based upon fact.

Benedict Arnold, the traitor, sank deep in the pit of
    shame,
Bartered for vengeance his honor, blackened for profit
    his fame;
Yet never a gallanter soldier, whatever his after crime,
Fought on the red field of honor than he in his early time.

Ah, I remember Stillwater, as it were yesterday!
Then first I shouldered a firelock, and set out the foe-
    men to slay.
The country was up all around us, racing and chasing
    Burgoyne,
And I had gone out with my neighbors, Gates and his
    forces to join.

Marched we with Poor and with Learned, ready and eager
    to fight;
There stood the foemen before us, cannon and men on
    the height;
Onward we trod with no shouting, forbidden to fire till
    the word;
As silent their long line of scarlet—not one of them
    whispered or stirred.

Suddenly, then, from among them smoke rose and spread
    on the breeze;
Grapeshot flew over us sharply, cutting the limbs from
    the trees;
But onward we pressed till the order of Cilley fell full
    on the ear;
Then we leveled our pieces and fired them, and rushed
    up the slope with a cheer.

Fiercely we charged on their center, and beat back the
    stout grenadiers,
And wounded the brave Major Ackland, and grappled
    the swart cannoneers;

Five times we captured their cannons, and five times
    they took them again;
But the sixth time we had them, and with
    them a share of their men.

Our colonel who led us dismounted, high on a cannon he
    sprang;
Over the noise of our shouting clearly his joyous words
    rang;
"These are our own brazen beauties! Here to America's
    cause
I dedicate each, and to freedom!—foes to King George
    and his laws!"

Worn as we were with the struggle, wounded and bleeding
    and sore,
Some stood all pale and exhausted; some lay there stiff
    in their gore;
And round through the mass went a murmur, that grew
    to a whispering clear,
And then to reproaches outspoken—"If General Arnold
    were here!"

For Gates, in his folly and envy, had given the chief no
    command,
And far in the rear some had seen him horseless and
    moodily stand.
Knitting his forehead in anger, gnawing his red lip in
    pain,
Fretting himself like a bloodhound held back from his
    prey by a chain.

Hark, at our right there is cheering! there is the ruffle of
    drums!
Here is the well-known brown charger! Spurring it madly
    he comes!

Learned's brigade have espied him, rending the air with
    a cheer;
Woe to the terrified foeman, now that our leader is here!

Piercing the tumult behind him, Armstrong is out on his
    track;
Gates has dispatched his lieutenant to summon the fugitive
    back.
Armstrong might summon the tempest, order the whirl-
    wind to stay,
Issue commands to the earthquake—would they the man-
    date obey?

Wounds, they were healed in a moment! weariness in-
    stantly gone!
Forward he pointed his saber—led us, not ordered us on.
Down on the Hessians we thundered, he, like a madman
    ahead;
Vainly they strove to withstand us; raging, they shivered
    and fled.

On to their earthworks we drove tnem, shaking with
    ire and dismay;
There they made stand with a purpose to beat back the
    tide of the day.
Onward we followed, then faltered; deadly their balls
    whistled free.
Where was our death-daring leader? Arnold, our hope,
    where was he?

He? He was everywhere riding! hither and thither his
    form,
On the brown charger careering, showed us the path of
    the storm;

Over the roar of the cannon, over the musketry's crash,
Sounded his voice, while his saber lit up the way with
its flash.

Throwing quick glances around him, reining a moment
his steed—
"Brooks, that redoubt!" was his order; "let the rest
follow my lead!
Mark where the smoke-cloud is parting! see where the
gun-barrels glance!
Livingston, forward! On, Wesson, charge them! Let
Morgan advance!"

"Forward!" he shouted, and, spurring on through the
sally-port then,
Fell sword in hand on the Hessians, closely behind him
our men.
Back shrank the foemen in terror; off went their forces
pellmell,
Firing one Parthian volley; struck by it, Arnold, he fell.

Ours was the day. Up we raised him; spurted the blood
from his knee—
"Take my cravat, boys, and bind it; I am not dead yet,"
said he.
"What! did you follow me, Armstrong? Pray, do you
think it quite right,
Leaving your duties out yonder, to risk your dear self in
the fight?"

"General Gates sent his orders"—faltering the aid-de-
camp spoke—
"You're to return, lest some rashness—" Fiercely the
speech Arnold broke:

9

"Rashness! Why, yes, tell the general the rashness he
   dreaded is done!
Tell him his kinsfolk are beaten! tell him the battle is
   won!"

Oh, that a soldier so glorious, ever victorious in fight,
Passed from a daylight of honor into the terrible night!—
Fell as the mighty archangel, ere the earth glowed in
   space, fell—
Fell from the patriot's heaven down to the loyalist's hell!

64

KEENAN'S CHARGE [1]

George Parsons Lathrop

The sun had set;
The leaves with dew were wet,—
Down fell a bloody dusk
Where "Stonewall's" corps, like a beast of prey,
Tore through with angry tusk.

"They've trapped us, boys!"
Rose from our flank a voice.
With rush of steel and smoke.
On came the rebels straight,
Eager as love, and wild as hate;
And our line reeled and broke;

---

1. At the battle of Chancellorsville, May 1, 2, and 3, 1863, the
Confederates under General Lee turned back the Union army under
General Hooker. On the second day of the fight General Pleasanton,
in order to gain time to place some guns, ordered Major Keenan with
four hundred Pennsylvania cavalrymen to charge ten thousand advancing Confederates under "Stonewall" Jackson. The story of the charge
is told in the poem.

Broke and fled.
Not one stayed,—but the dead!
With curses, shrieks, and cries,
Horses, and wagons, and men
Tumbled back through the shuddering glen,
And above us the fading skies.

There's some hope, still,—
Those batteries parked on the hill!
"Battery, wheel" ('mid the roar),
"Pass pieces; fix prolonge [2] to fire
Retiring. Trot!" In the panic dire
A bugle rings "Trot!"—and no more.

The horses plunged,
The cannon lurched and lunged,
To join the hopeless rout.
But suddenly rose a form
Calmly in front of the human storm,
With a stern commanding shout:

"Align [3] those guns!"
(We knew it was Pleasanton's.)
The cannoneers bent to obey,
And worked with a will at his word,
And the black guns moved as if they had heard.
But, ah, the dread delay!

"To wait is crime;
O God, for ten minutes' time!"
The general looked around.
There Keenan sat, like a stone,
With his three hundred horse alone,
Less shaken than the ground.

2. **Prolonge.** A rope of three pieces for drawing a gun carriage.
3. **Align.** Range in line.

"Major, your men?"
"Are soldiers, general."   "Then,
Charge, major! Do your best;
Hold the enemy back, at all cost,
Till my guns are placed;—else the army is lost.
You die to save the rest!"

By the shrouded gleam of the western skies
Brave Keenan looked into Pleasanton's eyes
For an instant,—clear, and cool, and still;
Then, with a smile, he said: "I will."

"Cavalry, charge!"   Not a man of them shrank.
Their sharp, full cheer, from rank on rank,
Rose joyously, with a willing breath,—
Rose like a greeting hail to death.

Then forward they sprang, and spurred, and clashed;
Shouted the officers, crimson-sashed;
Rode well the men, each brave as his fellow,
In their faded coats of the blue and yellow;
And above in the air, with an instinct true,
Like a bird of war their pennon flew.

With clank of scabbard, and thunder of steeds,
And blades that shine like sunlit reeds,
And strong brown faces bravely pale
For fear their proud attempt shall fail,
Three hundred Pennsylvanians close
On twice ten thousand gallant foes.

Line after line the troopers came
To the edge of the woods that was ringed with flame
Rode in, and sabered, and shot,—and fell;
Nor came one back his wounds to tell.

And full in the midst rose Keenan, tall,
In the gloom like a martyr awaiting his fall,
While the circle-stroke of his saber, swung
Round his head, like a halo there, luminous hung.

Line after line, aye, whole platoons,
Struck dead in their saddles, of brave dragoons,
By the maddened horses were onward borne,
And into the vortex flung, trampled and torn;
As Keenan fought with his men, side by side.
So they rode, till there were no more to ride.

And over them, lying there shattered and mute,
What deep echo rolls?—'T is a death-salute
From the cannon in place; for, heroes, you braved
Your fate not in vain; the army was saved!

Over them now,—year following year,—
Over their graves the pine cones fall,
And the whippoorwill chants his specter call;
But they stir not again, they raise no cheer;
They have ceased. But their glory shall never cease,
Nor their light be quenched in the light of peace.
The rush of their charge is resounding still
That saved the army at Chancellorsville.

65

GREENCASTLE JENNY [1]

HELEN GRAY CONE

Oh, Greencastle streets were a stream of steel
   With the slanted muskets the soldiers bore,
And the scared earth muttered and shook to feel
   The tramp and the rumble of Longstreet's [2] Corps;
The bands were blaring *The Bonny Blue Flag,*
   And the banners borne were a motley many;
And watching the gray column wind and drag
   Was a slip of a girl—we'll call her Jenny.

A slip of a girl—what needs her name?—
   With her cheeks aflame and her lips aquiver,
As she leaned and looked with a loyal shame
   On the steady flow of the steely river:
Till a storm grew black in her hazel eyes
   Time had not tamed, nor a lover sighed for;
And she ran and she girded her, apron-wise,
   With the flag she loved and her brothers died for.

Out of the doorway they saw her start
   (Pickett's [3] Virginians were marching through),
The hot little foolish hero-heart
   Armored with stars and the sacred blue.
Clutching the folds of red and white
   Stood she and bearded those ranks of theirs,
Shouting shrilly with all her might,
   "Come and take it, the man that dares!"

---

1. The incident narrated in the poem occurred as the Confederate army was on its way towards Gettysburg. The name of the girl is not known.

2. **Longstreet.** A brilliant Confederate general.

3. **Pickett.** The Confederate general who led in the famous charge at Gettysburg, after which battle the Confederate army was compelled to retreat.

Pickett's Virginians were passing through;
  Supple as steel and brown as leather,
Rusty and dusty of hat and shoe,
  Wonted to hunger and war and weather;
Peerless, fearless, an army's flower!
  Sterner soldiers the world saw never,
Marching lightly, that summer hour,
  To death and failure and fame forever.

Rose from the rippling ranks a cheer;
  Pickett saluted, with bold eyes beaming,
Sweeping his hat like a cavalier,
  With his tawny locks in the warm wind streaming.
Fierce little Jenny! her courage fell,
  As the firm lines flickered with friendly laughter,
And Greencastle streets gave back the yell
  That Gettysburg slopes gave back soon after.

So they cheered for the flag they fought
  With the generous glow of the stubborn fighter,
Loving the brave as the brave men ought,
  And never a finger was raised to fright her:
So they marched, though they knew it not,
  Through the fresh green June to the shock infernal,
To the hell of the shell and the plunging shot,
  And the charge that has won them a name eternal.

And she felt at last, as she hid her face,
  There had lain at the root of her childish daring
A trust in the men of her own brave race,
  And a secret faith in the foe's forbearing.
And she sobbed, till the roll of the rumbling gun
  And the swinging tramp of the marching men
Were a memory only, and day was done,
  And the stars in the fold of the blue again.
(*Thank God that the day of the sword is done,*
  And the stars in the fold of the blue again!)

66

VIVE LA FRANCE![1]

CHARLOTTE HOLMES CRAWFORD

Franceline rose in the dawning gray,
And her heart would dance though she knelt to pray,
For her man Michel had holiday,
    Fighting for France.

She offered her prayer by the cradle-side,
And with baby palms folded in hers she cried:
"If I have but one prayer, dear, crucified
    Christ—save France!

"But if I have two, then, by Mary's grace,
Carry me safe to the meeting-place,
Let me look once again on my dear love's face,
    Save him for France!"

She crooned to her boy: "Oh, how glad he'll be,
Little three-months old, to set eyes on thee!
For, 'Rather than gold, would I give,' wrote he,
    'A son to France.'

"Come, now, be good, little stray *sauterelle*,[2]
For we're going by-by to thy papa Michel,
But I'll not say where for fear thou wilt tell,
    Little pigeon of France!

"Six days' leave and a year between!
But what would you have? In six days clean,
Heaven was made," said Franceline,
    "Heaven and France."

1. Vive la France. Long live France! Written in 1916.
2. Sauterelle. Grasshopper.

She came to the town of the nameless name,
To the marching troops in the street she came,
And she held high her boy like a taper flame
    Burning for France.

Fresh from the trenches and gray with grime,
Silent they marched like a pantomime;
"But what need of music? My heart beats time—
    Vive la France!"

His regiment comes. Oh, then where is he?
"There is dust in my eyes, for I cannot see,—
Is that my Michel to the right of thee,
    Soldier of France?"

Then out of the ranks a comrade fell,—
"Yesterday—'twas a splinter of shell—
And he whispered thy name, did thy poor Michel,
    Dying for France."

The tread of the troops on the pavement throbbed
Like a woman's heart of its last joy robbed,
As she lifted her boy to the flag, and sobbed:
    "*Vive la France!*"

67

THE HELL-GATE OF SOISSONS [1]

Herbert Kaufman

My name is Darino, the poet. You have heard? *Oui,
Comédie Française.* [2]
Perchance it has happened, *mon ami,* [3] you know of my
unworthy lays.
Ah, then you must guess how my fingers are itching to
talk to a pen;
For I was at Soissons, and saw it, the death of the twelve
Englishmen.

My leg, *malheureusement,* [4] I left it behind on the banks
of the Aisne.
Regret? I would pay with the other to witness their valor
again.
A trifle, indeed I assure you, to give for the honor to tell
How that handful of British, undaunted, went into the
Gateway of Hell.

Let me draw you a plan of the battle. Here we French
and your Engineers stood;
Over there a detachment of German sharp-shooters lay
hid in a wood.
A *mitrailleuse* [5] battery planted on top of this well-chosen
ridge
Held the road for the Prussians and covered the direct
approach to the bridge.

1. **Soissons.** A city on the Aisne river, France, along which was
much severe fighting in the early part of the war begun in 1914.
2. **Oui,** etc. The poet was probably connected with this well-known
theater.
3. **Mon ami.** My friend.
4. **Malheureusement.** Unfortunately.
5. **Mitrailleuse.** Machine gun.

It was madness to dare the dense murder that spewed
    from those ghastly machines.
(Only those who have danced to its music can know what
    the *mitrailleuse* means.)
But the bridge on the Aisne was a menace; our safety
    demanded its fall:
"Engineers,—volunteers!" In a body, the Royals [6] stood
    out at the call.

Death at best was the fate of that mission—to their glory
    not one was dismayed.
A party was chosen—and seven survived till the powder
    was laid,
And *they* died with their fuses unlighted. Another
    detachment! Again
A sortie is made—all too vainly. The bridge still com-
    manded the Aisne.

We were fighting two foes—Time and Prussia—the
    moments were worth more than the troops.
We *must* blow up the bridge. A lone soldier darts out
    from the Royals and swoops
For the fuse! Fate seems with us. We cheer him; he
    answers—our hopes are reborn!
A ball rips his visor—his khaki shows red where another
    has torn.

Will he live—will he last—will he make it? *Hélas!* [7] And
    so near the goal!
A second, he dies! then a third one! A fourth! Still the
    Germans take toll!

---

6. Royals. A special detachment of English engineers.
7. Hélas. Alas!

A fifth, *magnifique!* [8] It is magic! How does he escape
them? He may . . . .
Yes, he *does!* See, the match flares! A rifle rings out
from the wood and says "Nay!"

Six, seven, eight, nine take their places, six, seven, eight,
nine brave their hail;
Six, seven, eight, nine—how we count them! But the
sixth, seventh, eighth, and ninth fail!
A tenth! *Sacré nom!* [9] But these English are soldiers—
they know how to try;
(He fumbles the place where his jaw was)—they show,
too, how heroes can die.

Ten we count—ten who ventured unquailing—ten there
were—and ten are no more!
Yet another salutes and superbly essays where the ten
failed before.
God of Battles, look down and protect him! Lord, his
heart is as Thine—let him live!
But *mitrailleuse* splutters and stutters, and riddles him
into a sieve.

Then I thought of my sins, and sat waiting the charge
that we could not withstand.
And I thought of my beautiful Paris, and gave a last
look at the land,
At France, my *belle France,* [10] in her glory of blue sky
and green field and wood.
Death with honor, but never surrender. And to die with
such men—it was good.

8. **Magnifique.** Magnificent.
9. **Sacré nom.** Sacred name!
10. **Belle France.** Beautiful France.

They are forming—the bugles are blaring—they will cross
in a moment and then . . . .
When out of the line of the Royals (your island, *mon ami,*
breeds men)
Burst a private, a tawny-haired giant—it was hopeless,
but, *ciel!* [11] how he ran!
Bon Dieu [12] please remember the pattern, and make many
more on his plan!

No cheers from our ranks, and the Germans, they halted
in wonderment too;
See, he reaches the bridge; ah! he lights it! I am dream-
ing, it *cannot* be true.
Screams of rage! *Fusillade!* [13] They have killed him!
Too late though, the good work is done.
By the valor of twelve English martyrs, the Hell-Gate
of Soissons is won!

68

THE ITALIAN IN ENGLAND [1]

ROBERT BROWNING

That second time they hunted me
From hill to plain, from shore to sea,
And Austria, hounding far and wide
Her blood-hounds through the country-side,

11. **Ciel.** Heaven.
12. **Bon Dieu.** Good God.
13. **Fusillade.** A general discharge of firearms.
1. For many years Italy struggled for freedom from Austria, and
for unification. Metternich, prime minister of Austria, was one of
Italy's most determined and hated enemies. The Charles in the poem,
a historical character, was an Italian generally considered a traitor.
The speaker is an Italian patriot in England, telling of one of his narrow escapes. "The incident is not historical, though something of the
kind might well have happened to any of the Italian patriots in their
revolt against Austrian domination."—Berdoe, *Browning Encyclopedia.*

Breathed hot and instant on my trace,—
I made six days a hiding-place
Of that dry green old aqueduct
Where I and Charles, when boys, have plucked
The fire-flies from the roof above,
Bright creeping through the moss they love:
—How long it seems since Charles was lost!
Six days the soldiers crossed and crossed
The country in my very sight;
And when that peril ceased at night,
The sky broke out in red dismay
With signal fires; well, there I lay
Close covered o'er in my recess,
Up to the neck in ferns and cress,
Thinking on Metternich our friend,
And Charles's miserable end,
And much beside, two days; the third,
Hunger o'ercame me when I heard
The peasants from the village go
To work among the maize; you know,
With us in Lombardy, they bring
Provisions packed on mules, a string
With little bells that cheer their task,
And casks, and boughs on every cask
To keep the sun's heat from the wine;
These I let pass in jingling line,
And, close on them, dear noisy crew,
The peasants from the village, too;
For at the very rear would troop
Their wives and sisters in a group
To help, I knew. When these had passed
I threw my glove to strike the last,
Taking the chance: she did not start,
Much less cry out, but stooped apart,
One instant rapidly glanced round,
And saw me beckon from the ground;

A wild bush grows and hides my crypt;
She picked my glove up while she stripped
A branch off, then rejoined the rest
With that; my glove lay in her breast.
Then I drew breath: they disappeared:
It was for Italy I feared.

    An hour, and she returned alone
Exactly where my glove was thrown.
Meanwhile came many thoughts; on me
Rested the hopes of Italy;
I had devised a certain tale
Which, when 'twas told her, could not fail
Persuade a peasant of its truth;
I meant to call a freak of youth
This hiding, and give hopes of pay,
And no temptation to betray.
But when I saw that woman's face,
Its calm simplicity of grace,
Our Italy's own attitude
In which she walked thus far, and stood,
Planting each naked foot so firm,
To crush the snake and spare the worm—
At first sight of her eyes, I said,

"I am that man upon whose head
They fix the price, because I hate
The Austrians over us: the State
Will give you gold—oh, gold so much!—
If you betray me to their clutch,
And be your death, for aught I know,
If once they find you saved their foe.
Now, you must bring me food and drink,
And also paper, pen and ink,
And carry safe what I shall write
To Padua, which you'll reach at night

Before the duomo [2] shuts; go in,
And wait till Tenebræ [3] begin;
Walk to the third confessional,
Between the pillar and the wall,
And kneeling whisper, *Whence comes peace?*
Say it a second time, then cease;
And if the voice inside returns,
*From Christ and Freedom; what concerns
The cause of Peace?*—for answer, slip
My letter where you placed your lip;
Then come back happy we have done
Our mother service—I, the son,
As you the daughter of our land!"

Three mornings more, she took her stand
In the same place, with same eyes:
I was no surer of sunrise
Than of her coming. We conferred
Of her own prospects, and I heard
She had a lover—stout and tall,
She said—then let her eyelids fall,
"He could do much"—as if some doubt
Entered her heart,—then, passing out,
"She could not speak for others, who
Had other thoughts; herself she knew":
And so she brought me drink and food.
After four days, the scouts pursued
Another path; at last arrived
The help my Paduan friends contrived
To furnish me: she brought the news.
For the first time I could not choose
But kiss her hand, and lay my own
Upon her head—"This faith was shown

2. **Duomo.** Cathedral.
3. **Tenebræ.** A service at which it is customary gradually to darken the church by extinguishing candles lighted at the beginning.

To Italy, our mother; she
Uses my hand and blesses thee."
She followed down to the sea-shore;
I left and never saw her more.

How very long since I have thought
Concerning—much less wished for—aught
Beside the good of Italy,
For which I live and mean to die!
I never was in love; and since
Charles proved false, what shall now convince
My inmost heart I have a friend?
However, if I pleased to spend
Real wishes on myself—say, three—
I know at least what one should be.
I would grasp Metternich until
I felt his red wet throat distill
In blood through these two hands. And next
—Nor much for that am I perplexed—
Charles, perjured traitor, for his part,
Should die slow of a broken heart
Under his new employers. Last
—Ah, there, what should I wish? For fast
Do I grow old and out of strength.
If I resolved to seek at length
My father's house again, how scared
They all would look, and unprepared!
My brothers live in Austria's pay
—Disowned me long ago, men say;
And all my early mates who used
To praise me so—perhaps induced
More than one early step of mine—
Are turning wise: while some opine
"Freedom grows license," some suspect
"Haste breeds delay," and recollect

They always said, such premature
Beginnings never could endure!
So, with a sullen "All's for best,"
The land seems settling to its rest.
I think then, I should wish to stand
This evening in that dear, lost land,
Over the sea the thousand miles,
And know if yet that woman smiles
With the calm smile; some little farm
She lives in there, no doubt: what harm
If I sat on the door-side bench,
And, while her spindle made a trench
Fantastically in the dust,
Inquired of all her fortunes—just
Her children's ages and their names,
And what may be the husband's aims
For each of them. I'd talk this out,
And sit there, for an hour about,
Then kiss her hand once more, and lay
Mine on her head, and go my way.

So much for idle wishing—how
It steals the time! To business now.

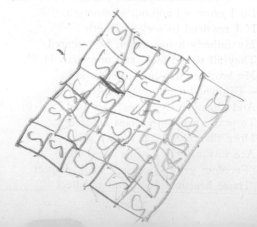

69

THE PRISONER OF CHILLON [1]

LORD BYRON

I

My hair is gray, but not with years,
 Nor grew it white
 In a single night,
As men's have grown from sudden fears;
My limbs are bowed, though not with toil,
 But rusted with a vile repose,
For they have been a dungeon's spoil,
 And mine has been the fate of those
To whom the goodly earth and air,
Are banned, and barred—forbidden fare;
But this was for my father's faith
I suffered chains and courted death;
That father perished at the stake
For tenets [2] he would not forsake;
And for the same his lineal race
In darkness found a dwelling place;
We were seven—who now are one,
 Six in youth, and one in age,
Finished as they had begun,
 Proud of Persecution's rage;
One in fire, and two in field,
Their belief with blood have sealed:

1. François de Bonnivard, a French reformer, aided the Genevese against Charles III of Savoy. He was imprisoned in the Castle of Chillon, on the shores of Lake Geneva, Switzerland, for six years, 1530-1536. He had no brothers in prison with him. Byron has invented much of the story in the poem to intensify the picture, and thus make a stronger case against tyranny.

2. **Tenets.** Beliefs.

Dying as their father died,
For the God their foes denied;—
Three were in a dungeon cast,
Of whom this wreck is left the last.

II

There are seven pillars of Gothic mold
In Chillon's dungeons deep and old,
There are seven columns massy and gray,
Dim with a dull imprisoned ray,
A sunbeam which hath lost its way,
And through the crevice and the cleft
Of the thick wall is fallen and left:
Creeping o'er the floor so damp,
Like a marsh's meteor lamp:
And in each pillar there is a ring,
  And in each ring there is a chain;
That iron is a cankering thing,
  For in these limbs its teeth remain,
With marks that will not wear away
Till I have done with this new day,
Which now is painful to these eyes,
Which have not seen the sun so rise
For years—I cannot count them o'er,
I lost their long and heavy score
When my last brother drooped and died,
And I lay living by his side.

III

They chained us each to a column stone,
And we were three—yet, each alone;
We could not move a single pace,
We could not see each other's face,

But with that pale and livid light
That made us strangers in our sight:
And thus together—yet apart,
Fettered in hand, but joined in heart,
'T was still some solace, in the dearth
Of the pure elements of earth,
To hearken to each other's speech,
And each turn comforter to each
With some new hope or legend old,
Or song heroically bold;
But even these at length grew cold.
Our voices took a dreary tone,
An echo of the dungeon stone,
  A grating sound—not full and free
  As they of yore were wont to be;
  It might be fancy—but to me
They never sounded like our own.

IV

I was the eldest of the three,
  And to uphold and cheer the rest
  I ought to do—and did my best—
And each did well in his degree.
  The youngest, whom my father loved,
Because our mother's brow was given
To him—with eyes as blue as heaven,
  For him my soul was sorely moved:
And truly might it be distressed
To see such bird in such a nest;
For he was beautiful as day—
  (When day was beautiful to me
  As to young eagles being free)—
  A polar day, which will not see
A sunset till its summer's gone,
  Its sleepless summer of long light,

The snow-clad offspring of the sun:
  And thus he was as pure and bright,
And in his natural spirit gay,
With tears for naught but others' ills,
And then they flowed like mountain rills,
Unless he could assuage the woe
Which he abhorred to view below.

v

The other was as pure of mind,
But formed to combat with his kind;
Strong in his frame, and of a mood
Which 'gainst the world in war had stood,
And perished in the foremost rank
  With joy:—but not in chains to pine:
His spirit withered with their clank,
  I saw it silently decline—
  And so perchance in sooth did mine:
But yet I forced it on to cheer
Those relics of a home so dear.
He was a hunter of the hills,
  Had followed there the deer and wolf;
  To him this dungeon was a gulf,
And fettered feet the worst of ills.

VI

Lake Leman [3] lies by Chillon's walls:
A thousand feet in depth below
Its massy waters meet and flow;
Thus much the fathom-line was sent
From Chillon's snow-white battlement,

---

3. **Lake Leman.** Lake Geneva.

Which round about the wave inthrals:
A double dungeon wall and wave
Have made—and like a living grave.
Below the surface of the lake
The dark vault lies wherein we lay:
We heard it ripple night and day;
  Sounding o'er our heads it knocked;
And I have felt the winter's spray
Wash through the bars when winds were high
And wanton in the happy sky;
  And then the very rock hath rocked,
  And I have felt it shake, unshocked,
Because I could have smiled to see
The death that would have set me free.

VII

I said my nearer brother pined,
I said his mighty heart declined,
He loathed and put away his food;
It was not that 't was coarse and rude,
For we were used to hunter's fare,
And for the like had little care:
The milk drawn from the mountain goat
Was changed for water from the moat,
Our bread was such as captive's tears
Have moistened many a thousand years,
Since man first pent his fellow men
Like brutes within an iron den;
But what were these to us or him?
These wasted not his heart or limb;
My brother's soul was of that mold
Which in a palace had grown cold,
Had his free breathing been denied
The range of the steep mountain's side.

But why delay the truth?—he died.
I saw, and could not hold his head,
Nor reach his dying hand—nor dead,—
Though hard I strove, but strove in vain,
To rend and gnash my bonds in twain.
He died, and they unlocked his chain,
And scooped for him a shallow grave
Even from the cold earth of our cave.
I begged them, as a boon, to lay
His corse in dust whereon the day
Might shine—it was a foolish thought,
But then within my brain it wrought,
That even in death his freeborn breast
In such a dungeon could not rest.
I might have spared my idle prayer—
They coldly laughed, and laid him there:
The flat and turfless earth above
The being we so much did love;
His empty chain above it leant,
Such murder's fitting monument!

VIII

But he, the favorite and the flower,
Most cherished since his natal hour,
His mother's image in fair face,
The infant love of all his race,
His martyred father's dearest thought,
My latest care, for whom I sought
To hoard my life, that his might be
Less wretched now, and one day free;
He, too, who yet had held untired
A spirit natural or inspired—
He, too, was struck, and day by day
Was withered on the stalk away.

Oh, God! it is a fearful thing
To see the human soul take wing
In any shape, in any mood:—
I've seen it rushing forth in blood,
I've seen it on the breaking ocean
Strive with a swol'n convulsive motion,
I've seen the sick and ghastly bed
Of Sin delirious with its dread:
But these were horrors—this was woe
Unmixed with such—but sure and slow;
He faded, and so calm and meek,
So softly worn, so sweetly weak,
So tearless, yet so tender—kind,
And grieved for those he left behind;
Withal the while a cheek whose bloom
Was as a mockery of the tomb,
Whose tints as gently sunk away
As a departing rainbow's ray—
An eye of most transparent light,
That almost made the dungeon bright,
And not a word of murmur, not
A groan o'er his untimely lot,—
A little talk of better days,
A little hope my own to raise,
For I was sunk in silence—lost
In this last loss, of all the most;
And then the sighs he would suppress
Of fainting nature's feebleness,
More slowly drawn, grew less and less:
I listened, but I could not hear—
I called, for I was wild with fear;
I knew 't was hopeless, but my dread
Would not be thus admonishéd;
I called, and thought I heard a sound—
I burst my chain with one strong bound,

And rushed to him:—I found him not,
I only stirred in this black spot,
I only lived—*I* only drew
The accursed breath of dungeon-dew;
The last, the sole, the dearest link
Between me and the eternal brink,
Which bound me to my failing race,
Was broken in this fatal place.
One on the earth, and one beneath—
My brothers—both had ceased to breathe.
I took that hand which lay so still,
Alas! my own was full as chill;
I had not strength to stir, or strive,
But felt that I was still alive—
A frantic feeling, when we know
That what we love shall ne'er be so.
　　I know not why
　　　I could not die,
I had no earthly hope—but faith,
And that forbade a selfish death.

IX

What next befell me then and there
　I know not well—I never knew—
First came the loss of light, and air,
　And then of darkness too:
I had no thought, no feeling—none—
Among the stones I stood a stone,
And was, scarce conscious what I wist,
As shrubless crags within the mist;
For all was blank, and bleak, and gray;
It was not night—it was not day,
It was not even the dungeon-light,
So hateful to my heavy sight,

But vacancy absorbing space,
And fixedness, without a place;
There were no stars, no earth, no time,
No check, no change, no good, no crime,
But silence, and a stirless breath
Which neither was of life nor death;
A sea of stagnant idleness,
Blind, boundless mute, and motionless!

x

A light broke in upon my brain,—
  It was the carol of a bird;
It ceased, and then it came again,
  The sweetest song ear ever heard,
And mine was thankful till my eyes
Ran over with the glad surprise,
And they that moment could not see
I was the mate of misery;
But then by dull degrees came back
My senses to their wonted track;
I saw the dungeon walls and floor
Close slowly round me as before,
I saw the glimmer of the sun
Creeping as it before had done,
But through the crevice where it came
That bird was perched, as fond and tame,
  And tamer than upon the tree;
A lovely bird, with azure wings,
And song that said a thousand things,
  And seemed to say them all for me!
I never saw its like before,
I ne'er shall see its likeness more:
It seemed like me to want a mate,
But was not half so desolate,

And it was come to love me when
None lived to love me so again,
And cheering from my dungeon's brink,
Had brought me back to feel and think.
I know not if it late were free,
    Or broke its cage to perch on mine,
But knowing well captivity,
    Sweet bird! I could not wish for thine!
Or if it were, in wingéd guise,
A visitant from Paradise;
For—Heaven forgive that thought! the while
Which made me both to weep and smile;
I sometimes deemed that it might be
My brother's soul come down to me;
But then at last away it flew,
And then 't was mortal well I knew,
For he would never thus have flown,
And left me twice so doubly lone,—
Lone as the corse within its shroud,
Lone as a solitary cloud,
    A single cloud on a sunny day,
While all the rest of heaven is clear,
A frown upon the atmosphere,
That hath no business to appear
    When skies are blue, and earth is gay.

XI

A kind of change came in my fate,
My keepers grew compassionate;
I know not what had made them so,
They were inured to sights of woe,
But so it was:—my broken chain
With links unfastened did remain,
And it was liberty to stride
Along my cell from side to side,

And up and down, and then athwart,
And tread it over every part;
And round the pillars one by one,
Returning where my walk begun,
Avoiding only, as I trod,
My brothers' graves without a sod;
For if I thought with heedless tread
My step profaned their lowly bed,
My breath came gaspingly and thick,
And my crushed heart fell blind and sick.

XII

I made a footing in the wall,
　It was not therefrom to escape,
For I had buried one and all
　Who loved me in a human shape;
And the whole earth would henceforth be
A wider prison unto me:
No child, no sire, no kin had I,
No partner in my misery;
I thought of this, and I was glad,
For thought of them had made me mad;
But I was curious to ascend
To my barred windows, and to bend
Once more, upon the mountains high,
The quiet of a loving eye.

XIII

I saw them—and they were the same,
They were not changed like me in frame;
I saw their thousand years of snow
On high—their wide long lake below,
And the blue Rhone in fullest flow;

I heard the torrents leap and gush
O'er channelled rock and broken bush;
I saw the white-walled distant town,
And whiter sails go skimming down;
And then there was a little isle,
Which in my very face did smile,
   The only one in view;
A small green isle, it seemed no more,
Scarce broader than my dungeon floor,
But in it there were three tall trees,
And o'er it blew the mountain breeze,
And by it there were waters flowing,
And on it there were young flowers growing,
   Of gentle breath and hue.
The fish swam by the castle wall,
And they seemed joyous each and all;
The eagle rode the rising blast,
Methought he never flew so fast
As then to me he seemed to fly,
And then new tears came in my eye,
And I felt troubled—and would fain
I had not left my recent chain;
And when I did descend again,
The darkness of my dim abode
Fell on me as a heavy load;
It was as is a new-dug grave,
Closing o'er one we sought to save,—
And yet my glance, too much oppressed,
Had almost need of such a rest.

XIV

It might be months, or years, or days,
   I kept no count—I took no note,
I had no hope my eyes to raise,
   And clear them of their dreary mote:

At last men came to set me free,
  I asked not why, and recked not where;
It was at length the same to me,
Fettered or fetterless to be,
  I learned to love despair.
And thus when they appeared at last,
And all my bonds aside were cast,
These heavy walls to me had grown
A hermitage—and all my own!
And half I felt as they were come
To tear me from a second home:
With spiders I had friendship made,
And watched them in their sullen trade,
Had seen the mice by moonlight play,
And why should I feel less than they?
We were all inmates of one place,
And I, the monarch of each race,
Had power to kill—yet, strange to tell!
In quiet we had learned to dwell—
My very chains and I grew friends,
So much a long communion tends
To make us what we are:—even I
Regained my freedom with a sigh.

70

HORATIUS [1]

A LAY MADE ABOUT THE YEAR OF THE CITY CCCLX

THOMAS BABINGTON MACAULAY

I

Lars Porsena [2] of Clusium
  By the Nine Gods [3] he swore
That the great house of Tarquin
  Should suffer wrong no more.
By the Nine Gods he swore it,
  And named a trysting day,
And bade his messengers ride forth,
East and west and south and north,
  To summon his array.

II

East and west and south and north
  The messengers ride fast,
And tower and town and cottage
  Have heard the trumpet's blast.

1. Because of their tyranny, the Tarquins were banished from Rome, 509 B. C. "The banished King Tarquinius, however, soon marched with a vast Etruscan army against Rome, and drove the Romans, who had advanced beyond the Tiber to meet him, back into the city. The Romans destroyed the wooden bridge, by which they effected their retreat, and thus cut off the pursuit of the Etruscans." —Abbot's *Italy*. The various places mentioned are in Italy or on neighboring shores. Macaulay says of the *Lays of Ancient Rome*, of which this is one:

"In the poems the author speaks, not in his own person, but in the persons of ancient minstrels who know only what Roman citizens born three or four hundred years before the Christian era may be supposed to have known, and who are in nowise above the passions and prejudices of their age and nation."

2. **Lars Porsena.** Emperor of the ancient Etruscans.

3. **Nine Gods.** The nine great gods of the Etruscans, who alone had the power of hurling the thunderbolt.

Shame on the false Etruscan
  Who lingers in his home,
When Porsena of Clusium
  Is on the march for Rome!

III

The horsemen and the footmen
  Are pouring in amain
From many a stately market-place,
  From many a fruitful plain;
From many a lonely hamlet,
  Which, hid by beech and pine,
Like an eagle's nest, hangs on the crest
  Of purple Apennine;

IV

From lordly Volaterræ,
  Where scowls the far-famed hold
Piled by the hands of giants
  For godlike kings of old;
From sea-girt Populonia,
  Whose sentinels descry
Sardinia's snowy mountain-tops
  Fringing the southern sky;

V

From the proud mart of Pisæ,
  Queen of the western waves,
Where ride Massilia's triremes [4]
  Heavy with fair-haired slaves;

---

4. **Triremes.** Warships with three banks of oars.

10

From where sweet Clanis wanders
  Through corn and vines and flowers;
From where Cortona lifts to heaven
  Her diadem of towers.

VI

Tall are the oaks whose acorns
  Drop in dark Auser's rill;
Fat are the stags that champ the boughs
  Of the Ciminian hill;
Beyond all streams Clitumnus
  Is to the herdsman dear;
Best of all pools the fowler loves
  The great Volsinian mere.[5]

VII

But now no stroke of woodman
  Is heard by Auser's rill;
No hunter tracks the stag's green path
  Up the Ciminian hill;
Unwatched along Clitumnus
  Grazes the milk-white steer;
Unharmed the water-fowl may dip
  In the Volsinian mere.

VIII

The harvests of Arretium
  This year old men shall reap;
This year young boys in Umbro
  Shall plunge the struggling sheep;

5. **Mere.** Sea, lake.

And in the vats of Luna
    This year the must [6] shall foam
Round the white feet of laughing girls,
    Whose sires have marched to Rome.

IX

There be thirty chosen prophets,
    The wisest of the land,
Who alway by Lars Porsena
    Both morn and evening stand;
Evening and morn the Thirty [7]
    Have turned the verses [8] o'er,
Traced from the right on linen white
    By mighty seers of yore.

X

And with one voice the Thirty
    Have their glad answer given:
"Go forth, go forth, Lars Porsena;
    Go forth, beloved of Heaven;
Go, and return in glory
    To Clusium's royal dome,
And hang round Nurscia's [9] altars
    The golden shields of Rome."

XI

And now hath every city
    Sent up her tale of men;
The foot are fourscore thousand,
    The horse are thousands ten.

6. **Must.** Grape juice.
7. **Thirty.** Priests, augurs, who interpreted the prophecies recorded in the sacred books.
8. **Verses.** Prophecies recorded in verse.
9. **Nurscia.** Goddess of the Volscians.

Before the gates of Sutrium
  Is met the great array.
A proud man was Lars Porsena
  Upon this trysting day.

XII

For all the Etruscan armies
  Were ranged beneath his eye,
And many a banished Roman,
  And many a stout ally;
And with a mighty following
  To join the muster came
The Tusculan Mamilius,
  Prince of the Latian name.

XIII

But by the yellow Tiber
  Was tumult and affright;
From all the spacious champaign
  To Rome men took their flight.
A mile around the city
  The throng stopped up the ways;
A fearful sight it was to see
  Through two long nights and days.

XIV

For aged folk on crutches,
  And women great with child,
And mothers sobbing over babes
  That clung to them and smiled,
And sick men borne in litters
  High on the necks of slaves,
And troops of sunburnt husbandmen
  With reaping-hooks and staves,

XV

And droves of mules and asses
　Laden with skins of wine,
And endless flocks of goats and sheep,
　And endless herds of kine,
And endless trains of wagons,
　That creaked beneath the weight
Of corn-sacks and of household goods,
　Choked every roaring gate.

XVI

Now from the rock Tarpeian [10]
　Could the wan burghers spy
The line of blazing villages
　Red in the midnight sky.
The Fathers of the City
　They sat all night and day,
For every hour some horseman came
　With tidings of dismay.

XVII

To eastward and to westward
　Have spread the Tuscan bands;
Nor house nor fence nor dovecote
　In Crustumerium stands.
Verbenna down to Ostia
　Hath wasted all the plain;
Astur hath stormed Janiculum, [11]
　And the stout guards are slain.

10. **Tarpeian.** A high rock from which traitors were hurled to death.
11. **Janiculum.** A high hill across the Tiber.

XVIII

I wis, in all the Senate
  There was no heart so bold
But sore it ached and fast it beat,
  When that ill news was told.
Forthwith up rose the Consul,
  Up rose the Fathers [12] all;
In haste they girded up their gowns,
  And hied them to the wall.

XIX

They held a council standing
  Before the River-Gate;
Short time was there, ye well may guess,
  For musing or debate.
Out spake the Consul roundly:
  "The bridge must straight go down;
For, since Janiculum is lost,
  Naught else can save the town."

XX

Just then a scout came flying,
  All wild with haste and fear:
"To arms! to arms! Sir Consul;
  Lars Porsena is here."
On the low hills to westward
  The Consul fixed his eye,
And saw the swarthy storm of dust
  Rise fast along the sky.

12. **Fathers.** Senators.

XXI

And nearer fast and nearer
  Doth the red whirlwind come;
And louder still and still more loud,
From underneath that rolling cloud,
Is heard the trumpet's war-note proud,
  The trampling and the hum.
And plainly and more plainly
  Now through the gloom appears,
Far to left and far to right,
In broken gleams of dark-blue light,
The long array of helmets bright,
  The long array of spears.

XXII

And plainly and more plainly,
  Above that glimmering line,
Now might ye see the banners
  Of twelve fair cities shine;
But the banner of proud Clusium
  Was highest of them all,
The terror of the Umbrian,
  The terror of the Gaul.

XXIII

And plainly and more plainly
  Now might the burghers know,
By port and vest, by horse and crest,
  Each warlike Lucumo.
There Cilnius of Arretium
  On his fleet roan was seen;

And Astur of the fourfold shield,
Girt with the brand none else may wield,
Tolumnius with the belt of gold,
And dark Verbenna from the hold
    By reedy Thrasymene.

XXIV

Fast by the royal standard,
    O'erlooking all the war,
Lars Porsena of Clusium
    Sat in his ivory car.
By the right wheel rode Mamilius,
    Prince of the Latian name;
And by the left false Sextus,
    That wrought the deed of shame.

XXV

But when the face of Sextus
    Was seen among the foes,
A yell that rent the firmament
    From all the town arose.
On the house-tops was no woman
    But spat towards him and hissed,
No child but screamed out curses
    And shook its little fist.

XXVI

But the Consul's brow was sad,
    And the Consul's speech was low,
And darkly looked he at the wall,
    And darkly at the foe.
"Their van will be upon us
    Before the bridge goes down;
And if they once may win the bridge,
    What hope to save the town?"

XXVII

Then out spake brave Horatius,
　The Captain of the Gate:
"To every man upon this earth
　Death cometh soon or late.
And how can man die better
　Than facing fearful odds,
For the ashes of his fathers
　And the temples of his Gods,

XXVIII

"And for the tender mother
　Who dandled him to rest,
And for the wife who nurses
　His baby at her breast,
And for the holy maidens
　Who feed the eternal flame,
To save them from false Sextus
　That wrought the deed of shame?

XXIX

"Hew down the bridge, Sir Consul,
　With all the speed ye may;
I, with two more to help me,
　Will hold the foe in play.
In yon strait path a thousand
　May well be stopped by three.
Now who will stand on either hand,
　And keep the bridge with me?"

XXX

Then out spake Spurius Lartius—
  A Ramnian [13] proud was he:
"Lo, I will stand at thy right hand,
  And keep the bridge with thee."
And out spake strong Herminius—
  Of Titian blood was he:
"I will abide on thy left side,
  And keep the bridge with thee."

XXXI

"Horatius," quoth the Consul,
  "As thou sayest, so let it be."
And straight against that great array
  Forth went the dauntless Three.
For Romans in Rome's quarrel
  Spared neither land nor gold,
Nor son nor wife, nor limb nor life,
  In the brave days of old.

XXXII

Then none was for a party;
  Then all were for the State;
Then the great man helped the poor,
  And the poor man loved the great;
Then lands were fairly portioned;
  Then spoils were fairly sold:
The Romans were like brothers
  In the brave days of old.

13. **Ramnian, Titian.** Two of the original three tribes of Rome.
Horatius belonged to the third tribe, the Luceres.

XXXIII

Now Roman is to Roman
　　More hateful than a foe;
And the Tribunes [14] beard the high,
　　And the Fathers grind the low.
As we wax hot in faction,
　　In battle we wax cold;
Wherefore men fight not as they fought
　　In the brave days of old.

XXXIV

Now while the Three were tightening
　　Their harness on their backs,
The Consul was the foremost man
　　To take in hand an axe;
And Fathers mixed with Commons
　　Seized hatchet, bar, and crow,
And smote upon the planks above,
　　And loosed the props below.

XXXV

Meanwhile the Tuscan army,
　　Right glorious to behold,
Came flashing back the noonday light,
Rank behind rank, like surges bright
　　Of a broad sea of gold.
Four hundred trumpets sounded
　　A peal of warlike glee,
As that great host, with measured tread,
And spears advanced and ensigns spread,
Rolled slowly towards the bridge's head,
　　Where stood the dauntless Three.

14. **Tribunes.** Officers appointed to protect the interests of the
common people.

XXXVI

The Three stood calm and silent,
  And looked upon the foes,
And a great shout of laughter
  From all the vanguard rose;
And forth three chiefs came spurring
  Before that deep array;
To earth they sprang, their swords they drew,
And lifted high their shields, and flew
  To win the narrow way;

XXXVII

Aunus from green Tifernum,
  Lord of the Hill of Vines;
And Seius, whose eight hundred slaves
  Sicken in Ilva's mines;
And Picus, long to Clusium
  Vassal in peace and war,
Who led to fight his Umbrian powers
From that gray crag where, girt with towers,
The fortress of Nequinum lowers
  O'er the pale waves of Nar.

XXXVIII

Stout Lartius hurled down Aunus
  Into the stream beneath;
Herminius struck at Seius,
  And clove him to the teeth;
At Picus brave Horatius
  Darted one fiery thrust,
And the proud Umbrian's gilded arms
  Clashed in the bloody dust.

XXXIX

Then Ocnus of Falerii
   Rushed on the Roman Three;
And Lausulus of Urgo,
   The rover of the sea;
And Aruns of Volsinium,
   Who slew the great wild boar,
The great wild boar that had his den
Amidst the reeds of Cosa's fen,
And wasted fields and slaughtered men
   Along Albinia's shore.

XL

Herminius smote down Aruns;
   Lartius laid Ocnus low;
Right to the heart of Lausulus
   Horatius sent a blow.
"Lie there," he cried, "fell pirate!
   No more, aghast and pale,
From Ostia's walls the crowd shall mark
The track of thy destroying bark.
No more Campania's hinds shall fly
To woods and caverns, when they spy
   Thy thrice accursed sail."

XLI

But now no sound of laughter
   Was heard among the foes;
A wild and wrathful clamor
   From all the vanguard rose.
Six spears' length from the entrance
   Halted that deep array,
And for a space no man came forth
   To win the narrow way.

XLII

But hark! the cry is "Astur!"
  And lo! the ranks divide,
And the great Lord of Luna
  Comes with his stately stride.
Upon his ample shoulders
  Clangs loud the fourfold shield,
And in his hand he shakes the brand
  Which none but he can wield.

XLIII

He smiled on those bold Romans
  A smile serene and high;
He eyed the flinching Tuscans,
  And scorn was in his eye.
Quoth he, "The she-wolf's litter
  Stands savagely at bay;
But will ye dare to follow,
  If Astur clears the way?"

XLIV

Then, whirling up his broadsword
  With both hands to the height,
He rushed against Horatius,
  And smote with all his might.
With shield and blade Horatius
  Right deftly turned the blow.
The blow, though turned, came yet too nigh;
It missed his helm, but gashed his thigh;
The Tuscans raised a joyful cry
  To see the red blood flow.

XLV

He reeled, and on Herminius
   He leaned one breathing-space;
Then, like a wildcat mad with wounds,
   Sprang right at Astur's face;
Through teeth and skull and helmet
   So fierce a thrust he sped,
The good sword stood a hand-breadth out
   Behind the Tuscan's head.

XLVI

And the great Lord of Luna
   Fell at that deadly stroke,
As falls on Mount Alvernus
   A thunder-smitten oak.
Far o'er the crashing forest
   The giant arms lie spread;
And the pale augurs, muttering low,
   Gaze on the blasted head.

XLVII

On Astur's throat Horatius
   Right firmly pressed his heel,
And thrice and four times tugged amain,
   Ere he wrenched out the steel.
"And see," he cried, "the welcome,
   Fair guests, that waits you here!
What noble Lucumo [15] comes next
   To taste our Roman cheer?"

15. **Lucumo.** Any Etruscan prince.

XLVIII

But at his haughty challenge
    A sullen murmur ran,
Mingled of wrath and shame and dread,
    Along that glittering van.
There lacked not men of prowess
    Nor men of lordly race;
For all Etruria's noblest
    Were round the fatal place.

XLIX

But all Etruria's noblest
    Felt their hearts sink to see
On the earth the bloody corpses,
    In the path the dauntless Three;
And from the ghastly entrance
    Where those bold Romans stood
All shrank, like boys who, unaware,
Ranging the woods to start a hare,
Come to the mouth of the dark lair
Where, growling low, a fierce old bear
    Lies amidst bones and blood.

L

Was none who would be foremost
    To lead such dire attack;
But those behind cried "Forward!"
    And those before cried "Back!"
And backward now and forward
    Wavers the deep array;
And on the tossing sea of steel
To and fro the standards reel,
And the victorious trumpet-peal
    Dies fitfully away.

LI

Yet one man for one moment
  Stood out before the crowd;
Well known was he to all the Three,
  And they gave him greeting loud:
"Now welcome, welcome, Sextus!
  Now welcome to thy home!
Why dost thou stay and turn away?
  Here lies the road to Rome."

LII

Thrice looked he at the city,
  Thrice looked he at the dead;
And thrice came on in fury,
  And thrice turned back in dread,
And, white with fear and hatred,
  Scowled at the narrow way,
Where, wallowing in a pool of blood,
  The bravest Tuscans lay.

LIII

But meanwhile axe and lever
  Have manfully been plied,
And now the bridge hangs tottering
  Above the boiling tide.
"Come back, come back, Horatius!"
  Loud cried the Fathers all.
"Back, Lartius! back, Herminius!
  Back, ere the ruin fall!"

LIV

Back darted Spurius Lartius,
  Herminius darted back;
And, as they passed, beneath their feet
  They felt the timbers crack.

But when they turned their faces,
   And on the farther shore
Saw brave Horatius stand alone,
   They would have crossed once more.

LV

But with a crash like thunder
   Fell every loosened beam,
And, like a dam, the mighty wreck
   Lay right athwart the stream.
And a long shout of triumph
   Rose from the walls of Rome,
As to the highest turret-tops
   Was splashed the yellow foam.

LVI

And, like a horse unbroken
   When first he feels the rein,
The furious river struggled hard,
   And tossed his tawny mane,
And burst the curb and bounded,
   Rejoicing to be free,
And, whirling down in fierce career
Battlement and plank and pier,
   Rushed headlong to the sea.

LVII

Alone stood brave Horatius,
   But constant still in mind,
Thrice thirty thousand foes before
   And the broad flood behind.
"Down with him!" cried false Sextus,
   With a smile on his pale face.
"Now yield thee," cried Lars Porsena,
   "Now yield thee to our grace."

LVIII

Round turned he, as not deigning
   Those craven ranks to see;
Naught spake he to Lars Porsena,
   To Sextus naught spake he;
But he saw on Palatinus [16]
   The white porch of his home,
And he spake to the noble river
   That rolls by the towers of Rome.

LIX

"O Tiber! father Tiber!
   To whom the Romans pray,
A Roman's life, a Roman's arms,
   Take thou in charge this day!"
So he spake, and speaking sheathed
   The good sword by his side,
And with his harness on his back
   Plunged headlong in the tide.

LX

No sound of joy or sorrow
   Was heard from either bank,
But friends and foes in dumb surprise,
With parted lips and straining eyes,
   Stood gazing where he sank;
And when above the surges
   They saw his crest appear,
All Rome sent forth a rapturous cry,
And even the ranks of Tuscany
   Could scarce forbear to cheer.

16. **Palatinus.** One of the Seven Hills of Rome.

LXI

But fiercely ran the current,
　Swollen high by months of rain;
And fast his blood was flowing,
　And he was sore in pain,
And heavy with his armor,
　And spent with changing blows;
And oft they thought him sinking,
　But still again he rose.

LXII

Never, I ween, did swimmer,
　In such an evil case,
Struggle through such a raging flood
　Safe to the landing place;
But his limbs were borne up bravely
　By the brave heart within,
And our good father Tiber
　Bore bravely up his chin.

LXIII

"Curse on him!" quoth false Sextus;
　"Will not the villain drown?
But for this stay, ere close of day
　We should have sacked the town!"
"Heaven help him!" quoth Lars Porsena,
　"And bring him safe to shore;
For such a gallant feat of arms
　Was never seen before."

LXIV

And now he feels the bottom;
　Now on dry earth he stands;
Now round him throng the Fathers
　To press his gory hands;

And now, with shouts and clapping
And noise of weeping loud,
He enters through the River-Gate,
Borne by the joyous crowd.

LXV

They gave him of the corn-land [17]
That was of public right,
As much as two strong oxen
Could plow from morn till night;
And they made a molten image
And set it up on high,
And there it stands unto this day
To witness if I lie.

LXVI

It stands in the Comitium,[18]
Plain for all folk to see,
Horatius in his harness
Halting upon one knee;
And underneath is written
In letters all of gold
How valiantly he kept the bridge
In the brave days of old.

LXVII

And still his name sounds stirring
Unto the men of Rome,
As the trumpet-blast that cries to them
To charge the Volscian home;

17. **Corn-land.** Lands belonging to the state.
18. **Comitium.** An open space adjoining the Forum.

And wives still pray to Juno [19]
  For boys with hearts as bold
As his who kept the bridge so well
  In the brave days of old.

LXVIII

And in the nights of winter,
  When the cold north winds blow,
And the long howling of the wolves
  Is heard amidst the snow;
When round the lonely cottage
  Roars loud the tempest's din,
And the good logs of Algidus
  Roar louder yet within;

LXIX

When the oldest cask is opened,
  And the largest lamp is lit;
When the chestnuts glow in the embers,
  And the kid turns on the spit;
When young and old in circle
  Around the firebrands close;
When the girls are weaving baskets,
  And the lads are shaping bows;

LXX

When the goodman mends his armor,
  And trims his helmet's plume;
When the goodwife's shuttle merrily
  Goes flashing through the loom;
With weeping and with laughter
  Still is the story told,
How well Horatius kept the bridge
  In the brave days of old.

19. **Juno.** Roman goddess; protectress of women.

71

RIZPAH [1]

ALFRED TENNYSON

I

Wailing, wailing, wailing, the wind over land and sea—
And Willy's voice in the wind, "O mother, come out to me!"
Why should he call me tonight, when he knows that I cannot go?
For the downs [2] are as bright as day, and the full moon stares at the snow.

II

We should be seen, my dear; they would spy us out of the town.
The loud black nights for us, and the storm rushing over the down,
When I cannot see my own hand, but am led by the creak of the chain,
And grovel and grope for my son till I find myself drenched with the rain.

III

Anything fallen again? nay—what was there left to fall?
I have taken them home, I have number'd the bones, I have hidden them all.

---

1. The story of this poem is very similar to the story of Rizpah in the Bible, 2 *Samuel* 21; 1-14. In the Bible story Rizpah had two sons hanged. She was not allowed to take down the bodies, but she "took sackcloth and spread it for her upon the rock, from the beginning of the harvest until water dropped upon them out of heaven, and suffered neither the birds of the air to rest on them by day, nor the beasts of the field by night." Tennyson founded his poem on an incident related in a penny magazine.

2. **Downs.** A tract of open upland.

What am I saying? and what are *you?* do you come as
a spy?

Falls? what falls? who knows? As the tree falls so
must it lie.

IV

Who let her in? how long has she been? you—what have
you heard?

Why did you sit so quiet? you never have spoken a word.

O—to pray with me—yes—a lady—none of their spies—

But the night has crept into my heart, and begun to darken
my eyes.

V

Ah—you, that have lived so soft, what should *you* know
of the night,

The blast and the burning shame and the bitter frost and
the fright?

I have done it, while you were asleep—you were only
made for the day.

I have gather'd my baby together—and now you may go
your way.

VI

Nay—for it's kind of you, Madam, to sit by an old dying
wife.

But say nothing hard of my boy, I have only an hour of
life.

I kiss'd my boy in the prison, before he went out to die.

"They dared me to do it," he said, and he never has told
me a lie.

I whipt him for robbing an orchard once when he was
but a child—

"The farmer dared me to do it," he said; he was always
so wild—

And idle—and couldn't be idle—my Willy—he never
    could rest.
The King should have made him a soldier, he would have
    been one of his best.

VII

But he lived with a lot of wild mates, and they never
    would let him be good;
They swore that he dare not rob the mail, and he swore
    that he would;
And he took no life, but he took one purse, and when all
    was done
He flung it among his fellows—"I'll none of it," said my
    son.

VIII

I came into court to the judge and the lawyers. I told
    them my tale,
God's own truth—but they kill'd him, they kill'd him for
    robbing the mail.
They hang'd him in chains for a show—we had always
    borne a good name—
To be hang'd for a thief—and then put away—isn't that
    enough shame?
Dust to dust—low down—let us hide! but they set him
    so high
That all the ships of the world could stare at him, passing
    by.
God 'ill pardon the hell-black raven and horrible fowls
    of the air,
But not the black heart of the lawyer who kill'd him and
    hang'd him there.

IX

And the jailer forced me away. I had bid him my last
　　goodbye;
They had fasten'd the door of his cell. "O mother!" I
　　heard him cry.
I couldn't get back tho' I tried, he had something further
　　to say,
And now I never shall know it. The jailer forced me
　　away.

X

Then since I couldn't but hear that cry of my boy that
　　was dead,
They seized me and shut me up: they fasten'd me down
　　on my bed.
"Mother, O mother!"—he call'd in the dark to me year
　　after year—
They beat me for that, they beat me—you know that I
　　couldn't but hear;
And then at the last they found I had grown so stupid
　　and still
They let me abroad again—but the creatures had worked
　　their will.

XI

Flesh of my flesh was gone, but bone of my bone was
　　left—
I stole them all from the lawyers—and you, will you call
　　it a theft?—
My baby, the bones that had suck'd me, the bones that had
　　laugh'd and had cried—
Theirs? O no! they are mine—not theirs—they had moved
　　in my side.

XII

Do you think I was scared by the bones? I kiss'd 'em, I
  buried 'em all—
I can't dig deep, I am old—in the night by the churchyard
  wall.
My Willy 'ill rise up whole when the trumpet of judgment 'ill sound;
But I charge you never to say that I laid him in holy
  ground.[3]

XIII

They would scratch him up—they would hang him again
  on the cursed tree.
Sin? O yes—we are sinners, I know—let all that be,
And read me a Bible verse of the Lord's good will toward
  men—
"Full of compassion and mercy, the Lord"—let me hear
  it again;
"Full of compassion and mercy—long-suffering." Yes,
  O yes!
For the lawyer is born but to murder—the Saviour lives
  but to bless.
*He'*ll never put on the black cap except for the worst of
  the worst,
And the first may be last—I have heard it in church—and
  the last may be first.
Suffering—O long-suffering—yes, as the Lord must know,
Year after year in the mist and the wind and the shower
  and the snow.

3. **Holy ground.** Criminals were not allowed Christian burial.

XIV

Heard, have you? what? they have told you he never repented his sin.

How do they know it? are *they* his mother? are *you* of his kin?

Heard! have you ever heard, when the storm on the downs began,

The wind that 'ill wail like a child and the sea that 'ill moan like a man?

XV

Election, Election and Reprobation [4]—it's all very well.

But I go tonight to my boy, and I shall not find him in Hell.

For I cared so much for my boy that the Lord has look'd into my care,

And He means me I'm sure to be happy with Willy, I know not where.

XVI

And if *he* be lost—but to save *my* soul, that is all your desire:

Do you think that I care for *my* soul if my boy be gone to the fire?

I have been with God in the dark—go, go, you may leave me alone—

You never have borne a child—you are just as hard as a stone.

4. **Election, Reprobation.** The reference is to the belief that God selects certain persons to be saved and others to be lost regardless of personal merits or faults.

XVII

Madam, I beg your pardon! I think that you mean to
 be kind,
But I cannot hear what you say for my Willy's voice in
 the wind—
The snow and the sky so bright—he used but to call in
 the dark,
And he calls to me now from the church and not from the
 gibbet—for hark!
Nay—you can hear it yourself—it is coming—shaking
 the walls—
Willy—the moon's in a cloud—Good-night. I am going.
 He calls.

72

KING ROBERT OF SICILY

HENRY WADSWORTH LONGFELLOW

Robert of Sicily, brother of Pope Urbane
And Valmond, Emperor of Allemaine,[1]
Appareled in magnificent attire,
With retinue of many a knight and squire,
On St. John's eve,[2] at vespers, proudly sat
And heard the priests chant the Magnificat.[3]
And as he listened, o'er and o'er again
Repeated, like a burden or refrain,
He caught the words, *"Deposuit potentes
De sede, et exaltavit humiles";*

1. **Allemaine.** Germany.
2. **St. John's Eve.** June 23.
3. **Magnificat.** The song of the Virgin Mary.

And slowly lifting up his kingly head
He to a learned clerk beside him said,
"What mean these words?" The clerk made answer meet,
"He has put down the mighty from their seat,
And has exalted them of low degree."
Thereat King Robert muttered scornfully,
" 'Tis well that such seditious words are sung
Only by priests and in the Latin tongue;
For unto priests and people be it known,
There is no power can push me from my throne!"
And leaning back, he yawned and fell asleep,
Lulled by the chant monotonous and deep.

When he awoke, it was already night;
The church was empty, and there was no light,
Save where the lamps, that glimmered few and faint,
Lighted a little space before some saint.
He started from his seat and gazed around,
But saw no living thing and heard no sound.
He groped towards the door, but it was locked;
He cried aloud, and listened, and then knocked,
And uttered awful threatenings and complaints,
And imprecations upon men and saints.
The sounds re-echoed from the roof and walls
As if dead priests were laughing in their stalls!

At length the sexton, hearing from without
The tumult of the knocking and the shout,
And thinking thieves were in the house of prayer,
Came with his lantern, asking, "Who is there?"
Half choked with rage, King Robert fiercely said,
"Open: 'tis I, the King! Art thou afraid?"
The frightened sexton, muttering, with a curse,
"This is some drunken vagabond, or worse!"
Turned the great key and flung the portal wide;
A man rushed by him at a single stride,

Haggard, half naked, without hat or cloak,
Who neither turned, nor looked at him, nor spoke,
But leaped into the blackness of the night,
And vanished like a specter from his sight.

Robert of Sicily, brother of Pope Urbane
And Valmond, Emperor of Allemaine,
Despoiled of his magnificent attire,
Bare-headed, breathless, and besprent with mire,
With sense of wrong and outrage desperate,
Strode on and thundered at the palace gate;
Rushed through the court-yard, thrusting in his rage
To right and left each seneschal [4] and page,
And hurried up the broad and sounding stair,
His white face ghastly in the torches' glare.
From hall to hall he passed with breathless speed;
Voices and cries he heard, but did not heed,
Until at last he reached the banquet-room,
Blazing with light, and breathing with perfume.

There on the dais sat another king,
Wearing his robes, his crown, his signet-ring,
King Robert's self in features, form, and height,
But all transfigured with angelic light!
It was an Angel; and his presence there
With a divine effulgence filled the air,
An exaltation, piercing the disguise,
Though none the hidden Angel recognize.

A moment speechless, motionless, amazed,
The throneless monarch on the Angel gazed,
Who met his looks of anger and surprise
With the divine compassion of his eyes;
Then said, "Who art thou? and why com'st thou here?"
To which King Robert answered, with a sneer,

4. **Seneschal.** A steward.

"I am the King, and come to claim my own
From an impostor, who usurps my throne!"
And suddenly, at these audacious words,
Up sprang the angry guests, and drew their swords;
The Angel answered, with unruffled brow,
"Nay, not the King, but the King's Jester, thou
Henceforth shalt wear the bells and scalloped cape,
And for thy counsellor shalt lead an ape;
Thou shalt obey my servants when they call,
And wait upon my henchmen in the hall!"

Deaf to King Robert's threats and cries and prayers,
They thrust him from the hall and down the stairs;
A group of tittering pages ran before,
And as they opened wide the folding-door,
His heart failed, for he heard, with strange alarms,
The boisterous laughter of the men-at-arms,
And all the vaulted chamber roar and ring
With the mock plaudits of "Long live the King!"

Next morning, waking with the day's first beam,
He said within himself, "It was a dream!"
But the straw rustled as he turned his head,
There were the cap and bells beside his bed,
Around him rose the bare, discolored walls,
Close by, the steeds were champing in their stalls,
And in the corner, a revolting shape,
Shivering and chattering sat the wretched ape.
It was no dream; the world he loved so much
Had turned to dust and ashes at his touch!

Days came and went; and now returned again
To Sicily the old Saturnian [5] reign;
Under the Angel's governance benign
The happy island danced with corn and wine,

5. Saturnian. A reference to the reign of Saturn, known as the
golden age.

And deep within the mountain's burning breast
Enceladus,[6] the giant, was at rest.

Meanwhile King Robert yielded to his fate,
Sullen and silent and disconsolate.
Dressed in the motley garb that Jesters wear,
With looks bewildered and a vacant stare,
Close shaven above the ears, as monks are shorn,
By courtiers mocked, by pages laughed to scorn,
His only friend the ape, his only food
What others left,—he still was unsubdued.
And when the Angel met him on his way,
And half in earnest, half in jest, would say,
Sternly, though tenderly, that he might feel
The velvet scabbard held a sword of steel,
"Art thou the King?" the passion of his woe
Burst from him in resistless overflow,
And, lifting high his forehead, he would fling
The haughty answer back, "I am, I am the King!"

Almost three years were ended; when there came
Ambassadors of great repute and name
From Valmond, Emperor of Allemaine,
Unto King Robert, saying that Pope Urbane
By letter summoned them forthwith to come
On Holy Thursday to his city of Rome.
The Angel with great joy received his guests,
And gave them presents of embroidered vests,
And velvet mantles with rich ermine lined,
And rings and jewels of the rarest kind.
Then he departed with them o'er the sea
Into the lovely land of Italy,
Whose loveliness was more resplendent made
By the mere passing of that cavalcade,

6. **Enceladus.** One of the giants who conspired against Jupiter,
and was finally buried alive under Mt. Etna.

With plumes, and cloaks, and housings, and the stir
Of jeweled bridle and of golden spur.

And lo! among the menials, in mock state,
Upon a piebald steed, with shambling gait,
His cloak of fox-tails flapping in the wind,
The solemn ape demurely perched behind,
King Robert rode, making huge merriment
In all the country towns through which they went.

The Pope received them with great pomp, and blare
Of bannered trumpets, on Saint Peter's square,
Giving his benediction and embrace,
Fervent, and full of apostolic grace.
While with congratulations and with prayers
He entertained the Angel unawares,
Robert, the Jester, bursting through the crowd,
Into their presence rushed, and cried aloud,
"I am the King! Look, and behold in me
Robert, your brother, King of Sicily!
This man, who wears my semblance to your eyes,
Is an impostor in a King's disguise.
Do you not know me? does no voice within
Answer my cry, and say we are akin?"
The Pope in silence, but with troubled mien,
Gazed at the Angel's countenance serene;
The Emperor, laughing, said, "It is strange sport
To keep a madman for thy Fool at court!"
And the poor, baffled Jester in disgrace
Was hustled back among the populace.

In solemn state the Holy Week went by,
And Easter Sunday gleamed upon the sky;
The presence of the Angel, with its light,
Before the sun rose, made the city bright,
And with new fervor filled the hearts of men,
Who felt that Christ indeed had risen again.

Even the Jester, on his bed of straw,
With haggard eyes the unwonted splendor saw,
He felt within a power unfelt before,
And, kneeling humbly on his chamber floor,
He heard the rushing garments of the Lord
Sweep through the silent air, ascending heavenward.

And now the visit ending, and once more
Valmond returning to the Danube's shore,
Homeward the Angel journeyed, and again
The land was made resplendent with his train,
Flashing along the towns of Italy
Unto Salerno, and from there by sea.
And when once more within Palermo's wall,
And, seated on the throne in his great hall,
He heard the Angelus [7] from convent towers,
As if the better world conversed with ours,
He beckoned to King Robert to draw nigher,
And with a gesture bade the rest retire;
And when they were alone, the Angel said,
"Art thou the King?" Then bowing down his head,
King Robert crossed both hands upon his breast,
And meekly answered him: "Thou knowest best!
My sins as scarlet are; let me go hence,
And in some cloister's school of penitence,
Across those stones, that pave the way to heaven,
Walk barefoot, till my guilty soul is shriven!"

The Angel smiled, and from his radiant face
A holy light illumined all the place,
And through the open window, loud and clear,
They heard the monks chant in the chapel near,
Above the stir and tumult of the street:
"He has put down the mighty from their seat,

7. **Angelus.** The Angelus bell, rung in connection with devotions commemorating Christ's incarnation

And has exalted them of low degree!"
And through the chant a second melody
Rose like the throbbing of a single string:
"I am an Angel, and thou art the King!"

King Robert, who was standing near the throne,
Lifted his eyes, and lo! he was alone!
But all appareled as in day of old,
With ermined mantle and with cloth of gold;
And when his courtiers came, they found him there
Kneeling upon the floor, absorbed in silent prayer.

73

JUGGLING JERRY

George Meredith

Pitch here the tent, while the old horse grazes:
    By the old hedge-side we'll halt a stage.
It's nigh my last above the daisies:
    My next leaf'll be man's blank page.
Yes, my old girl! and it's no use crying:
    Juggler, constable, king, must bow.
One that outjuggles all's been spying
    Long to have me, and he has me now.

We've traveled times to this old common:
    Often we've hung our pots in the gorse.[1]
We've had a stirring life, old woman!
    You, and I, and the old gray horse.

1. **Gorse.** Furze, a spiny, evergreen shrub.

Races, and fairs, and royal occasions,
   Found us coming to their call:
Now they'll miss us at our stations:
   There's a Juggler outjuggles all!

Up goes the lark, as if all were jolly!
   Over the duck-pond the willow shakes.
Easy to think that grieving's folly,
   When the hand's firm as driven stakes!
Ay, when we're strong, and braced, and manful,
   Life's a sweet fiddle: but we're a batch
Born to become the Great Juggler's [2] han'ful:
   Balls he shies up, and is safe to catch.

Here's where the lads of the village cricket:
   I was a lad not wide from here:
Couldn't I whip off the bale from the wicket?
   Like an old world those days appear!
Donkey, sheep, geese, and thatched ale-house— I know
     them!
   They are old friends of my halts, and seem,
Somehow, as if kind thanks I owe them:
   Juggling don't hinder the heart's esteem.

Juggling's no sin, for we must have victual:
   Nature allows us to bait for the fool.
Holding one's own makes us juggle no little;
   But, to increase it, hard juggling's the rule.
You that are sneering at my profession,
   Haven't you juggled a vast amount?
There's the Prime Minister,[3] in one Session,
   Juggles more games than my sins'll count.

---

2. **The Great Juggler.** Death.
3. **Prime Minister.** The man at the head of the party in control of
the English government.

I've murdered insects with mock thunder:
  Conscience, for that, in men don't quail.
I've made bread from the bump of wonder:
  That's my business, and there's my tale.
Fashion and rank all praised the professor:
  Ay! and I've had my smile from the Queen: [4]
Bravo, Jerry! she meant: God bless her!
  Ain't this a sermon on that scene?

I've studied men from my topsy-turvy
  Close, and, I reckon, rather true.
Some are fine fellows: some, right scurvy:
  Most, a dash between the two.
But it's a woman, old girl, that makes me
  Think more kindly of the race:
And it's a woman, old girl, that shakes me
  When the Great Juggler I must face.

We two were married, due and legal:
  Honest we've lived since we've been one.
Lord! I could then jump like an eagle:
  You danced bright as a bit o' the sun.
Birds in a May-bush we were! right merry!
  All night we kiss'd, we juggled all day.
Joy was the heart of Juggling Jerry!
  Now from his old girl he's juggled away.

It's past parsons to console us:
  No, nor no doctor fetch for me:
I can die without my bolus; [5]
  Two of a trade, lass, never agree!
Parson and Doctor!—don't they love rarely,
  Fighting the devil in other men's fields!
Stand up yourself and match him fairly:
  Then see how the rascal yields!

4. **Queen.** Queen Victoria.
5. **Bolus.** A large pill, as for a horse. He means he can die
without the aid of a doctor.

I, lass, have lived no gipsy, flaunting
   Finery while his poor helpmate grubs:
Coin I've stored, and you won't be wanting:
   You sha'n't beg from the troughs and tubs.
Nobly you've stuck to me, though in his kitchen
   Many a Marquis would hail you Cook!
Palaces you could have ruled and grown rich in,
   But your old Jerry you never forsook.

Hand up the chirper! [6] ripe ale winks in it;
   Let's have comfort and be at peace.
Once a stout draught made me light as a linnet.
   Cheer up! the Lord must have his lease.
May be—for none see in that black hollow—
   It's just a place where we're held in pawn,
And, when the Great Juggler makes as to swallow,
   It's just the sword-trick—I ain't quite gone.

Yonder came smells of the gorse, so nutty,
   Gold-like and warm: it's the prime of May.
Better than mortar, brick, and putty,
   Is God's house on a blowing day.
Lean me more up the mound; now I feel it:
   All the old heath-smells! Ain't it strange?
There's the world laughing, as if to conceal it!
   But He's by us, juggling the change.

I mind it well, by the sea-beach lying,
   Once—it's long gone—when two gulls we beheld,
Which, as the moon got up, were flying
   Down a big wave that sparked and swelled.
Crack went a gun: one fell: the second
   Wheeled round him twice, and was off for new luck:
There in the dark her white wing beckon'd:—
   Drop me a kiss—I'm the bird dead-struck!

6. **Chirper.** A vessel containing ale.

74

PAN IN WALL STREET [1]

Edmund Clarence Stedman

Just where the Treasury's marble front
    Looks over Wall Street's [2] mingled nations;
Where Jews and Gentiles most are wont
    To throng for trade and last quotations;
Where, hour by hour, the rates of gold
    Outrival, in the ears of people,
The quarter-chimes, serenely tolled
    From Trinity's [3] undaunted steeple,—

Even there I heard a strange, wild strain
    Sound high above the modern clamor,
Above the cries of greed and gain,
    The curbstone war, the auction's hammer;
And swift, on Music's misty ways,
    It led, from all this strife for millions,
To ancient, sweet-do-nothing days
    Among the kirtle-robed Sicilians.

And as it stilled the multitude,
    And yet more joyous rose, and shriller,
I saw the minstrel where he stood
    At ease against a Doric pillar:
One hand a droning organ played,
    The other held a Pan's-pipe (fashioned
Like those of old) to lips that made
    The reeds give out that strain impassioned.

    1. **Pan.** The Greek god of pastures, flocks, and forests; usually represented with the head and body of a man and the horns, ears, and legs of a goat.
    2. **Wall Street.** The chief financial center of the United States.
    3. **Trinity.** A church almost in the heart of the financial district of New York.

'T was Pan himself had wandered here
   A-strolling through this sordid city,
And piping to the civic ear
   The prelude of some pastoral ditty!
The demigod had crossed the seas,—
   From haunts of shepherd, nymph, and satyr,
And Syracusan times,—to these
   Far shores and twenty centuries later.

A ragged cap was on his head;
   But—hidden thus—there was no doubting
That, all with crispy locks o'erspread,
   His gnarlèd horns were somewhere sprouting;
His club-feet, cased in rusty shoes,
   Were crossed, as on some frieze you see them,
And trousers patched of divers hues,
   Concealed his crooked shanks beneath them.

He filled the quivering reeds with sound,
   And o'er his mouth their changes shifted,
And with his goat's-eyes looked around
   Where'er the passing current drifted;
And soon, as on Trinacrian hills [4]
   The nymphs and herdsmen ran to hear him,
Even now the tradesmen from their tills,
   With clerks and porters, crowded near him.

The bulls [5] and bears [6] together drew
   From Jauncey Court and New Street Alley,
As erst, if pastorals be true,
   Came beasts from every wooded valley;

---

4. **Trinacrian hills.** The hills of Sicily.
5. **Bulls.** A term applied to those who push prices up in the
stock market
6. **bears.** Those who try to lower the price of stocks.

And random passers stayed to list,—
  A boxer Ægon,[7] rough and merry,
A Broadway Daphnis,[8] on his tryst
  With Nais [9] at the Brooklyn Ferry.

A one-eyed Cyclops [10] halted long
  In tattered cloak of army pattern,
And Galatea [11] joined the throng,—
  A blowsy apple-vending slattern;
While old Silenus [12] staggered out
  From some new-fangled lunch-house handy,
And bade the piper, with a shout,
  To strike up Yankee Doodle Dandy!

A newsboy and a peanut-girl
  Like little Fauns [13] began to caper;
His hair was all in tangled curl,
  Her tawny legs were bare and taper;
And still the gathering larger grew,
  And gave its pence and crowded nigher,
While aye the shepherd-minstrel blew
  His pipe, and struck the gamut higher.

O heart of Nature, beating still
  With throbs her vernal passion taught her,—
Even here, as on the vine-clad hill,
  Or by the Arethusan [14] water!

---

 7. **Aegon.** A fabulous giant.
 8. **Daphnis.** A beautiful Sicilian shepherd.
 9. **Nais.** A water nymph.
10. **Cyclops.** Savage, one-eyed giants.
11. **Galatea.** A sea nymph.
12. **Silenus.** The foster father of Bacchus, god of wine and revelry.
13. **Fauns.** Rural deities, half goat, half man.
14. **Arethusan.** From Arethusa, a wood nymph who was changed
into a stream.

New forms may fold the speech, new lands
   Arise within these ocean-portals,
But Music waves eternal wands,—
   Enchantress of the souls of mortals!

So thought I,—but among us trod
   A man in blue, with legal baton,
And scoffed the vagrant demigod,
   And pushed him from the step I sat on.
Doubting I mused upon the cry,
   "Great Pan is dead!"—and all the people
Went on their ways:—and clear and high
   The quarter sounded from the steeple.

75

FLEURETTE

(*The Wounded Canadian Speaks*)

1916

ROBERT W. SERVICE

My leg? It's off at the knee.
Do I miss it? Well, some. You see
I've had it since I was born;
And lately a devilish corn.
(I rather chuckle with glee
To think how I've fooled that corn.)

But I'll hobble around all right.
It isn't that, it's my face.
Oh, I know I'm a hideous sight,
Hardly a thing in place.

Sort of gargoyle,[1] you'd say.
Nurse won't give me a glass,
But I see the folks as they pass
Shudder and turn away;
Turn away in distress . . .
Mirror enough, I guess.
I'm gay! You bet I *am* gay;
But I wasn't a while ago.
If you'd seen me even today,
The darndest picture of woe,
With this Caliban [2] mug of mine,
So ravaged and raw and red,
Turned to the wall—in fine
Wishing that I was dead . . .
What has happened since then,
Since I lay with my face to the wall,
The most despairing of men?
Listen! I'll tell you all.

That *poilu* [3] across the way,
With the shrapnel wound on his head,
Has a sister: she came today
To sit a while by his bed.
All morning I heard him fret:
"Oh, when will she come, Fleurette?"

Then sudden, a joyous cry;
The tripping of little feet;
The softest, tenderest sigh;
A voice so fresh and sweet;

1. **Gargoyle.** A grotesquely carved stone spout.
2. **Caliban.** A creature half man, half monster, in Shakespeare's *The Tempest.*
3. **Poilu.** French soldier.

Clear as a silver bell,
Fresh as the morning dews:
"C'est toi, c'est toi, Marcel!
Mon frere, comme je suis heureuse!" [4]

So over the blanket's rim
I raised my terrible face,
And I saw—how I envied him!
A girl of such delicate grace;
Sixteen, all laughter and love;
As gay as a linnet, and yet
As tenderly sweet as a dove;
Half woman, half child—Fleurette.

Then I turned to the wall again.
(I was awfully blue, you see),
And I thought with a bitter pain:
"Such visions are not for me."
So there like a log I lay,
All hidden, I thought from view,
When sudden I heard her say:
"Ah! Who is that *malheureux?"* [5]
Then briefly I heard him tell
(However he came to know)
How I'd smothered a bomb that fell
Into the trench, and so
None of my men were hit,
Though it busted me up a bit.

Well, I didn't quiver an eye,
And he chattered and there she sat;
And I fancied I heard her sigh—

4. C'est toi, etc. It is you, it is you, Marcel! My brother, how
happy I am.
5. Malheureux. Unhappy man.

But I wouldn't just swear to that.
And maybe she wasn't so bright,
Though she talked in a merry strain,
And I closed my eyes ever so tight,
Yet I saw her ever so plain:
Her dear little tilted nose,
Her delicate, dimpled chin,
Her mouth like a budding rose,
And the glistening pearls within;
Her eyes like the violet:
Such a rare little queen—Fleurette.

And at last when she rose to go,
The light was a little dim,
And I ventured to peep, and so
I saw her graceful and slim,
And she kissed him and kissed him, and oh
How I envied and envied him!

So when she was gone I said
In rather a dreary voice
To him of the opposite bed:
"Ah, friend, how you must rejoice!
But me, I'm a thing of dread.
For me nevermore the bliss,
The thrill of a woman's kiss."

Then I stopped, for lo! she was there,
And a great light shone in her eyes.
And me! I could only stare,
I was taken so by surprise,
When gently she bent her head:
"May I kiss you, sergeant?" she said.

Then she kissed my burning lips,
With her mouth like a scented flower,
And I thrilled to the finger-tips,
And I hadn't even the power
To say: "God bless you, dear!
And I felt such a precious tear
Fall on my withered cheek,
And darn it! I couldn't speak.

And so she went sadly away,
And I know that my eyes were wet.
Ah, not to my dying day
Will I forget, forget!
Can you wonder now I am gay?
God bless her, that little Fleurette!

76

GRAND-PÈRE

ROBERT W. SERVICE

And so when he reached my bed
The General made a stand:
"My brave young fellow," he said,
  "I would shake your hand."

So I lifted my arm, the right,
With never a hand at all;
Only a stump, a sight
  Fit to appall.

"Well, well. Now that's too bad!
That's sorrowful luck," he said;
"But there! You give me, my lad,
  The left instead"

So from under the blanket's rim
   I raised and showed him the other,
A snag as ugly and grim
    As its ugly brother.

He looked at each jagged wrist;
   He looked but he did not speak;
And then he bent down and kissed
    Me on either cheek.

You wonder now I don't mind
   I hadn't a hand to offer. . .
They tell me (you know I'm blind)
    'T was Grand-père Joffre.

77

HOW OSWALD DINED WITH GOD [1]

Edwin Markham

Over Northumbria's lone, gray lands,
   Over the frozen marl,[2]
Went flying the fogs from the fens and sands,
   And the wind with a wolfish snarl.

Frosty and stiff by the gray York wall
   Stood the rusty grass and the yarrow:[3]
Gone wings and songs to the southland, all—
   Robin and starling and sparrow.

1. "Oswald, 'the most Christian King of the Northumbrians,' was born about 604 A. D., shortly after the time of King Arthur. The moral power that reached its height in King Alfred had its first dawn in the character of Oswald."—Edwin Markham.

2. **Marl.** Earth.

3. **Yarrow.** A plant of the aster family.

Weary with weaving the battle-woof,
  Came the king and his thanes to the Hall:
Feast-fires reddened the beams of the roof,
  Torch flames waved from the wall.

Bright was the gold that the table bore,
  Where platters and beakers shone:
Whining hounds on the sanded floor
  Looked hungrily up for a bone.

Laughing, the king took his seat at the board,
  With his gold-haired queen at his right:
War-men sitting around them roared
  Like a crash of the shields in fight.

Loud rose laughter and lusty cheer,
  And gleemen [4] sang loud in their throats,
Telling of swords and the whistling spear,
  Till their red beards shook with the notes.

Varlets [5] were bringing the smoking boar,
  Ladies were pouring the ale,
When the watchman called from the great hall door:
  "O King, on the wind is a wail.

"Feebly the host of the hungry poor
  Lift hands at the gate with a cry:
Grizzled and gaunt they come over the moor,
  Blasted by earth and sky."

"Ho!" cried the king to the thanes, "make speed—
  Carry this food to the gates,
Off with the boar and the cask of mead—
  Leave but a loaf on the plates."

4. **Gleemen.** Musicians.
5. **Varlets.** Attendants.

Still came a cry from the hollow night:
  "King, this is one day's feast;
But days are coming with famine and blight;
  Wolf winds howl from the east!"

Hot from the king's heart leaped a deed,
  High as his iron crown:
(Noble souls have a deathless need
  To stoop to the lowest down.)

"Thanes, I swear by Godde's Bride
  This is a cursèd thing—
Hunger for the folk outside,
  Gold inside for the king!"

Whirling his war-ax over his head,
  He cleft each plate into four.
"Gather them up, O thanes," he said,
  "For the work-folk at the door.

"Give them this for the morrow's meat,
  Then shall we feast in accord:
Our half of the loaf will then be sweet—
  Sweet as the bread of the Lord!"

78

HOW THE GREAT GUEST CAME

EDWIN MARKHAM

I

Before the Cathedral in grandeur rose,
At Ingelburg where the Danube goes;
Before its forest of silver spires
Went airily up to the clouds and fires;
Before the oak had ready a beam,
While yet the arch was stone and dream—
There where the altar was later laid,
Conrad the cobbler plied his trade.

II

Doubled all day on his busy bench,
Hard at his cobbling for master and hench,
He pounded away at a brisk rat-tat,
Shearing and shaping with pull and pat,
Hide well hammered and pegs sent home,
Till the shoe was fit for the Prince of Rome.
And he sang as the threads went to and fro:
"Whether 'tis hidden or whether it show,
Let the work be sound, for the Lord will know."

III

Tall was the cobbler, and gray and thin,
And a full moon shone where the hair had been.
His eyes peered out, intent and afar,
As looking beyond the things that are.
He walked as one who is done with fear,
Knowing at last that God is near.

Only the half of him cobbled the shoes:
The rest was away for the heavenly news.
Indeed, so thin was the mystic screen
That parted the Unseen from the Seen,
You could not tell, from the cobbler's theme
If his dream were truth or his truth were dream.

IV

It happened one day at the year's white end,
Two neighbors called on their old-time friend;
And they found the shop, so meager and mean,
Made gay with a hundred boughs of green.
Conrad was stitching with face ashine,
But suddenly stopped as he twitched a twine:
"Old friends, good news! At dawn today,
As the cocks were scaring the night away,
The Lord appeared in a dream to me,
And said, 'I am coming your guest to be!'
So I've been busy with feet astir,
Strewing the floor with branches of fir.
The wall is washed and the shelf is shined,
And over the rafter the holly twined.
He comes today, and the table is spread
With milk and honey and wheaten bread."

V

His friends went home; and his face grew still
As he watched for the shadow across the sill.
He lived all the moments o'er and o'er,
When the Lord should enter the lowly door—
The knock, the call, the latch pulled up,
The lighted face, the offered cup.
He would wash the feet where the spikes had been;
He would kiss the hands where the nails went in;

And then at last he would sit with Him
And break the bread as the day grew dim.

VI

While the cobbler mused, there passed his pane
A beggar drenched by the driving rain.
He called him in from the stony street
And gave him shoes for his bruiséd feet.
The beggar went and there came a crone,
Her face with wrinkles of sorrow sown.
A bundle of fagots bowed her back,
And she was spent with the wrench and rack.
He gave her his loaf and steadied her load
As she took her way on the weary road.
Then came to his door a little child,
Lost and afraid in the world so wild,
In the big, dark world. Catching it up,
He gave it the milk in the waiting cup,
And led it home to its mother's arms,
Out of the reach of the world's alarms.

VII

The day went down in the crimson west
And with it the hope of the blesséd Guest,
And Conrad sighed as the world turned gray:
"Why is it, Lord, that your feet delay?
Did You forget that this was the day?"
Then soft in the silence a Voice he heard:
"Lift up your heart, for I kept my word.
Three times I came to your friendly door;
Three times my shadow was on your floor.
I was the beggar with bruiséd feet;
I was the woman you gave to eat;
I was the child on the homeless street!"

79

THE FOOL'S PRAYER

EDWARD ROWLAND SILL

The royal feast was done; the King
  Sought some new sport to banish care,
And to his jester cried: "Sir Fool,
  Kneel now, and make for us a prayer!"

The jester doffed his cap and bells,
  And stood the mocking court before;
They could not see the bitter smile
  Behind the painted grin he wore.

He bowed his head, and bent his knee
  Upon the monarch's silken stool;
His pleading voice arose: "O Lord,
  Be merciful to me, a fool!

"No pity, Lord, could change the heart
  From red with wrong to white as wool:
The rod must heal the sin; but, Lord,
  Be merciful to me, a fool!

" 'Tis not by guilt the onward sweep
  Of truth and right, O Lord, we stay;
'Tis by our follies that so long
  We hold the earth from heaven away.

"These clumsy feet, still in the mire,
  Go crushing blossoms without end;
These hard, well-meaning hands we thrust
  Among the heartstrings of a friend.

"The ill-timed truth we might have kept—
  Who knows how sharp it pierced and stung!
The word we had not sense to say—
  Who knows how grandly it had rung!

"Our faults no tenderness should ask,
  The chastening stripes must cleanse them all;
But for our blunders—Oh, in shame
  Before the eyes of heaven we fall.

"Earth bears no balsam for mistakes;
  Men crown the knave, and scourge the tool
That did his will; but Thou, O Lord,
  Be merciful to me, a fool!"

The room was hushed; in silence rose
  The King, and sought his gardens cool,
And walked apart, and murmured low,
  "Be merciful to me, a fool!"

80

OPPORTUNITY

Edward Rowland Sill

This I beheld, or dreamed it in a dream:—
There spread a cloud of dust along a plain;
And underneath the cloud, or in it, raged
A furious battle, and men yelled, and swords
Shocked upon swords and shields. A prince's banner
Wavered, then staggered back, hemmed in by foes.
A craven hung along the battle's edge,
And thought, "Had I a sword of keener steel—
That blue blade that the king's son bears,—but this

Blunt thing—!" he snapt and flung it from his hand,
And lowering crept away and left the field.
Then came the king's son, wounded, sore bestead,
And weaponless, and saw the broken sword,
Hilt-buried in the dry and trodden sand,
And ran and snatched it, and with battle-shout
Lifted afresh he hewed his enemy down,
And saved a great cause that heroic day.

81

THE REVERIE OF POOR SUSAN

William Wordsworth

At the corner of Wood Street, when daylight appears,
Hangs a Thrush that sings loud, it has sung for three
    years:
Poor Susan has pass'd by the spot, and has heard
In the silence of morning the song of the bird.

'Tis a note of enchantment; what ails her? She sees
A mountain ascending, a vision of trees;
Bright volumes of vapor through Lothbury glide,
And a river flows on through the vale of Cheapside.[1]

Green pastures she views in the midst of the dale
Down which she so often has tripp'd with her pail;
And a single small cottage, a nest like a dove's,
The one only dwelling on earth that she loves.

She looks, and her heart is in heaven: but they fade,
The mist and the river, the hill and the shade;
The stream will not flow, and the hill will not rise,
And the colors have all pass'd away from her eyes!

1. **Wood Street, Lothbury, Cheapside.** London streets.

82

COLUMBUS

Joaquin Miller

Behind him lay the gray Azores,
   Behind the Gates of Hercules;[1]
Before him not the ghost of shores,
   Before him only shoreless seas.
The good mate said: "Now must we pray,
   For lo! the very stars are gone.
Brave Adm'r'l, speak, what shall I say?"
   "Why, say: 'Sail on! sail on! and on!'"

"My men grow mutinous day by day;
   My men grow ghastly wan and weak."
The stout mate thought of home; a spray
   Of salt wave washed his swarthy cheek.
"What shall I say, brave Adm'r'l, say,
   If we sight naught but seas at dawn?"
"Why, you shall say at break of day:
   'Sail on! sail on! sail on! and on!'"

They sailed and sailed, as winds might blow,
   Until at last the blanched mate said:
"Why, now not even God would know
   Should I and all my men fall dead.
These very winds forget their way,
   For God from these dread seas is gone.
Now speak, brave Adm'r'l, speak and say"—
   He said: "Sail on! sail on! and on!"

1. **Gates of Hercules.** The Straits of Gibraltar.

They sailed. They sailed. Then spake the mate:
  "This mad sea shows his teeth tonight.
He curls his lip, he lies in wait,
  With lifted teeth, as if to bite!
Brave Adm'r'l, say but one good word:
  What shall we do when hope is gone?"
The words leapt like a leaping sword:
  "Sail on! sail on! sail on! and on!"

Then, pale and worn, he kept his deck,
  And peered through darkness. Ah, that night
Of all dark nights! And then a speck—
  A light! A light! A light! A light!
It grew, a starlit flag unfurled!
  It grew to be Time's burst of dawn.
He gained a world; he gave that world
  Its grandest lesson: "On! sail on!"

83

ABOU BEN ADHEM

Leigh Hunt

Abou Ben Adhem (may his tribe increase!)
Awoke one night from a deep dream of peace,
And saw within the moonlight in his room,
Making it rich and like a lily in bloom,
An angel writing in a book of gold:—
Exceeding peace had made Ben Adhem bold,
And to the presence in the room he said,
"What writest thou?" The vision raised its head,
And, with a look made of all sweet accord,
Answered, "The names of those who love the Lord."

"And is mine one?" said Abou. "Nay, not so,"
Replied the angel. Abou spoke more low,
But cheerly still; and said, "I pray thee, then,
Write me as one that loves his fellow-men."

The angel wrote, and vanished. The next night
It came again, with a great wakening light,
And showed the names whom love of God had blessed,—
And, lo! Ben Adhem's name led all the rest!

84

THE LEGEND BEAUTIFUL

HENRY WADSWORTH LONGFELLOW

"Hadst thou stayed, I must have fled!"
That is what the Vision said.
In his chamber all alone,
Kneeling on the floor of stone,
Prayed the Monk in deep contrition
For his sins of indecision,
Prayed for greater self-denial
In temptation and in trial;
It was noonday by the dial,
And the Monk was all alone.

Suddenly, as if it lightened,
An unwonted splendor brightened
All within him and without him
In that narrow cell of stone;
And he saw the Blessed Vision
Of our Lord, with light Elysian
Like a vesture wrapped about Him,
Like a garment round Him thrown.

Not as crucified and slain,
Not in agonies of pain,
Not with bleeding hands and feet,
Did the Monk his Master see;
But as in the village street,
In the house or harvest-field,
Halt and lame and blind He healed,
When He walked in Galilee.

In an attitude imploring,
Hands upon his bosom crossed,
Wondering, worshiping, adoring,
Knelt the Monk in rapture lost.
Lord, he thought, in heaven that reignest,
Who am I, that thus thou deignest
To reveal thyself to me?
Who am I, that from the center
Of thy glory thou shouldst enter
This poor cell, my guest to be?

Then amid his exaltation,
Loud the convent bell appalling,
From its belfry calling, calling,
Rang through court and corridor
With persistent iteration
He had never heard before.
It was now the appointed hour
When alike in shine or shower,
Winter's cold or summer's heat,
To the convent portals came
All the blind and halt and lame,
All the beggars of the street,
For their daily dole of food
Dealt them by the brotherhood;
And their almoner was he
Who upon his bended knee,

Rapt in silent ecstasy
Of divinest self-surrender,
Saw the Vision and the Splendor.
Deep distress and hesitation
Mingled with his adoration;
Should he go or should he stay?
Should he leave the poor to wait
Hungry at the convent gate,
Till the Vision passed away?
Should he slight his radiant guest,
Slight this visitant celestial,
For a crowd of ragged, bestial
Beggars at the convent gate?
Would the Vision there remain?
Would the Vision come again?
Then a voice within his breast
Whispered, audible and clear
As if to the outward ear:
"Do thy duty; that is best;
Leave unto thy Lord the rest!"

Straightway to his feet he started,
And with longing look intent
On the Blessed Vision bent,
Slowly from his cell departed,
Slowly on his errand went.

At the gate the poor were waiting,
Looking through the iron grating,
With that terror in the eye
That is only seen in those
Who amid their wants and woes
Hear the sound of doors that close,
And of feet that pass them by;
Grown familiar with disfavor,
Grown familiar with the savor

Of the bread by which men die!
But today, they know not why,
Like the gate of Paradise
Seemed the convent gate to rise,
Like a sacrament divine
Seemed to them the bread and wine.
In his heart the Monk was praying,
Thinking of the homeless poor,
What they suffer and endure;
What we see not, what we see;
And the inward voice was saying:
"Whatsoever thing thou doest
To the least of mine and lowest,
That thou doest unto me!"

Unto me! but had the Vision
Come to him in beggar's clothing,
Come a mendicant imploring,
Would he then have knelt adoring,
Or have listened with derision,
And have turned away with loathing?

Thus his conscience put the question,
Full of troublesome suggestion,
As at length, with hurried pace,
Towards his cell he turned his face,
And beheld the convent bright
With a supernatural light,
Like a luminous cloud expanding
Over floor and wall and ceiling.

But he paused with awe-struck feeling
At the threshold of his door,
For the Vision still was standing
As he left it there before,

When the convent bell appalling,
From its belfry calling, calling,
Summoned him to feed the poor.
Through the long hour intervening
It had waited his return,
And he felt his bosom burn,
Comprehending all the meaning,
When the Blessed Vision said,
"Hadst thou stayed, I must have fled!"

85

"HE FELL AMONG THIEVES"

HENRY NEWBOLT

"Ye have robbed," said he, "ye have slaughtered and
        made an end;
    Take your ill-got plunder, and bury the dead:
What will ye more of your guest and sometime friend?"
    "Blood for our blood," they said.

He laughed: "If one may settle the score for five
    I am ready; but let the reckoning stand till day:
I have loved the sunlight as dearly as any alive."
    "You shall die at dawn," said they.

He flung his empty revolver down the slope;
    He climbed alone to the eastward edge of the trees;
All night long in a dream untroubled of hope
    He brooded, clasping his knees.

He did not hear the monotonous roar that fills
    The ravine where the Yassin River sullenly flows;
He did not see the starlight on the Laspur hills,
    Or far Afghan snows.

He saw the April on his books aglow,
    The wistaria trailing in at the window wide;
He heard his father's voice from the terrace below
    Calling him down to ride.

He saw the gray little church across the park,
    The mounds that hide the loved and honored dead;
The Norman arch, the chancel softly dark,
    The brasses black and red.[1]

He saw the School Close,[2] sunny and green,
    The runner beside him, the stand by the parapet wall,
The distant tape, and the crowd roaring between
    His own name over all.

He saw the dark wainscot and timbered roof,
    The long tables, and the faces merry and keen;
The College Eight and their trainer dining aloof,
    The Dons [3] on the dais serene.

He watched the liner's stem plowing the foam,
    He felt her trembling speed and the thrash of her screw;
He heard her passengers' voices talking of home,
    He saw the flag she flew.

And now it was dawn. He rose strong on his feet,
    And strode to his ruined camp below the wood:
He drank the breath of the morning cool and sweet;
    His murderers round him stood.

Light on the Laspur hills was broadening fast,
    The blood-red snow-peaks chilled to a dazzling white;
He turned, and saw the golden circle at last,
    Cut by the Eastern height.

1. **Brasses.** Brass memorial tablets.
2 **School close.** Athletic field.
3. **Dons.** The college professors.

"O glorious Life, Who dwellest in earth and sun,
　I have lived, I praise and adore Thee."
　　　　　　　　　　　　　A sword swept.
Over the pass the voices one by one
　Faded, and the hill slept.

86

THE BOY AND THE ANGEL [1]

Robert Browning

Morning, evening, noon and night,
"Praise God!" sang Theocrite.

Then to his poor trade he turned,
Whereby the daily meal was earned.

Hard he labored, long and well;
O'er his work the boy's curls fell.

But ever, at each period,
He stopped and sang, "Praise God!"

Then back again his curls he threw,
And cheerful turned to work anew.

Said Blaise, the listening monk, "Well done;
I doubt not thou art heard, my son:

"As well as if thy voice today
Were praising God, the Pope's great way.

---

1. Browning is fond of the idea that "all service ranks the same with God." In this story the simple, loving praise of little Theocrite, the craftsman, is even sweeter than praise from the Pope himself.

12

"This Easter Day, the Pope at Rome
Praises God from Peter's dome."

Said Theocrite, "Would God that I
Might praise him that great way, and die!"

Night passed, day shone,
And Theocrite was gone.

With God a day endures alway,
A thousand years are but a day.

God said in heaven, "Nor day nor night
Now brings the voice of my delight."

Then Gabriel, like a rainbow's birth,
Spread his wings and sank to earth;

Entered, in flesh, the empty cell,
Lived there, and played the craftsman well;

And morning, evening, noon, and night,
Praised God in place of Theocrite.

And from a boy, to youth he grew:
The man put off the stripling's hue:

The man matured and fell away
Into the season of decay:

And ever o'er the trade he bent,
And ever lived on earth content.

(He did God's will; to him, all one
If on the earth or in the sun.)

God said, "A praise is in mine ear;
There is no doubt in it, no fear:

"So sing old worlds, and so
New worlds that from my footstool go.

"Clearer loves sound other ways:
I miss my little human praise."

Then forth sprang Gabriel's wings, off fell
The flesh disguise, remained the cell.

'Twas Easter Day: he flew to Rome,
And paused above Saint Peter's dome.

In the tiring-room close by
The great outer gallery,

With his holy vestments dight,
Stood the new Pope, Theocrite:

And all his past career
Came back upon him clear,

Since when, a boy, he plied his trade,
Till on his life the sickness weighed;

And in his cell, when death drew near,
An angel in a dream brought cheer:

And rising from the sickness drear
He grew a priest, and now stood here.

To the East with praise he turned,
And on his sight the angel burned.

I bore thee from thy craftsman's cell,
And set thee here; I did not well.

"Vainly I left my angel-sphere,
Vain was thy dream of many a year.

"Thy voice's praise seemed weak; it dropped—
Creation's chorus stopped!

"Go back and praise again
The early way, while I remain.

"With that weak voice of our disdain,
Take up creation's pausing strain.

"Back to the cell and poor employ:
Resume the craftsman and the boy!"

Theocrite grew old at home;
A new Pope dwelt in Peter's dome.

One vanished as the other died:
They sought God side by side.

87

TITHONUS [1]

ALFRED TENNYSON

The woods decay, the woods decay and fall,
The vapors weep their burthen to the ground,
Man comes and tills the field and lies beneath,
And after many a summer dies the swan.
Me only cruel immortality
Consumes: I wither slowly in thine arms,
Here at the quiet limit of the world,
A white-hair'd shadow roaming like a dream
The ever-silent spaces of the East,
Far-folded mists, and gleaming halls of morn.

Alas! for this gray shadow, once a man—
So glorious in his beauty and thy choice,
Who madest him thy chosen, that he seem'd
To his great heart none other than a God!
I ask'd thee, "Give me immortality."
Then didst thou grant mine asking with a smile,
Like wealthy men who care not how they give.
But thy strong Hours indignant work'd their wills,
And beat me down and marr'd and wasted me,
And tho' they could not end me, left me maim'd
To dwell in presence of immortal youth,
Immortal age beside immortal youth,
And all I was, in ashes. Can thy love,

1. "Aurora, goddess of the dawn, fell in love with Tithonus, son
of the king of Troy. She stole him away, and prevailed on Jupiter
to grant him immortality; but forgetting to have youth joined in the
gift, after some time she discovered that he was growing old. When
his hair was white she left his society. In time he lost the power of
using his limbs. Finally she turned him into a grasshopper."—Gayley's
Classic Myths.

Thy beauty, make amends, tho' even now,
Close over us, the silver star, thy guide,
Shines in those tremulous eyes that fill with tears
To hear me? Let me go: take back thy gift:
Why should a man desire in any way
To vary from the kindly race of men,
Or pass beyond the goal of ordinance
Where all should pause, as is most meet for all?

A soft air fans the cloud apart; there comes
A glimpse of that dark world where I was born.
Once more the old mysterious glimmer steals
From thy pure brows, and from thy shoulders pure,
And bosom beating with a heart renew'd.
Thy cheek begins to redden thro' the gloom,
Thy sweet eyes brighten slowly close to mine,
Ere yet they blind the stars, and the wild team
Which love thee, yearning for thy yoke, arise,
And shake the darkness from their loosen'd manes,
And beat the twilight into flakes of fire.

Lo! ever thus thou growest beautiful
In silence, then before thine answer given
Departest, and thy tears are on my cheek.

Why wilt thou ever scare me with thy tears,
And make me tremble lest a saying learnt,
In days far-off, on that dark earth, be true?
"The Gods themselves cannot recall their gifts."

Ay me! ay me! with what another heart
In days far-off, and with what other eyes
I used to watch—if I be he that watch'd—
The lucid outline forming round thee; saw
The dim curls kindle into sunny rings;
Changed with thy mystic change, and felt my blood

Glow with the glow that slowly crimson'd all
Thy presence and thy portals, while I lay,
Mouth, forehead, eyelids, growing dewy-warm
With kisses balmier than half-opening buds
Of April, and could hear the lips that kiss'd
Whispering I knew not what of wild and sweet,
Like that strange song I heard Apollo [2] sing,
While Ilion [3] like a mist rose into towers.

Yet hold me not for ever in thine East:
How can my nature longer mix with thine?
Coldly thy rosy shadows bathe me, cold
Are all thy lights, and cold my wrinkled feet
Upon thy glimmering thresholds, when the steam
Floats up from those dim fields about the homes
Of happy men that have the power to die,
And grassy barrows of the happier dead.
Release me, and restore me to the ground;
Thou seëst all things, thou wilt see my grave:
Thou wilt renew thy beauty morn by morn;
I earth in earth forget these empty courts,
And thee returning on thy silver wheels

2. Apollo. The god of music.
3. Ilion. Troy.

88

THE ANGELS OF BUENA VISTA [1]

JOHN GREENLEAF WHITTIER

Speak and tell us, our Ximena,[2] looking northward far
    away,
O'er the camp of the invaders, o'er the Mexican array,
Who is losing? who is winning? are they far or come
    they near?
Look abroad, and tell us, sister, whither rolls the storm
    we hear.

"Down the hills of Angostura still the storm of battle
    rolls;
Blood is flowing, men are dying; God have mercy on their
    souls!"
Who is losing? who is winning?—"Over hill and over
    plain,
I see but smoke of cannon clouding through the mountain
    rain."

Holy Mother! keep our brothers! Look, Ximena, look
    once more:
"Still I see the fearful whirlwind rolling darkly as before,
Bearing on, in strange confusion, friend and foeman,
    foot and horse,
Like some wild and troubled torrent sweeping down its
    mountain course."

---

1. "A letter written from Mexico during the Mexican war, when detailing some of the incidents at the terrible fight of Buena Vista, mentioned that Mexican women were seen hovering near the field of death, for the purpose of giving aid and succor to the wounded. One poor woman was found surrounded by maimed and suffering of both armies, ministering to the wants of Americans as well as Mexicans with impartial tenderness."—Whittier.

2. **Ximena**, pronounced Zimáynya.

Look forth once more, Ximena! "Ah! the smoke has
    rolled away;
And I see the Northern rifles gleaming down the ranks of
    gray.
Hark! that sudden blast of bugles! there the troop of
    Minon wheels;
There the Northern horses thunder, with the cannon at
    their heels.

"Jesu, pity! how it thickens! now retreat and now
    advance!
Right against the blazing cannon shivers Puebla's charg-
    ing lance!
Down they go, the brave young riders; horse and foot
    together fall;
Like a plowshare in the fallow, through them plow the
    Northern ball."

Nearer came the storm and nearer, rolling fast and
    frightful on:
Speak, Ximena, speak and tell us, who has lost, and who
    has won?
"Alas! alas! I know not; friend and foe together fall,
O'er the dying rush the living: pray, my sisters, for them
    all!"

"Lo! the wind the smoke is lifting: Blessed Mother, save
    my brain!
I can see the wounded crawling slowly out from heaps of
    slain.
Now they stagger, blind and bleeding; now they fall, and
    strive to rise;
Hasten, sisters, haste and save them, lest they die before
    our eyes!"

"Oh my heart's love! oh my dear one! lay thy poor head
    on my knee;
Dost thou know the lips that kiss thee? Canst thou hear
    me? canst thou see?
Oh, my husband, brave and gentle! oh, my Bernal, look
    once more
On the blessed cross before thee! mercy! mercy! all is
    o'er!"

Dry thy tears, my poor Ximena; lay thy dear one down to
    rest;
Let his hands be meekly folded, lay the cross upon his
    breast;
Let his dirge be sung hereafter, and his funeral masses
    said;
Today, thou poor bereaved one, the living ask thy aid.

Close beside her, faintly moaning, fair and young, a
    soldier lay,
Torn with shot and pierced with lances, bleeding slow his
    life away;
But, as tenderly before him, the lorn Ximena knelt,
She saw the Northern eagle shining on his pistol belt.

With a stifled cry of horror straight she turned away her
    head;
With a sad and bitter feeling looked she back upon her
    dead;
But she heard the youth's low moaning, and his struggling
    breath of pain,
And she raised the cooling water to his parching lips again.

Whispered low the dying soldier, pressed her hand and
    faintly smiled:
Was that pitying face his mother's? did she watch beside
    her child?

All his stranger words with meaning her woman's heart
supplied;
With her kiss upon his forehead "Mother!" murmured
he, and died!

"A bitter curse upon them, poor boy, who led thee forth,
From some gentle, sad-eyed mother, weeping, lonely, in
the North!"
Spake the mournful Mexic woman, as she laid him with
her dead,
And turned to soothe the living, and bind the wounds
which bled.

Look forth once more, Ximena! "Like a cloud before
the wind
Rolls the battle down the mountains, leaving blood and
death behind;
Ah! they plead in vain for mercy; in the dust the wounded
strive;
Hide your faces, holy angels! oh, thou Christ of God,
forgive!"

Sink, oh Night, among thy Mountains! let the cool, gray
shadows fall;
Dying brothers, fighting demons, drop thy curtain over
all!
Through the thickening winter twilight, wide apart the
battle rolled,
In its sheath the saber rested, and the cannon's lips grew
cold.

But the noble Mexic women still their holy task pursued,
Through that long, dark night of sorrow, worn and faint
and lacking food;

Over weak and suffering brothers, with a tender care they
    hung,
And the dying foeman blessed them in a strange and
    Northern tongue.

Not wholly lost, oh Father! is this evil world of ours;
Upward, through its blood and ashes, spring afresh the
    Eden flowers;
From its smoking hell of battle, Love and Pity send their
    prayer,
And still thy white-winged angels hover dimly in our air!

89

THE HOST OF THE AIR [1]

William Butler Yeats

O'Driscoll drove with a song,
The wild duck and the drake,
From the tall and the tufted reeds
Of the drear Hart Lake.

And he saw how the reeds grew dark
At the coming of night tide,
And dreamed of the long dim hair
Of Bridget his bride.

1. "The gods of ancient Ireland, the Sidhe, still ride the country
as of old. The Sidhe have much to do with the wind. When the
country people see the leaves whirling on the road they bless themselves, because they believe the Sidhe to be passing by. If anyone
becomes too much interested in them and sees them overmuch, he
loses all interest in ordinary things. They are said to steal brides
just after their marriage, and sometimes in a blast of wind. The
story in the poem is founded on an old Gaelic ballad."—William Butler Yeats.

He heard while he sang and dreamed
A piper piping away,
And never was piping so sad,
And never was piping so gay.

And he saw young men and young girls
Who danced on a level place
And Bridget his bride among them,
With a sad and a gay face.

The dancers crowded about him,
And many a sweet thing said,
And a young man brought him red wine
And a young girl white bread.

But Bridget drew him by the sleeve,
Away from the merry bands,
To old men playing at cards
With a twinkling of ancient hands.

The bread and the wine had a doom,
For these were the host of the air; [2]
He sat and played in a dream
Of her long dim hair.

He played with the merry old men
And thought not of evil chance,
Until one bore Bridget his bride
Away from the merry dance.

He bore her away in his arms,
The handsomest young man there,
And his neck and his breast and his arms
Were drowned in her long dim hair.

2. **The host of the air.** The Sidhe.

O'Driscoll scattered the cards
And out of his dream awoke:
Old men and young men and young girls
Were gone like a drifting smoke;

But he heard high up in the air
A piper piping away,
And never was piping so sad,
And never was piping so gay.

90

THE LADY OF SHALOTT [1]

ALFRED TENNYSON

PART I

On either side the river lie
Long fields of barley and of rye,
That clothe the wold [2] and meet the sky;
And thro' the field the road runs by
    To many-tower'd Camelot; [3]
And up and down the people go,
Gazing where the lilies blow
Round an island there below,
    The island of Shalott.

---

1. Mr. Stopford Brooke says in *Tennyson, His Art and Relation to Modern Life*, that this poem was never intended to have any special meaning. He calls it "simplicity in a mask of mysticism." Tennyson, however, calls the passage beginning with the line "Or when the moon was overhead" the key to the symbolism of the tale. He says, "The new-born love for some one in the wide world from which she has been so long secluded, takes her out of the region of shadows into that of realities."

2. **Wold.** A plain or low hill.

3. **Camelot.** The city of King Arthur's court.

Willows whiten, aspens quiver,
Little breezes dusk and shiver
Thro' the wave that runs for ever
By the island in the river
 Flowing down to Camelot.
Four gray walls, and four gray towers,
Overlook a space of flowers,
And the silent isle imbowers
 The Lady of Shalott.

By the margin, willow-veil'd
Slide the heavy barges trail'd
By slow horses; and unhail'd
The shallop flitteth silken-sail'd
 Skimming down to Camelot:
But who hath seen her wave her hand?
Or at the casement seen her stand?
Or is she known in all the land,
 The Lady of Shalott?

Only reapers, reaping early
In among the bearded barley,
Hear a song that echoes cheerly
From the river winding clearly,
 Down to tower'd Camelot:
And by the moon the reaper weary,
Piling sheaves in uplands airy,
Listening, whispers " 'Tis the fairy
 Lady of Shalott."

PART II

There she weaves by night and day
A magic web with colors gay.
She has heard a whisper say,
A curse is on her if she stay

To look down to Camelot.
She knows not what the curse may be,
And so she weaveth steadily,
And little other care hath she,
    The Lady of Shalott.

And moving thro' a mirror clear
That hangs before her all the year,
Shadows of the world appear.
There she sees the highway near
    Winding down to Camelot:
There the river eddy whirls,
And there the surly village-churls,
And the red cloaks of market girls,
    Pass onward from Shalott.

Sometimes a troop of damsels glad,
An abbot on an ambling pad,
Sometimes a curly shepherd-lad,
Or long-hair'd page in crimson clad,
    Goes by to tower'd Camelot:
And sometimes thro' the mirror blue
The knights come riding two and two:
She hath no loyal knight and true,
    The Lady of Shalott.

But in her web she still delights
To weave the mirror's magic sights,
For often thro' the silent nights
A funeral, with plumes and lights
    And music, went to Camelot:
Or when the moon was overhead,
Came two young lovers lately wed;
"I am half sick of shadows," said
    The Lady of Shalott.

PART III

A bow-shot from her bower-eaves,
He rode between the barley-sheaves,
The sun came dazzling thro' the leaves,
And flamed upon the brazen greaves [4]
  Of bold Sir Lancelot.[5]
A red-cross knight for ever kneel'd
To a lady in his shield,
That sparkled on the yellow field,
  Beside remote Shalott.

The gemmy bridle glitter'd free,
Like to some branch of stars we see
Hung in the golden Galaxy.[6]
The bridle bells rang merrily
  As he rode down to Camelot:
And from his blazon'd baldric [7] slung
A mighty silver bugle hung,
And as he rode his armor rung,
  Beside remote Shalott.

All in the blue unclouded weather
Thick-jewel'd shone the saddle-leather,
The helmet and the helmet-feather
Burn'd like one burning flame together,
  As he rode down to Camelot.
As often thro' the purple night,
Below the starry clusters bright,
Some bearded meteor, trailing light,
  Moves over still Shalott.

4. **Greaves.** Armor for the legs below the knees.
5. **Sir Lancelot.** The chief of Arthur's Knights of the Round Table.
6. **Galaxy.** The Milky Way.
7. **Blazon'd baldric.** A richly ornamented belt worn over one shoulder and across the breast.

His broad clear brow in sunlight glow'd;
On burnish'd hooves his war-horse trode;
From underneath his helmet flow'd
His coal-black curls as on he rode,
  As he rode down to Camelot.
From the bank and from the river
He flash'd into the crystal mirror,
"Tirra lirra," by the river
  Sang Sir Lancelot.

She left the web, she left the loom,
She made three paces thro' the room,
She saw the water-lily bloom,
She saw the helmet and the plume,
  She look'd down to Camelot.
Out flew the web and floated wide;
The mirror crack'd from side to side;
"The curse is come upon me," cried
  The Lady of Shalott.

PART IV

In the stormy east-wind straining,
The pale yellow woods were waning,
The broad stream in his banks complaining,
Heavily the low sky raining
  Over tower'd Camelot;
Down she came and found a boat
Beneath a willow left afloat,
And round about the prow she wrote
  The Lady of Shalott.

And down the river's dim expanse
Like some bold seër in a trance,
Seeing all his own mischance—
With a glassy countenance
  Did she look to Camelot.

And at the closing of the day
She loosed the chain, and down she lay;
The broad stream bore her far away,
  The Lady of Shalott.

Lying, robed in snowy white
That loosely flew to left and right—
The leaves upon her falling light—
Thro' the noises of the night
  She floated down to Camelot:
And as the boat-head wound along
The willowy hills and fields among,
They heard her singing her last song,
  The Lady of Shalott.

Heard a carol, mournful, holy,
Chanted loudly, chanted lowly,
Till her blood was frozen slowly,
And her eyes were darken'd wholly,
  Turn'd to tower'd Camelot.
For ere she reach'd upon the tide
The first house by the water-side,
Singing in her song she died,
  The Lady of Shalott.

Under tower and balcony,
By garden-wall and gallery,
A gleaming shape she floated by,
Dead-pale between the houses high,
  Silent into Camelot.
Out upon the wharfs they came,
Knight and burgher, lord and dame,
And round the prow they read her name,
  The Lady of Shalott.

Who is this? and what is here?
And in the lighted palace near
Died the sound of royal cheer;
And they cross'd themselves for fear,
  All the knights at Camelot:
But Lancelot mused a little space;
He said, "She has a lovely face;
God in his mercy lend her grace,
  The Lady of Shalott.

91

LA BELLE DAME SANS MERCI [1]

John Keats

O what can ail thee, knight-at-arms,
  Alone and palely loitering?
The sedge has wither'd from the lake,
  And no birds sing.

O what can ail thee, knight-at-arms!
  So haggard and so woe-begone?
The squirrel's granary is full,
  And the harvest's done.

I see a lily on thy brow
  With anguish moist and fever-dew,
And on thy cheeks a fading rose
  Fast withereth too.

---

1. In many ways this poem presents an interesting contrast to the "The Lady of Shalott." The poems are alike, however, in their mystic atmosphere. La Belle Dame, etc. The beautiful lady without mercy.

I met a lady in the meads,
 Full beautiful—a faery's child,
Her hair was long, her foot was light,
 And her eyes were wild.

I made a garland for her head,
 And bracelets too, and fragrant zone;
She look'd at me as she did love,
 And made sweet moan.

I set her on my pacing steed
 And nothing else saw all day long,
For sidelong would she bend, and sing
 A faery's song.

She found me roots of relish sweet,
 And honey wild and manna-dew,
And sure in language strange she said,
 "I love thee true."

She took me to her elfin grot,
 And there she wept and sigh'd full sore;
And there I shut her wild, wild eyes
 With kisses four.

And there she lull'd me asleep,
 And there I dream'd—Ah! woe betide!
The latest dream I ever dream'd
 On the cold hill's side.

I saw pale kings and princes too,
 Pale warriors, death-pale were they all:
They cried—"La belle Dame sans Merci
 Hath thee in thrall!"

I saw their starved lips in the gloam
  With horrid warning gapéd wide,
And I awoke and found me here
  On the cold hill's side.

And this is why I sojourn here
  Alone and palely loitering,
Though the sedge is wither'd from the lake,
  And no birds sing.

92

THE HAYSTACK IN THE FLOODS

WILLIAM MORRIS

Had she come all the way for this,
To part at last without a kiss?
Yea, had she borne the dirt and rain
That her own eyes might see him slain
Beside the haystack in the floods?

Along the dripping leafless woods,
The stirrup touching either shoe,
She rode astride as troopers do;
With kirtle kilted to her knee,
To which the mud splash'd wretchedly;
And the wet dripp'd from every tree
Upon her head and heavy hair,
And on her eyelids broad and fair;
The tears and rain ran down her face.

By fits and starts they rode apace,
And very often was his place
Far off from her; he had to ride
Ahead, to see what might betide

When the roads cross'd; and sometimes, when
There rose a murmuring from his men,
Had to turn back with promises;
Ah me! she had but little ease;
And often for pure doubt and dread
She sobb'd, made giddy in the head
By the swift riding; while, for cold,
Her slender fingers scarce could hold
The wet reins; yea, and scarcely, too,
She felt the foot within her shoe
Against the stirrup: all for this,
To part at last without a kiss
Beside the haystack in the floods.

For when they near'd that old soak'd hay,
They saw across the only way
That Judas, Godmar, and the three
Red running lions dismally
Grinn'd from his pennon, under which
In one straight line along the ditch
They counted thirty heads.

                    So then,
While Robert turn'd round to his men,
She saw at once the wretched end,
And, stooping down, tried hard to rend
Her coif [1] the wrong way from her head,
And hid her eyes; while Robert said:
"Nay, love, 'tis scarcely two to one,
At Poictiers [2] where we made them run
So fast—why, sweet my love, good cheer,
The Gascon frontier is so near,
Nought after this."

1. **Coif.** A close fitting cap, like a small hood.
2. **Poictiers.** A battle in which the Black Prince of England de
feated the French and captured King John, 1356.

But, "O," she said,

"My God! my God! I have to tread
The long way back without you; then
The court at Paris; those six men;
The gratings of the Chatelet;[3]
The swift Seine on some rainy day
Like this, and people standing by,
And laughing, while my weak hands try
To recollect how strong men swim.
All this, or else a life with him,
For which I should be damned at last,
Would God that this next hour were past!"

He answer'd not, but cried his cry,
"St. George for Marny!" cheerily;
And laid his hand upon her rein.
Alas! no man of all his train
Gave back that cheery cry again;
And, while for rage his thumb beat fast
Upon his sword-hilt, some one cast
About his neck a kerchief long,
And bound him.

Then they went along

To Godmar; who said: "Now, Jehane,
Your lover's life is on the wane
So fast, that, if this very hour
You yield not as my paramour,
He will not see the rain leave off—
Nay, keep your tongue from gibe and scoff,
Sir Robert, or I slay you now."
She laid her hand upon her brow,
Then gazed upon the palm, as though
She thought her forehead bled, and—"No."

---

3. **Chatelet.** A prison of Paris.

She said, and turn'd her head away,
As there were nothing else to say,
And everything were settled: red
Grew Godmar's face from chin to head;
"Jehane, on yonder hill there stands
My castle, guarding well my lands:
What hinders me from taking you,
And doing what I list to do
To your fair wilful body, while
Your knight lies dead?"

            A wicked smile
Wrinkled her face, her lips grew thin,
A long way out she thrust her chin:
"You know that I should strangle you
While you were sleeping; or bite through
Your throat, by God's help—ah!" she said,
"Lord Jesus, pity your poor maid!
For in such wise they hem me in,
I cannot choose but sin and sin,
Whatever happens; yet I think
They could not make me eat or drink,
And so should I just reach my rest."

"Nay, if you do not my behest,
O Jehane! though I love you well,"
Said Godmar, "would I fail to tell
All that I know?" "Foul lies," she said.
"Eh? lies, my Jehane? by God's head,
At Paris folks would deem them true!
Do you know, Jehane, they cry for you,
'Jehane the brown! Jehane the brown!
Give us Jehane to burn or drown!'—
Eh—gag me, Robert!—sweet my friend,
This were indeed a piteous end

For those long fingers, and long feet,
And long neck, and smooth shoulders sweet;
An end that few men would forget
That saw it—So, an hour yet:
Consider, Jehane, which to take
Of life or death!"

        So, scarce awake,
Dismounting, did she leave that place,
And totter some yards; with her face
Turn'd upward to the sky she lay,
Her head on a wet heap of hay,
And fell asleep: and while she slept,
And did not dream, the minutes crept
Round to the twelve again; but she,
Being waked at last, sigh'd quietly,
And strangely childlike came, and said:
"I will not." Straightway Godmar's head,
As though it hung on strong wires, turn'd
Most sharply round, and his face burn'd.

For Robert—both his eyes were dry,
He could not weep, but gloomily
He seem'd to watch the rain; yea, too,
His lips were firm; he tried once more
To touch her lips; she reach'd out, sore
And vain desire so tortured them,
The poor gray lips, and now the hem
Of his sleeve brush'd them.

        With a start
Up Godmar rose, thrust them apart;
From Robert's throat he loosed the bands
Of silk and mail; with empty hands
Held out, she stood and gazed, and saw
The long bright blade without a flaw

Glide out from Godmar's sheath, his hand
In Robert's hair; she saw him bend
Back Robert's head; she saw him send
The thin steel down; the blow told well,
Right backward the knight Robert fell,
And moan'd as dogs do, being half dead,
Unwitting, as I deem; so then
Godmar turn'd grinning to his men,
Who ran, some five or six, and beat
His head to pieces at their feet.

Then Godmar turn'd again and said:
"So, Jehane, the first fitte [4] is read!
Take note, my lady, that your way
Lies backward to the Chatelet!"
She shook her head and gazed awhile
At her cold hands with a rueful smile,
As though this thing had made her mad.

This was the parting that they had
Beside the haystack in the floods.

---

4. **Fitte.** Parts of old ballads were called fittes. He speaks as if she were reading or acting a story.

93

VIGIL STRANGE I KEPT ON THE FIELD ONE NIGHT

<small>WALT WHITMAN</small>

Vigil strange I kept on the field one night;

When you my son and my comrade dropt at my side that
day,

One look I but gave which your dear eyes return'd with
a look I shall never forget,

One touch of your hand to mine, O boy, reach'd up as
you lay on the ground,

Then onward I sped in the battle, the even-contested
battle,

Till late in the night reliev'd to the place at last again
I made my way;

Found you in death so cold, dear comrade, found your
body, son of responding kisses (never again on earth
responding),

Bared your face in the starlight, curious the scene, cool
blew the moderate night-wind;

Long there and then in vigil I stood, dimly around me
the battlefield spreading,

Vigil wondrous and vigil sweet there in the fragrant
silent night;

But not a tear fell, not even a long-drawn sigh; long,
long I gazed,

Then on the earth partially reclining sat by your side
leaning my chin in my hands;

Passing sweet hours, immortal and mystic hours with you,
dearest comrade—not a tear, not a word;

Vigil of silence, love and death, vigil for you my son
and my soldier,

As onward silently stars aloft, eastward new ones upward stole;
Vigil final for you, brave boy, (I could not save you, swift was your death,
I faithfully loved you and cared for you living, I think we shall surely meet again,)
Till at latest lingering of the night, indeed just as the dawn appear'd,
My comrade I wrapt in his blanket, envelop'd well his form,
Folded the blanket well, tucked it carefully over head and carefully under feet,
And there and then and bathed by the rising sun, my son in his grave, in his rude-dug grave I deposited;
Ending my strange vigil with that, vigil of night and battlefield dim,
Vigil for boy of responding kisses (never again on earth responding),
Vigil for comrade swiftly slain, vigil I never forget, how as day brighten'd,
I rose from the chill ground and folded my soldier well in his blanket,
And buried him where he fell.

94

SHAMEFUL DEATH

William Morris

There were four of us about that bed;
   The mass-priest knelt at the side,
I and his mother stood at the head,
   Over his feet lay the bride;
We were quite sure that he was dead,
   Though his eyes were open wide.

He did not die in the night,
  He did not die in the day,
But in the morning twilight
  His spirit pass'd away,
When neither sun nor moon was bright,
  And the trees were merely gray.

He was not slain with the sword,
  Knight's axe, or the knightly spear,
Yet spoke he never a word
  After he came in here;
I cut away the cord
  From the neck of my brother dear.

He did not strike one blow,
  For the recreants came behind,
In a place where the hornbeams grow,
  A path right hard to find,
For the hornbeam boughs swing so,
  That the twilight makes it blind.

They lighted a great torch then,
  When his arms were pinion'd fast,
Sir John the knight of the Fen,
  Sir Guy of the Dolorous Blast,
With knights threescore and ten,
  Hung brave Lord Hugh at last.

I am threescore and ten,
  And my hair is all turn'd gray,
But I met Sir John of the Fen
  Long ago on a summer day,
And am glad to think of the moment when
  I took his life away.

I am threescore and ten,
   And my strength is mostly pass'd,
But long ago I and my men,
   When the sky was overcast,
And the smoke roll'd over the reeds of the fen,
   Slew Guy of the Dolorous Blast.

And now, knights all of you,
I pray you pray for Sir Hugh,
A good knight and a true,
And for Alice, his wife, pray too.

95

THE HIGHWAYMAN

ALFRED NOYES

PART ONE

I

The wind was a torrent of darkness among the gusty trees,
The moon was a ghostly galleon [1] tossed upon cloudy seas,
The road was a ribbon of moonlight over the purple moor,
And the highwayman came riding—
   Riding—riding—
The highwayman came riding, up to the old inn door.

II

He'd a French cocked hat on his forehead, a bunch of
   lace at his chin,
A coat of the claret velvet, and breeches of brown doe-
   skin;

1. **Galleon.** A sailing vessel, sometimes with three or four decks

They fitted with never a wrinkle: his boots were up to
    the thigh!
And he rode with a jeweled twinkle,
  His pistol butts a-twinkle,
His rapier hilt a-twinkle, under the jeweled sky.

III

Over the cobbles he clattered and clashed in the dark inn
    yard,
And he tapped with his whip on the shutters, but all was
    locked and barred;
He whistled a tune to the window, and who should be
    waiting there
But the landlord's black-eyed daughter,
  Bess, the landlord's daughter,
Plaiting a dark red love knot into her long black hair.

IV

And dark in the dark old inn yard a stable-wicket creaked
Where Tim the ostler listened; his face was white and
    peaked;
His eyes were hollows of madness, his hair like moldy hay,
But he loved the landlord's daughter,
  The landlord's red-lipped daughter,
Dumb as a dog he listened, and he heard the robber say—

V

"One kiss, my bonny sweetheart, I'm after a prize tonight,
But I shall be back with the yellow gold before the morn-
    ing light;
Yet, if they press me sharply, and harry me through the
    day,
Then look for me by moonlight,
  Watch for me by moonlight,
I'll come to thee by moonlight, though hell should bar
    the way."

VI

He rose upright in the stirrups; he scarce could reach her
    hand,
But she loosened her hair i' the casement! His face
    burned like a brand
As the black cascade of perfume came tumbling over his
    breast;
And he kissed its waves in the moonlight,
  (Oh, sweet black waves in the moonlight!)
Then he tugged at his rein in the moonlight, and galloped
    away to the West.

PART TWO

I

He did not come in the dawning; he did not come at noon;
And out o' the tawny sunset, before the rise o' the moon,
When the road was a gypsy's ribbon, looping the purple
    moor,
A redcoat troop came marching—
  Marching—marching—
King George's men came marching, up to the old inn door.

II

They said no word to the landlord, they drank his ale
    instead,
But they gagged his daughter and bound her to the foot
    of her narrow bed;
Two of them knelt at her casement, with muskets at their
    side!
There was death at every window;
  And hell at one dark window;
For Bess could see, through her casement, the road that
    he would ride.

III

They had tied her up to attention, with many a sniggering
jest;
They had bound a musket beside her, with the barrel
beneath her breast!
"Now keep good watch!" and they kissed her.
  She heard the dead man say
Look for me by moonlight;
  Watch for me by moonlight;
*I'll come to thee by moonlight, though hell should bar the
way!*

IV

She twisted her hands behind her; but all the knots held
good!
She writhed her hands till her fingers were wet with
sweat or blood!
They stretched and strained in the darkness, and the hours
crawled by like years,
Till, now, on the stroke of midnight,
  Cold on the stroke of midnight,
The tip of one finger touched it!   The trigger at least was
hers!

V

The tip of one finger touched it; she strove no more for
the rest!
Up, she stood up to attention, with the barrel beneath her
breast.
She would not risk their hearing; she would not strive
again;
For the road lay bare in the moonlight;
  Blank and bare in the moonlight;
And the blood of her veins in the moonlight throbbed to
her love's refrain.

VI

Tlot-tlot; tlot-tlot! Had they heard it? The horse-hoofs
    ringing clear;
Tlot-tlot, tlot-tlot, in the distance! Were they deaf that
    they did not hear?
Down the ribbon of moonlight, over the brow of the hill,
The highwayman came riding,
    Riding,—riding!
The redcoats looked to their priming! She stood up,
    straight and still!

VII

Tlot-tlot. in the frosty silence! *Tlot-tlot,* in the echoing
    night!
Nearer he came and nearer! Her face was like a light!
Her eyes grew wide for a moment; she drew one last
    deep breath,
Then her finger moved in the moonlight,
    Her musket shattered the moonlight,
Shattered her breast in the moonlight and warned him—
    with her death.

VIII

He turned; he spurred to the Westward; he did not know
    who stood
Bowed, with her head o'er the musket, drenched with her
    own red blood!
Not till the dawn he heard it, and slowly blanched to hear
How Bess, the landlord's daughter,
    The landlord's black-eyed daughter,
Had watched for her love in the moonlight, and died in
    the darkness there.

IX

Back, he spurred like a madman, shrieking a curse to
    the sky,
With the white road smoking behind him, and his rapier
    brandished high!
Blood-red were his spurs i' the golden noon; wine-red was
    his velvet coat;
When they shot him down on the highway,
    Down like a dog on the highway,
And he lay in his blood on the highway, with the bunch
    of lace at his throat.

   .   .   .   .   .   .

X

And still of a winter's night, they say, when the wind is in
    the trees,
When the moon is a ghostly galleon tossed upon cloudy
    seas,
When the road is a ribbon of moonlight over the purple
    moor,
A highwayman comes riding—
    Riding—riding—
A highwayman comes riding, up to the old inn door.

XI

Over the cobbles he clatters and clangs in the dark inn
    yard;
And he taps with his whip on the shutters, but all is
    locked and barred;
He whistles a tune to the window, and who should be
    waiting there
But the landlord's black-eyed daughter,
    Bess, the landlord's daughter,
Plaiting a dark red love knot into her long black hair.

96

THE SINGER IN THE PRISON

Walt Whitman

I

O sight of pity, shame and dole!
O fearful thought—a convict soul.

Rang the refrain along the hall, the prison,
Rose to the roof, the vaults of heaven above,
Pouring in floods of melody in tones so pensive sweet and
    strong the like whereof was never heard,
Reaching the far-off sentry and the armed guards, who
    ceas'd their pacing,
Making the hearer's pulses stop for ecstasy and awe.

II

The sun was low in the west one winter day,
When down a narrow aisle amid the thieves and outlaws
    of the land,
(There by the hundreds seated, sear-faced murderers,
    wily counterfeiters,
Gather'd to Sunday church in prison walls, the keepers
    round,
Plenteous, well-armed, watching with vigilant eyes,)
Calmly a lady walk'd holding a little innocent child by
    either hand,
Whom seating on their stools beside her on the platform,
She, first preluding with the instrument a low and musical
    prelude,
In voice surpassing all, sang forth a quaint old hymn.

A soul confined by bars and bands,
Cries, help! O help! and wrings her hands,
Blinded her eyes, bleeding her breast,
Nor pardon finds, nor balm of rest.

Ceaseless she paces to and fro,
O heart-sick days! O nights of woe!
Nor hand of friend, nor loving face,
Nor favor comes, nor word of grace.

It was not I that sinn'd the sin,
The ruthless body dragg'd me in;
Though long I strove courageously,
The body was too much for me.

Dear prison'd soul bear up a space,
For soon or late the certain grace;
To set thee free and bear thee home,
The heavenly pardoner death shall come.

> *Convict no more, nor shame, nor dole!*
> *Depart—a God-enfranchis'd soul!*

III

The singer ceas'd,
One glance swept from her clear calm eyes o'er all those
    upturn'd faces,
Strange sea of prison faces, a thousand varied, crafty,
    brutal, seam'd and beauteous faces,
Then rising, passing back along the narrow aisle between
    them,
While her gown touch'd them rustling in the silence,
She vanish'd with her children in the dusk.
While upon all, convicts and armed keepers ere they stirr'd
(Convict forgetting prison, keeper his loaded pistol),

A hush and pause fell down a wondrous minute,
With deep half-stifled sobs and sound of bad men bow'd
    and moved to weeping,
And youth's convulsive breathings, memories of home,
The mother's voice in lullaby, the sister's care, the happy
    childhood,
The long-pent spirit rous'd to reminiscence;
A wondrous minute then—but after in the solitary night,
    to many, many there,
Years after, even in the hour of death, the sad refrain,
    the tune, the voice, the words,
Resumed, the large calm lady walks the narrow aisle,
The wailing melody again, the singer in the prison sings,

> *O sight of pity, shame and dole!*
> *O fearful thought—a convict soul.*

97

THE WHITE SHIP [1]

DANTE GABRIEL ROSSETTI

By none but me can the tale be told,
The butcher of Rouen, poor Berold.
   (*Lands are swayed by a King on a throne.*)
'Twas a royal train put forth to sea,
Yet the tale can be told by none but me.
   (*The sea hath no King but God alone.*)

---

1. This narrative is based upon fact. Henry I of England was
returning from Normandy, France. To quote from the historian
Green: "His son William had, with a crowd of nobles, accompanied
the king on his return from Normandy; but the white ship in which
he had embarked lingered behind the rest of the royal fleet while
the young nobles, excited with wine, hung over the ship's side and
chased away with taunts the priest who came to give the customary
benediction. At last the guard of the king's treasure pressed the

King Henry held it as life's whole gain
That after his death his son should reign.

'Twas so in my youth I heard men say,
And my old age calls it back today.

King Henry of England's realm was he,
And Henry Duke of Normandy.

The times had changed when on either coast
"Clerkly Harry" [2] was all his boast.

Of ruthless strokes full many an one
He had struck to crown himself and his son;
And his elder brother's [3] eyes were gone.

And when to the chase his court would crowd,
The poor flung plowshares on his road,
And shrieked: "Our cry is from King to God!"

But all the chiefs of the English land
Had knelt and kissed the Prince's hand.

And next with his son he sailed to France
To claim the Norman allegiance:

And every baron in Normandy
Had taken the oath of fealty.

vessel's departure, and, driven by the arms of fifty rowers, it swept
swiftly out to sea. All at once the ship's side struck on a rock at
the mouth of the harbor, and in an instant it sank beneath the waves.
One terrible cry, ringing through the stillness of the night, was heard
by the royal fleet; but it was not till the morning that the fatal news
reached the king. He fell unconscious to the ground and rose never
to smile again."

2. **Clerkly Harry.** Henry I, surnamed Beauclerc, "the good
scholar."

3. **Elder brother.** Henry kept his elder brother Robert in prison
for thirty years.

'Twas sworn and sealed, and the day had come
When the King and the Prince might journey home:

For Christmas cheer is to home hearts dear,
And Christmas now was drawing near.

Stout Fitz-Stephen came to the King,—
A pilot famous in seafaring;

And he held to the King, in all men's sight,
A mark of gold for his tribute's right.

"Liege Lord! my father guided the ship
From whose boat your father's [4] foot did slip
When he caught the English soil in his grip,

"And cried: 'By this clasp I claim command
O'er every rood of English land!'

"He was borne to the realm you rule o'er now
In that ship with the archer carved at her prow:

"And thither I'll bear, an' it be my due,
Your father's son and his grandson too.

"The famed White Ship is mine in the bay,
From Harfleur's harbor she sails today,

"With masts fair-pennoned as Norman spears
And with fifty well-tried mariners."

Quoth the King: "My ships are chosen each one,
But I'll not say nay to Stephen's son.

4. Your father's foot, etc. William of Normandy, father of Henry
I, landed in England with an army in 1066.

"My son and daughter and fellowship
Shall cross the water in the White Ship."

The King set sail with the eve's south wind,
And soon he left that coast behind.

The Prince and all his, a princely show,
Remained in the good White Ship to go.

With noble knights and with ladies fair,
With courtiers and sailors gathered there,
Three hundred living souls we were:

And I Berold was the meanest hind [5]
In all that train to the Prince assign'd.

The Prince was a lawless shameless youth;
From his father's loins he sprang without ruth:

Eighteen years till then he had seen,
And the devil's dues in him were eighteen.

And now he cried: "Bring wine from below;
Let the sailors revel ere yet they row:

"Our speed shall o'ertake my father's flight
Though we sail from the harbor at midnight."

The rowers made good cheer without check;
The lords and ladies obeyed his beck;
The night was light, and they danced on the deck.

But at midnight's stroke they cleared the bay.
And the White Ship furrowed the water-way.

5. Hind. Peasant.

The sails were set, and the oars kept tune
To the double flight of the ship and the moon:

Swift and swifter the White Ship sped
Till she flew as the spirit flies from the dead:

As white as a lily glimmered she
Like a ship's fair ghost upon the sea.

And the Prince cried, "Friends, 'tis the hour to sing!
Is a songbird's course so swift on the wing?"

And under the winter stars' still throng,
From brown throats, white throats, merry and strong,
The knights and the ladies raised a song.

A song,—nay, a shriek that rent the sky,
That leaped o'er the deep!—the grievous cry
Of three hundred living that now must die.

An instant shriek that sprang to the shock
As the ship's keel felt the sunken rock.

'Tis said that afar—a shrill strange sigh—
The King's ships heard it, and knew not why.

Pale Fitz-Stephen stood by the helm
'Mid all those folk that the waves must whelm.

A great King's heir for the waves to whelm,
And the helpless pilot pale at the helm!

The ship was eager and sucked athirst,
By the stealthy stab of the sharp reef pierc'd:

And like the moil round a sinking cup
The waters against her crowded up.

A moment the pilot's senses spin,—
The next he snatched the Prince 'mid the din,
Cut the boat loose, and the youth leaped in.

A few friends leaped with him, standing near.
"Row! the sea's smooth and the night is clear!"

"What! none to be saved but these and I?"
"Row, row as you'd live! All here must die!"

Out of the churn of the choking ship,
Which the gulf grapples and the waves strip,
They struck with the strained oars' flash and dip.

'Twas then o'er the splitting bulwarks' brim
The Prince's sister screamed to him.

He gazed aloft, still rowing apace,
And through the whirled surf he knew **her face.**

To the toppling decks clave one and all
As a fly cleaves to a chamber-wall.

I Berold was clinging anear;
I prayed for myself and quaked with fear,
But I saw his eyes as he looked at her.

He knew her face and he heard her cry,
And he said, "Put back! she must not die!"

And back with the current's force they reel
Like a leaf that's drawn to a water-wheel.

'Neath the ship's travail they scarce might float,
But he rose and stood in the rocking boat.

Low the poor ship leaned on the tide:
O'er the naked keel as she best might slide,
The sister toiled to the brother's side.

He reached an oar to her from below,
And stiffened his arms to clutch her so.

But now from the ship some spied the boat,
And "Saved!" was the cry from many a throat.

And down to the boat they leaped and fell:
It turned as a bucket turns in a well,
And nothing was there but the surge and swell.

The Prince that was and the King to come,
There in an instant gone to his doom,

Despite of all England's bended knee
And mauger the Norman fealty!

He was a Prince of lust and pride;
He showed no grace till the hour he died.

When he should be King, he oft would vow,
He'd yoke the peasant to his own plow.
O'er him the ships score their furrows now.

God only knows where his soul did wake,
But I saw him die for his sister's sake.

By none but me can the tale be told,
The butcher of Rouen, poor Berold.
      (*Lands are swayed by a King on a throne.*)

'Twas a royal train put forth to sea,
Yet the tale can be told by none but me.
  (*The sea hath no King but God alone.*)

And now the end came o'er the waters' womb
Like the last great Day that's yet to come.

With prayers in vain and curses in vain,
The White Ship sundered on the mid-main;

And what were men and what was a ship
Were toys and splinters in the sea's grip.

I Berold was down in the sea;
And passing strange though the thing may be,
Of dreams then known I remember me.

Blithe is the shout on Harfleur's strand
When morning lights the sails to land:

And blithe is Harfleur's echoing gloam
When mothers call the children home:

And high do the bells of Rouen beat
When the Body of Christ [6] goes down the street.

These things and the like were heard and shown
In a moment's trance 'neath the sea alone;

And when I rose, 'twas the sea did seem,
And not these things, to be all a dream.

The ship was gone and the crowd was gone,
And the deep shuddered and the moon shone,

6. **Body of Christ.** The Holy Sacrament.

And in a strait grasp my arms did span
The mainyard rent from the mast where it ran;
And on it with me was another man.

Where lands were none 'neath the dim sea-sky,
We told our names, that man and I.

"O I am Godefroy de l'Aigle hight,
And son I am to a belted knight."

"And I am Berold the butcher's son
Who slays the beasts in Rouen town."

Then cried we upon God's name, as we
Did drift on the bitter winter sea.

But lo! a third man rose o'er the wave,
And we said, "Thank God! us three may He save!"

He clutched to the yard with panting stare,
And we looked and knew Fitz-Stephen there.

He clung, and "What of the Prince?" quoth he.
"Lost, lost!" we cried.   He cried, "Woe on me!"
And loosed his hold and sank through the sea.

And soul with soul again in that space
We two were together face to face:

And each knew each, as the moments sped,
Less for one living than for one dead:

And every still star overhead
Seemed an eye that knew we were but dead.

And the hours passed; till the noble's son
Sighed, "God be thy help! my strength's foredone!

"O farewell, friend, for I can no more!"
"Christ take thee!" I moaned; and his life was o'er.

Three hundred souls were all lost but one,
And I drifted over the sea alone.

At last the morning rose on the sea
Like an angel's wing that beat tow'rds me.

Sore numbed I was in my sheepskin coat;
Half dead I hung, and might nothing note,
Till I woke sun-warmed in a fisher-boat.

The sun was high o'er the eastern brim
As I praised God and gave thanks to Him.

That day I told my tale to a priest,
Who charged me, till the shrift were releas'd,
That I should keep it in mine own breast.

And with the priest I thence did fare
To King Henry's court at Winchester.

We spoke with the King's high chamberlain,
And he wept and mourned again and again,
As if his own son had been slain:

And round us ever there crowded fast
Great men with faces all aghast:

And who so bold that might tell the thing
Which now they knew to their lord the King?
Much woe I learnt in their communing.

The King had watched with a heart sore stirred
For two whole days, and this was the third:

And still to all his court would he say,
"What keeps my son so long away?"

And they said: "The ports lie far and wide
That skirt the swell of the English tide;

"And England's cliffs are not more white
Than her women are, and scarce so light
Her skies as their eyes are blue and bright;

"And in some port that he reached from France
The Prince has lingered for his pleasaunce."

But once the King asked: "What distant cry
Was that we heard 'twixt the sea and sky?"

And one said: "With suchlike shouts, pardie!
Do the fishers fling their nets at sea."

And one: "Who knows not the shrieking quest
When the sea-mew misses its young from the nest?"

'Twas thus till now they had soothed his dread,
Albeit they knew not what they said:

But who should speak today of the thing
That all knew there except the King?

Then pondering much they found a way,
And met round the King's high seat that day:

And the King sat with a heart sore stirred,
And seldom he spoke and seldom heard.

'Twas then through the hall the King was 'ware
Of a little boy with golden hair,

As bright as the golden poppy is
That the beach breeds for the surf to kiss:

Yet pale his cheek as the thorn in Spring,
And his garb black like the raven's wing.

Nothing heard but his foot through the hall,
For now the lords were silent all.

And the King wondered, and said, "Alack!
Who sends me a fair boy dressed in black?

"Why, sweet heart, do you pace through the hall
As though my court were a funeral?"

Then lowly knelt the child at the dais,
And looked up weeping in the King's face.

"O wherefore black, O King, ye may say,
For white is the hue of death today.

"Your son and all his fellowship
Lie low in the sea with the White Ship."

King Henry fell as a man struck dead;
And speechless still he stared from his bed
When to him next day my rede [7] I read.

There's many an hour must needs beguile
A King's high heart that he should smile,—

7. **Rede I read.** Tale I told.

Full many a lordly hour, full fain
Of his realm's rule and pride of his reign:—

But this King never smiled again.

By none but me can the tale be told,
The butcher of Rouen, poor Berold.
　　(*Lands are swayed by a King on a throne.*)
'Twas a royal train put forth to sea,
Yet the tale can be told by none but me.
　　(*The sea hath no King but God alone.*)

98

SOHRAB AND RUSTUM [1]

Matthew Arnold

And the first gray of morning fill'd the east,
And the fog rose out of the Oxus stream.
But all the Tartar camp along the stream
Was hush'd, and still the men were plunged in sleep;
Sohrab alone, he slept not; all night long
He had lain wakeful, tossing on his bed;

1. "Sohrab and Rustum" is an episode taken from the *Shah Nameh*, the Persian Book of Kings. Rustum is the hero of many exploits, in all of which he is aided by his wonderful horse Ruksh. Rustum is to Central Asia what King Arthur is to England, and Charlemagne to France. In his wanderings he fell in love with and married a beautiful girl, the daughter of a petty king. The restless Rustum, however, left for new adventures before the birth of their child Sohrab, a son. Word was sent to the father that the child was a daughter. When Sohrab grew up to manhood he too became a great warrior. His mother told him that he was the son of Rustum, and Sohrab started out in search of his father.

At the time of the episode given in this poem Sohrab was a warrior in the Tartar army under Peran-Wisa, hoping in the course of the battles to find his father. The poem tells the story of their meeting. The scene of the story is laid in Central Asia near the Oxus river. It is scarcely worth while to attempt here to identify the numerous proper names.

But when the gray dawn stole into his tent,
He rose, and clad himself, and girt his sword,
And took his horseman's cloak, and left his tent,
And went abroad into the cold wet fog,
Through the dim camp to Peran-Wisa's tent.

　　Through the black Tartar tents he passed, which stood
Clustering like bee-hives on the low flat strand
Of Oxus, where the summer-floods o'erflow
When the sun melts the snows in high Pamere;
Through the black tents he pass'd, o'er that low strand,
And to a hillock came, a little back
From the stream's brink—the spot where first a boat,
Crossing the stream in summer, scrapes the land.
The men of former times had crown'd the top
With a clay fort; but that was fall'n, and now
The Tartars built there Peran-Wisa's tent,
A dome of laths, and o'er it felts were spread.
And Sohrab came there, and went in, and stood
Upon the thick piled carpets in the tent,
And found the old man sleeping on his bed
Of rugs and felts, and near him lay his arms.
And Peran-Wisa heard him, though the step
Was dull'd; for he slept light, an old man's sleep;
And he rose quickly on one arm, and said:—

　　"Who art thou? for it is not yet clear dawn
Speak! is there news, or any night alarm?"
　　But Sohrab came to the bedside, and said:—
"Thou know'st me, Peran-Wisa! it is I.
The sun is not yet risen, and the foe
Sleep; but I sleep not; all night long I lie
Tossing and wakeful, and I come to thee.
For so did King Afrasiab bid me seek
Thy counsel, and to heed thee as thy son,
In Samarcand, before the army march'd;
And I will tell thee what my heart desires.
Thou knowest if, since from Ader-baijan first

I came among the Tartars and bore arms,
I have still served Afrasiab well, and shown,
At my boy's years, the courage of a man.
This too thou know'st, that while I still bear on
The conquering Tartar ensigns through the world,
And beat the Persians back on every field,
I seek one man, one man, and one alone—
Rustum, my father; who I hoped should greet,
Should one day greet, upon some well-fought field
His not unworthy, not inglorious son.
So I long hoped, but him I never find.
Come then, hear now, and grant me what I ask.
Let the two armies rest today; but I
Will challenge forth the bravest Persian lords
To meet me, man to man! if I prevail,
Rustum will surely hear it; if I fall—
Old man, the dead need no one, claim no kin.
Dim is the rumor of a common fight,
Where host meets host, and many names are sunk;
But of a single combat fame speaks clear."

   He spoke; and Peran-Wisa took the hand
Of the young man in his, and sigh'd, and said:—
   "O Sohrab, an unquiet heart is thine!
Canst thou not rest among the Tartar chiefs,
And share the battle's common chance with us
Who love thee, but must press for ever first,
In single fight incurring single risk,
To find a father thou hast never seen?
That were far best, my son, to stay with us
Unmurmuring; in our tents, while it is war,
And when 'tis truce, then in Afrasiab's towns.
But, if this one desire indeed rules all,
To seek out Rustum—seek him not through fight!
Seek him in peace, and carry to his arms,
O Sohrab, carry an unwounded son!
But far hence seek him, for he is not here.

For now it is not as when I was young,
When Rustum was in front of every fray;
But now he keeps apart, and sits at home,
In Seistan, with Zal, his father old.
Whether that his own mighty strength at last
Feels the abhorr'd approaches of old age,
Or in some quarrel with the Persian King.
There go!—Thou wilt not? Yet my heart forebodes
Danger or death awaits thee on this field.
Fain would I know thee safe and well, though lost
To us; fain therefore send thee hence, in peace
To seek thy father, not seek single fights
In vain;—but who can keep the lion's cub
From ravening, and who govern Rustum's son?
Go, I will grant thee what thy heart desires."

So said he, and dropp'd Sohrab's hand, and left
His bed, and the warm rugs whereon he lay;
And o'er his chilly limbs his woollen coat
He pass'd, and tied his sandals on his feet,
And threw a white cloak round him, and he took
In his right hand a ruler's staff, no sword;
And on his head he set his sheep-skin cap,
Black, glossy, curl'd, the fleece of Kara-Kul;
And rais'd the curtain of his tent, and call'd
His herald to his side, and went abroad.

The sun by this had risen, and clear'd the fog
From the broad Oxus and the glittering sands.
And from their tents the Tartar horsemen filed
Into the open plain; so Haman bade—
Haman, who next to Peran-Wisa ruled
The host, and still was in his lusty prime.
From their black tents, long files of horse, they stream'd;
As when some gray November morn the files,
In marching order spread, of long-necked cranes
Stream over Casbin and the southern slopes
Of Elburz, from the Aralian estuaries,

Or some frore [2] Caspian reed-bed, southward bound
For the warm Persian sea-board—so they stream'd.
The Tartars of the Oxus, the King's guard,
First, with black sheep-skin caps and with long spears;
Large men, large steeds; who from Bokhara come
And Khiva, and ferment the milk of mares.
Next, the more temperate Toorkmuns of the south,
The Tukas, and the lances of Salore,
And those from Attruck and the Caspian sands;
Light men and on light steeds, who only drink
The acrid milk of camels, and their wells.
And then a swarm of wandering horse, who came
From far, and a more doubtful service own'd;
The Tartars of Ferghana, from the banks
Of the Jaxartes, men with scanty beards
And close-set skull-caps; and those wilder hordes
Who roam o'er Kipchak and the northern waste,
Kalmucks and unkempt Kuzzacks, tribes who stray
Nearest the Pole, and wandering Kirghizzes,
Who come on shaggy ponies from Pamere;
These all filed out from camp into the plain.
And on the other side the Persians form'd;—
First a light cloud of horse, Tartars they seem'd,
The Ilyats of Khorassan; and behind,
The royal troops of Persia, horse and foot,
Marshall'd battalions bright in burnish'd steel.
But Peran-Wisa with his herald came,
Threading the Tartar squadrons to the front,
And with his staff kept back the foremost ranks.
And when Ferood, who led the Persians, saw
That Peran-Wisa kept the Tartars back,
He took his spear, and to the front he came,
And check'd his ranks, and fix'd them where they stood,
And the old Tartar came upon the sand

2. **Frore.** Frozen.

Betwixt the silent hosts, and spake, and said:—

"Ferood, and ye, Persians and Tartars, hear!
Let there be truce between the hosts today.
But choose a champion from the Persian lords
To fight our champion Sohrab, man to man."

As, in the country, on a morn in June,
When the dew glistens on the pearled ears,
A shiver runs through the deep corn for joy—
So, when they heard what Peran-Wisa said,
A thrill through all the Tartar squadrons ran
Of pride and hope for Sohrab, whom they loved.

But as a troop of pedlars, from Cabool,
Cross underneath the Indian Caucasus,
That vast sky-neighboring mountain of milk snow;
Crossing so high, that, as they mount, they pass
Long flocks of traveling birds dead on the snow,
Choked by the air, and scarce can they themselves
Slake their parch'd throats with sugar'd mulberries—
In single file they move, and stop their breaths,
For fear they should dislodge the o'erhanging snows—
So the pale Persians held their breath with fear.

And to Ferood his brother chiefs came up
To counsel; Gudurz and Zoarrah came,
And Feraburz, who ruled the Persian host
Second, and was the uncle of the King;
There came and counsell'd, and then Gudurz said:—

"Ferood, shame bids us take their challenge up,
Yet champion have we none to match this youth.
He has the wild stag's foot, the lion's heart.
But Rustum came last night; aloof he sits
And sullen, and has pitched his tents apart.
Him will I seek, and carry to his ear
The Tartar challenge, and this young man's name;
Haply he will forget his wrath, and fight.
Stand forth the while, and take their challenge up."

So spake he; and Ferood stood forth and cried:—

"Old man, be it agreed as thou hast said!
Let Sohrab arm, and we will find a man."

  He spake; and Peran-Wisa turn'd, and strode
Back through the opening squadrons to his tent.
But through the anxious Persians Gudurz ran,
And cross'd the camp which lay behind, and reach'd,
Out on the sands beyond it, Rustum's tents.
Of scarlet cloth they were, and glittering gay,
Just pitch'd; the high pavilion in the midst
Was Rustum's, and his men lay camp'd around.
And Gudurz enter'd Rustum's tent, and found
Rustum; his morning meal was done, but still
The table stood before him, charged with food—
A side of roasted sheep, and cakes of bread,
And dark green melons; and there Rustum sate
Listless, and held a falcon on his wrist,
And play'd with it; but Gudurz came and stood
Before him; and he look'd, and saw him stand,
And with a cry sprang up and dropp'd the bird,
And greeted Gudurz with both hands, and said:—

  "Welcome! these eyes could see no better sight.
What news? but sit down first, and eat and drink."

  But Gudurz stood in the tent-door, and said:—
"Not now! a time will come to eat and drink,
But not today; today has other needs.
The armies are drawn out, and stand at gaze;
For from the Tartars is a challenge brought
To pick a champion from the Persian lords
To fight their champion—and thou know'st his name—
Sohrab men call him, but his birth is hid.
O Rustum, like thy might is this young man's!
He has the wild stag's foot, the lion's heart;
And he is young, and Iran's chiefs are old,
Or else too weak; and all eyes turn to thee.
Come down and help us, Rustum, or we lose!"

  He spake; but Rustum answer'd with a smile:—

"Go to! if Iran's chiefs are old, then I
Am older; if the young are weak, the King
Errs strangely; for the King, for Kai Khosroo,
Himself is young, and honors younger men,
And lets the aged molder to their graves.
Rustum he loves no more, but loves the young—
The young may rise at Sohrab's vaunts, not I. *BOASTS*
For what care I, though all speak Sohrab's fame?
For would that I myself had such a son,
And not that one slight helpless girl I have—
A son so famed, so brave, to send to war,
And I to tarry with the snow-hair'd Zal,
My father, whom the robber Afghans vex,
And clip his borders short, and drive his herds,
And he has none to guard his weak old age.
There would I go, and hang my armor up,
And with my great name fence that weak old man,
And spend the goodly treasures I have got,
And rest my age, and hear of Sohrab's fame,
And leave to death the hosts of thankless kings,
And with these slaughterous hands draw sword no more."

He spoke, and smiled; and Gudurz made reply:—
"What then, O Rustum, will men say to this,
When Sohrab dares our bravest forth, and seeks
Thee most of all, and thou, whom most he seeks,
Hidest thy face? Take heed lest men should say:
Like some old miser, Rustum hoards his fame,
And shuns to peril it with younger men."

And, greatly moved, then Rustum made reply:—
"O Gudurz, wherefore dost thou say such words?
Thou knowest better words than this to say.
What is one more, one less, obscure or famed,
Valiant or craven, young or old, to me?
Are not they mortal, am not I myself?
But who for men of nought would do great deeds?
Come, thou shalt see how Rustum hoards his fame!

But I will fight unknown, and in plain arms;
Let not men say of Rustum, he was match'd
In single fight with any mortal man."

He spoke, and frown'd; and Gudurz turn'd, and ran
Back quickly through the camp in fear and joy—
Fear at his wrath, but joy that Rustum came.
But Rustum strode to his tent-door, and call'd
His followers in, and bade them bring his arms,
And clad himself in steel; the arms he chose
Were plain, and on his shield was no device,
Only his helm was rich, inlaid with gold,
And, from the fluted spine atop, a plume
Of horsehair waved, a scarlet horsehair plume.
So arm'd, he issued forth; and Ruksh, his horse,
Followed him like a faithful hound at heel—
Ruksh, whose renown was noised through all the earth,
The horse, whom Rustum on a foray once
Did in Bokhara by the river find
A colt beneath its dam, and drove him home,
And rear'd him; a bright bay, with lofty crest,
Dight [3] with a saddle-cloth of broider'd green
Crusted with gold, and on the ground were work'd
All beasts of chase, all beasts which hunters know.
So follow'd, Rustum left his tents, and cross'd
The camp, and to the Persian host appear'd.
And all the Persians knew him, and with shouts
Hail'd; but the Tartars knew not who he was.
And dear as the wet diver to the eyes
Of his pale wife who waits and weeps on shore,
By sandy Bahrein, in the Persian Gulf,
Plunging all day in the blue waves, at night,
Having made up his tale of precious pearls,
Rejoins her in their hut upon the sands—
So dear to the pale Persians Rustum came.

3. **Dight.** Equipped.

And Rustum to the Persian front advanced,
And Sohrab arm'd in Haman's tent, and came.
And as afield the reapers cut a swath
Down through the middle of a rich man's corn,
And on each side are squares of standing corn,
And in the midst a stubble, short and bare—
So on each side were squares of men, with spears
Bristling, and in the midst, the open sand.
And Rustum came upon the sand, and cast
His eyes toward the Tartar tents, and saw
Sohrab come forth, and eyed him as he came.

As some rich woman, on a winter's morn,
Eyes through her silken curtains the poor drudge
Who with numb blacken'd fingers makes her fire—
At cock-crow, on a starlit winter's morn,
When the frost flowers the whiten'd window-panes—
And wonders how she lives, and what the thoughts
Of that poor drudge may be; so Rustum eyed
The unknown adventurous youth, who from afar
Came seeking Rustum, and defying forth
All the most valiant chiefs; long he perused
His spirited air, and wonder'd who he was.
For very young he seem'd, tenderly rear'd;
Like some young cypress, tall, and dark, and straight,
Which in a queen's secluded garden throws
Its slight dark shadow on the moonlit turf,
By midnight, to a bubbling fountain's sound—
So slender Sohrab seem'd, so softly rear'd.
And a deep pity enter'd Rustum's soul
As he beheld him coming; and he stood,
And beckon'd to him with his hand, and said:—

"O thou young man, the air of Heaven is soft,
And warm, and pleasant; but the grave is cold!
Heaven's air is better than the cold dead grave.
Behold me! I am vast, and clad in iron,
And tried; and I have stood on many a field

Of blood, and I have fought with many a foe—
Never was that field lost, or that foe saved.
O Sohrab, wherefore wilt thou rush on death?
Be govern'd! quit the Tartar host, and come
To Iran, and be as my son to me,
And fight beneath my banner till I die!
There are no youths in Iran brave as thou."

So he spake, mildly; Sohrab heard his voice,
The mighty voice of Rustum, and he saw
His giant figure planted on the sand,
Sole, like some single tower, which a chief
Hath builded on the waste in former years
Against the robbers; and he saw that head,
Streak'd with its first gray hairs;—hope filled his soul,
And he ran forward and embraced his knees,
And clasp'd his hand within his own, and said:—

"O, by thy father's head; by thine own soul!
Art thou not Rustum? speak! art thou not he?"

But Rustum eyed askance the kneeling youth,
And turn'd away, and spake to his own soul:—

"Ah me, I muse what this young fox may mean!
False, wily, boastful, are these Tartar boys.
For if I now confess this thing he asks,
And hide it not, but say: *Rustum is here!*
He will not yield indeed, nor quit our foes,
But he will find some pretext not to fight,
And praise my fame, and proffer courteous gifts,
A belt or sword perhaps, and go his way.
And on a feast-tide, in Afrasiab's hall,
In Samarcand, he will arise and cry:
'I challenged once, when the two armies camp'd
Beside the Oxus, all the Persian lords
To cope with me in single fight; but they
Shrank, only Rustum dared; then he and I
Changed gifts, and went on equal terms away.'
So will he speak, perhaps, while men applaud;

Then were the chiefs of Iran shamed through me."
    And then he turn'd, and sternly spake aloud:—
"Rise! wherefore dost thou vainly question thus
Of Rustum? I am here, whom thou hast call'd
By challenge forth; make good thy vaunt, or yield!
Is it with Rustum only thou wouldst fight?
Rash boy, men look on Rustum's face and flee!
For well I know, that did great Rustum stand
Before thy face this day, and were reveal'd,
There would be then no talk of fighting more.
But being what I am, I tell thee this—
Do thou record it in thine inmost soul:
Either thou shalt renounce thy vaunt and yield,
Or else thy bones shall strew this sand, till winds
Bleach them, or Oxus with his summer-floods,
Oxus in summer wash them all away."
    He spoke; and Sohrab answer'd, on his feet:—
"Art thou so fierce? Thou wilt not fright me so!
I am no girl, to be made pale by words.
Yet this thou hast said well, did Rustum stand
Here on this field, there were no fighting then.
But Rustum is far hence, and we stand here.
Begin! thou art more vast, more dread than I,
And thou art proved, I know, and I am young—
But yet success sways with the breath of Heaven.
And though thou thinkest that thou knowest sure
Thy victory, yet thou canst not surely know.
For we are all, like swimmers in the sea,
Poised on the top of a huge wave of fate,
Which hangs uncertain to which side to fall.
And whether it will heave us up to land,
Or whether it will roll us out to sea,
Back out to sea, to the deep waves of death,
We know not, and no search will make us know;
Only the event will teach us in its hour."
    He spoke, and Rustum answered not, but hurl'd

His spear; down from the shoulder, down it came,
As on some partridge in the corn a hawk,
That long has tower'd in the airy clouds,
Drops like a plummet; Sohrab saw it come,
And sprang aside, quick as a flash; the spear
Hiss'd, and went quivering down into the sand,
Which it sent flying wide;—then Sohrab threw
In turn, and full struck Rustum's shield; sharp rang,
The iron plates rang sharp, but turn'd the spear.
And Rustum seized his club, which none but he
Could wield; an unlopp'd trunk it was, and huge,
Still rough—like those which men in treeless plains
To build them boats fish from the flooded rivers,
Hyphasis or Hydaspes, when, high up
By their dark springs, the wind in winter-time
Hath made in Himalayan forests wrack,
And strewn the channels with torn boughs—so huge
The club which Rustum lifted now, and struck
One stroke; but again Sohrab sprang aside,
Lithe as the glancing snake, and the club came
Thundering to earth, and leapt from Rustum's hand.
And Rustum follow'd his own blow, and fell
To his knees, and with his fingers clutched the sand;
And now might Sohrab have unsheathed his sword,
And pierced the mighty Rustum while he lay
Dizzy, and on his knees, and choked with sand;
But he look'd on, and smiled, nor bared his sword,
But courteously drew back, and spoke, and said:—

"Thou strik'st too hard! that club of thine will float
Upon the summer floods, and not my bones.
But rise, and be not wroth! not wroth am I;
No, when I see thee, wrath forsakes my soul.
Thou say'st thou art not Rustum; be it so!
Who art thou then, that canst so touch my soul?
Boy as I am, I have seen battles too—
Have waded foremost in their bloody waves,

And heard their hollow roar of dying men;
But never was my heart thus touch'd before.
Are they from Heaven, these softenings of the heart?
O thou old warrior, let us yield to Heaven!
Come, plant we here in earth our angry spears,
And make a truce, and sit upon this sand,
And pledge each other in red wine, like friends,
And thou shalt talk to me of Rustum's deeds.
There are enough foes in the Persian host,
Whom I may meet, and strike, and feel no pang;
Champions enough Afrasiab has, whom thou
May'st fight; fight *them,* when they confront thy spear:
But oh, let there be peace 'twixt thee and me!"

He ceased, but while he spake, Rustum had risen,
And stood erect, trembling with rage; his club
He left to lie, but had regain'd his spear,
Whose fiery point now in his mail'd right-hand
Blazed bright and baleful, like that autumn-star,
The baleful sign of fevers; dust had soil'd
His stately crest, and dimm'd his glittering arms.
His breast heaved, his lips foam'd, and twice his voice
Was choked with rage; at last these words broke way:—

"Girl! nimble with thy feet, not with thy hands!
Curl'd minion, dancer, coiner of sweet words!
Fight, let me hear thy hateful voice no more!
Thou art not in Afrasiab's gardens now
With Tartar girls, with whom thou art wont to dance;
But on the Oxus-sands, and in the dance
Of battle, and with me, who make no play
Of war; I fight it out, and hand to hand.
Speak not to me of truce, and pledge, and wine!
Remember all thy valor; try thy feints
And cunning! all the pity I had is gone;
Because thou hast shamed me before both the hosts
With thy light skipping tricks, and thy girl's wiles."

He spoke, and Sohrab kindled at his taunts,

And he too drew his sword; at once they rush'd
Together, as two eagles on one prey
Come rushing down together from the clouds,
One from the east, one from the west; their shields
Dash'd with a clang together, and a din
Rose, such as that the sinewy woodcutters
Make often in the forest's heart at morn,
Of hewing axes, crashing trees—such blows
Rustum and Sohrab on each other hail'd.
And you would say that sun and stars took part
In that unnatural conflict; for a cloud
Grew suddenly in Heaven, and dark'd the sun
Over the fighters' heads; and a wind rose
Under their feet, and moaning swept the plain,
And in a sandy whirlwind wrapp'd the pair.
In gloom they twain were wrapp'd, and they alone;
For both the on-looking hosts on either hand
Stood in broad daylight, and the sky was pure,
And the sun sparkled on the Oxus stream.
But in the gloom they fought, with bloodshot eyes
And laboring breath; first Rustum struck the shield
Which Sohrab held stiff out; the steel-spiked spear
Rent the tough plates, but fail'd to reach the skin,
And Rustum pluck'd it back with angry groan.
Then Sohrab with his sword smote Rustum's helm,
Nor clove its steel quite through; but all the crest
He shore away, and that proud horsehair plume,
Never till now defiled, sank to the dust;
And Rustum bow'd his head; but then the gloom
Grew blacker, thunder rumbled in the air,
And lightnings rent the cloud; and Ruksh, the horse,
Who stood at hand, utter'd a dreadful cry;—
No horse's cry was that, most like the roar
Of some pain'd desert-lion, who all day
Hath trail'd the hunter's javelin in his side,
And comes at night to die upon the sand.
14

The two hosts heard that cry, and quaked for fear,
And Oxus curdled as it cross'd his stream.
But Sohrab heard, and quail'd not, but rush'd on,
And struck again; and again Rustum bow'd
His head; but this time all the blade, like glass,
Sprang in a thousand shivers on the helm,
And in the hand the hilt remain'd alone.
Then Rustum raised his head; his dreadful eyes
Glared, and he shook on high his menacing spear,
And shouted: *Rustum!*—Sohrab heard that shout,
And shrank amazed; back he recoil'd one step,
And scanned with blinking eyes the advancing form;
And then he stood bewilder'd; and he dropp'd
His covering shield, and the spear pierced his side.
He reel'd, and staggering back, sank to the ground;
And then the gloom dispersed, and the wind fell,
And the bright sun broke forth, and melted all
The cloud; and the two armies saw the pair—
Saw Rustum standing, safe upon his feet,
And Sohrab, wounded, on the bloody sand.
    Then, with a bitter smile, Rustum began:—
"Sohrab, thou thoughtest in thy mind to kill
A Persian lord this day, and strip his corpse,
And bear thy trophies to Afrasiab's tent.
Or else that the great Rustum would come down
Himself to fight, and that thy wiles would move
His heart to take a gift, and let thee go.
And then that all the Tartar host would praise
Thy courage or thy craft, and spread thy fame,
To glad thy father in his weak old age.
Fool, thou art slain, and by an unknown man!
Dearer to the red jackals shalt thou be
Than to thy friends, and to thy father old."
    And, with a fearless mien, Sohrab replied:—
"Unknown thou art; yet thy fierce vaunt is vain.
Thou dost not slay me, proud and boastful man!

No! Rustum slays me, and this filial heart.
For were I match'd with ten such men as thee,
And I were that which till today I was,
They should be lying here, I standing there.
But that beloved name unnerved my arm—
That name, and something, I confess, in thee,
Which troubles all my heart, and made my shield
Fall; and thy spear transfix'd an unarm'd foe.
And now thou boastest, and insult'st my fate.
But hear thou this, fierce man, tremble to hear;
The mighty Rustum shall avenge my death!
My father, whom I seek through all the world,
He shall avenge my death, and punish thee!"

  As when some hunter in the spring hath found
A breeding eagle sitting on her nest,
Upon the craggy isle of a hill-lake,
And pierced her with an arrow as she rose,
And follow'd her to find her where she fell
Far off;—anon her mate comes winging back
From hunting, and a great way off descries
His huddling young left sole; at that, he checks
His pinion, and with short uneasy sweeps
Circles above his eyry, with loud screams
Chiding his mate back to her nest; but she
Lies dying, with the arrow in her side,
In some far stony gorge out of his ken,
A heap of fluttering feathers—never more
Shall the lake glass her, flying over it;
Never the black and dripping precipices
Echo her stormy scream as she sails by—
As that poor bird flies home, nor knows his loss,
So Rustum knew not his own loss, but stood
Over his dying son, and knew him not.

  But, with a cold, incredulous voice, he said:—
"What prate is this of fathers and revenge?
The mighty Rustum never had a son."

And, with a failing voice, Sohrab replied:—
"Ah yes, he had! and that lost son am I.
Surely the news will one day reach his ear,
Reach Rustum, where he sits, and tarries long,
Somewhere, I know not where, but far from here;
And pierce him like a stab, and make him leap
To arms, and cry for vengeance upon thee.
Fierce man, bethink thee, for an only son!
What will that grief, what will that vengeance be?
Oh, could I live, till I that grief have seen!
Yet him I pity not so much, but her,
My mother, who in Ader-baijan dwells
With that old king, her father, who grows gray
With age, and rules over the valiant Koords.
Her most I pity, who no more will see
Sohrab returning from the Tartar camp,
With spoils and honor, when the war is done.
But a dark rumor will be bruited up,
From tribe to tribe, until it reach her ear;
And then will that defenceless woman learn
That Sohrab will rejoice her sight no more,
But that in battle with a nameless foe,
By the far-distant Oxus, he is slain."

He spoke; and as he ceased, he wept aloud,
Thinking of her he left, and his own death.
He spoke; but Rustum listen'd, plunged in thought.
Nor did he yet believe it was his son
Who spoke, although he call'd back names he knew;
For he had had sure tidings that the babe,
Which was in Ader-baijan born to him,
Had been a puny girl, no boy at all—
So that sad mother sent him word, for fear
Rustum should seek the boy, to train in arms.
And so he deem'd that either Sohrab took,
By a false boast, the style of Rustum's son;
Or that men gave it him, to swell his fame.

So deem'd he; yet he listen'd, plunged in thought;
And his soul set to grief, as the vast tide
Of the bright rocking Ocean sets to shore
At the full moon; tears gather'd in his eyes;
For he remember'd his own early youth,
And all its bounding rapture; as, at dawn,
The shepherd from his mountain-lodge descries
A far, bright city, smitten by the sun,
Through many rolling clouds—so Rustum saw
His youth; saw Sohrab's mother, in her bloom;
And that old king, her father, who loved well
His wandering guest, and gave him his fair child
With joy; and all the pleasant life they led,
They three, in that long-distant summer-time—
The castle, and the dewy woods, and hunt
And hound, and morn on those delightful hills
In Ader-baijan. And he saw that Youth,
Of age and looks to be his own dear son,
Piteous and lovely, lying on the sand,
Like some rich hyacinth which by the scythe
Of an unskillful gardener has been cut,
Mowing the garden grass-plots near its bed,
And lies, a fragrant tower of purple bloom,
On the mown, dying grass—so Sohrab lay,
Lovely in death, upon the common sand.
And Rustum gazed on him with grief, and said:—

"O Sohrab, thou indeed art such a son
Whom Rustum, wert thou his, might well have loved.
Yet here thou errest, Sohrab, or else men
Have told thee false—thou art not Rustum's son.
For Rustum had no son; one child he had—
But one—a girl; who, with her mother now
Plies some light female task, nor dreams of us—
Of us she dreams not, nor of wounds, nor war."

But Sohrab answer'd him in wrath; for now
The anguish of the deep-fix'd spear grew fierce,

And he desired to draw forth the steel,
And let the blood flow free, and so to die—
But first he would convince his stubborn foe;
And, rising sternly on one arm, he said:—

"Man, who art thou who dost deny my words?
Truth sits upon the lips of dying men,
And falsehood, while I lived, was far from mine.
I tell thee, prick'd upon this arm I bear
That seal which Rustum to my mother gave,
That she might prick it on the babe she bore."

He spoke; and all the blood left Rustum's cheeks,
And his knees totter'd, and he smote his hand
Against his breast, his heavy mailèd hand,
That the hard iron corslet clank'd aloud;
And to his heart he press'd the other hand,
And in a hollow voice he spake, and said:—

"Sohrab, that were a proof which could not lie!
If thou show this, then art thou Rustum's son."

Then, with weak, hasty fingers, Sohrab loosed
His belt, and near the shoulder bared his arm,
And show'd a sign in faint vermilion points
Prick'd; as a cunning workman, in Pekin,
Pricks with vermilion some clear porcelain vase,
An emperor's gift—at early morn he paints,
And all day long, and, when night comes, the lamp
Lights up his studious forehead and thin hands—
So delicately prick'd the sign appear'd
On Sohrab's arm, the sign of Rustum's seal.
It was that griffin, which of old rear'd Zal,
Rustum's great father, whom they left to die,
A helpless babe, among the mountain rocks;
Him that kind creature found, and rear'd, and loved—
Then Rustum took it for his glorious sign.
And Sohrab bared that image on his arm,
And himself scann'd it long with mournful eyes,
And then he touch'd it with his hand and said:—

"How say'st thou? Is that sign the proper sign
Of Rustum's son, or of some other man's?"
He spoke; but Rustum gazed, and gazed, and stood
Speechless; and then he utter'd one sharp cry:
O boy—thy father!—and his voice choked there.
And then a dark cloud pass'd before his eyes,
And his head swam, and he sank down to earth.
But Sohrab crawl'd to where he lay, and cast
His arms about his neck, and kiss'd his lips,
And with fond, faltering fingers stroked his cheeks,
Trying to call him back to life; and life
Came back to Rustum, and he oped his eyes,
And they stood wide with horror; and he seized
In both his hands the dust which lay around,
And threw it on his head, and smirch'd his hair,—
His hair, and face, and beard, and glittering arms;
And strong convulsive groaning shook his breast,
And his sobs choked him; and he clutch'd his sword,
To draw it, and for ever let life out.
But Sohrab saw his thought, and held his hands,
And with a soothing voice he spake, and said:—

"Father, forbear! for I but meet today
The doom which at my birth was written down
In Heaven, and thou art Heaven's unconscious hand.
Surely my heart cried out that it was thou,
When first I saw thee; and thy heart spoke too,
I know it! but fate trod those promptings down
Under its iron heel; fate, fate engaged
The strife, and hurl'd me on my father's spear.
But let us speak no more of this! I find
My father; let me feel that I have found!
Come, sit beside me on this sand, and take
My head betwixt thy hands, and kiss my cheeks,
And wash them with thy tears, and say: *My son!*
Quick! quick! for numbered are my sands of life,
And swift; for like the lightning to this field

I came, and like the wind I go away—
Sudden, and swift, and like a passing wind.
But it was writ in Heaven that this should be."
  —So said he, and his voice released the heart
Of Rustum, and his tears broke forth; he cast
His arms round his son's neck, and wept aloud,
And kiss'd him. And awe fell on both the hosts,
When they saw Rustum's grief; and Ruksh, the horse,
With his head bowing to the ground and mane
Sweeping the dust, came near, and in mute woe
First to the one then to the other moved
His head, as if inquiring what their grief
Might mean; and from his dark, compassionate eyes,
The big warm tears roll'd down, and caked the sand.
But Rustum chid him with stern voice, and said:—
  "Ruksh, now thou grievest; but, O Ruksh, thy feet
Should first have rotted on their nimble joints,
Or ere they brought thy master to this field!"
  But Sohrab look'd upon the horse and said:—
"Is this, then, Ruksh? How often, in past days,
My mother told me of thee, thou brave steed,
My terrible father's terrible horse! and said,
That I should one day find thy lord and thee.
Come, let me lay my hand upon thy mane!
O Ruksh, thou art more fortunate than I;
For thou hast gone where I shall never go,
And snuff'd the breezes of my father's home.
And thou hast trod the sands of Seistan,
And seen the river of Helmund, and the Lake
Of Zirrah; and the aged Zal himself
Has often stroked thy neck, and given thee food,
Corn in a golden platter soaked with wine,
And said: *O Ruksh! bear Rustum well!*—but I
Have never known my grandsire's furrow'd face,
Nor seen his lofty house in Seistan,
Nor slaked my thirst at the clear Helmund stream;

But lodged among my father's foes, and seen
Afrasiab's cities only, Samarcand,
Bokhara, and lone Khiva in the waste,
And the black Toorkmun tents; and only drunk
The desert rivers, Moorghab and Tejend,
Kohik, and where the Kalmuks feed their sheep,
The northern Sir; and this great Oxus stream,
The yellow Oxus, by whose brink I die."
    Then, with a heavy groan, Rustum bewail'd:—
"Oh, that its waves were flowing over me!
Oh, that I saw its grains of yellow silt
Roll tumbling in the current o'er my head!"
    But, with a grave, mild voice, Sohrab replied:—
"Desire not that, my father! thou must live.
For some are born to do great deeds, and live,
As some are born to be obscured, and die.
Do thou the deeds I die too young to do,
And reap a second glory in thine age;
Thou art my father, and thy gain is mine.
But come; thou seest this great host of men
Which follow me; I pray thee, slay not these!
Let me entreat for them; what have they done?
They follow'd me, my hope, my fame, my star.
Let them all cross the Oxus back in peace.
But me thou must bear hence, not send with them,
But carry me with thee to Seistan,
And place me on a bed, and mourn for me,
Thou, and the snow-hair'd Zal, and all thy friends.
And thou must lay me in that lovely earth,
And heap a stately mound above my bones,
And plant a far-seen pillar over all.
That so the passing horseman on the waste
May see my tomb a great way off, and cry:
Sohrab, the mighty Rustum's son, lies there,
Whom his great father did in ignorance kill!
And I be not forgotten in my grave."
15

And, with a mournful voice, Rustum replied:—
"Fear not! as thou hast said, Sohrab, my son,
So shall it be; for I will burn my tents,
And quit the host, and bear thee hence with me,
And carry thee away to Seistan,
And place thee on a bed, and mourn for thee,
With the snow-headed Zal, and all my friends.
And I will lay thee in that lovely earth,
And heap a stately mound above thy bones,
And plant a far-seen pillar over all,
And men shall not forget thee in thy grave.
And I will spare thy host; yea, let them go!
Let them all cross the Oxus back in peace!
What should I do with slaying any more?
For would that all that I have ever slain
Might be once more alive; my bitterest foes,
And they who were call'd champions in their time,
And through whose death I won that fame I have—
And I were nothing but a common man,
A poor, mean soldier, and without renown,
So thou mightest live too, my son, my son!
Or rather would that I, even I myself,
Might now be lying on this bloody sand,
Near death, and by an ignorant stroke of thine,
Not thou of mine! and I might die, not thou;
And I, not thou, be borne to Seistan;
And Zal might weep above my grave, not thine;
And say: *O son, I weep thee not too sore,*
For willingly, I know, thou met'st thine end!
But now in blood and battles was my youth,
And full of blood and battles is my age,
And I shall never end this life of blood."
    Then, at the point of death, Sohrab replied:—
"A life of blood indeed, thou dreadful man!
But thou shalt yet have peace; only not now,
Not yet! but thou shalt have it on that day,

When thou shalt sail in a high-masted ship,
Thou and the other peers of Kai Khosroo,
Returning home over the salt blue sea,
From laying thy dear master in his grave."
And Rustum gazed in Sohrab's face, and said:—
"Soon be that day, my son, and deep that sea!
Till then, if fate so wills, let me endure."

He spoke; and Sohrab smiled on him, and took
The spear, and drew it from his side, and eased
His wound's imperious anguish; but the blood
Came welling from the open gash, and life
Flow'd with the stream;—all down his cold, white side
The crimson torrent ran, dim now and soil'd,
Like the soil'd tissue of white violets,
Left, freshly gather'd, on their native bank,
By children whom their nurses call with haste
Indoors from the sun's eye; his head droop'd low,
His limbs grew slack; motionless, white, he lay—
White, with eyes closed; only when heavy gasps,
Deep heavy gasps quivering through all his frame,
Convulsed him back to life, he open'd them,
And fixed them feebly on his father's face;
Till now all strength was ebb'd, and from his limbs
Unwillingly, the spirit fled away,
Regretting the warm mansion which it left,
And youth, and bloom, and this delightful world.

So, on the bloody sand, Sohrab lay dead;
And the great Rustum drew his horseman's cloak
Down o'er his face, and sate by his dead son.
As those black granite pillars, once high-rear'd
By Jemshid in Persepolis, to bear
His house, now mid their broken flights of steps
Lie prone, enormous, down the mountain side—
So in the sand lay Rustum by his son.

And night came down over the solemn waste,
And the two gazing hosts, and that sole pair,

And darken'd all; and a cold fog, with night,
Crept from the Oxus. Soon a hum arose,
As of a great assembly loosed, and fires
Began to twinkle through the fog; for now
Both armies moved to camp, and took their meal;
The Persians took it on the open sands
Southward, the Tartars by the river marge;
And Rustum and his son were left alone.

But the majestic river floated on,
Out of the mist and hum of that low land,
Into the frosty starlight, and there moved,
Rejoicing, through the hush'd Chorasmian waste,
Under the solitary moon;—he flow'd
Right for the polar star, past Orgunjè,
Brimming, and bright, and large; then sands begin
To hem his watery march, and dam his streams,
And split his currents; that for many a league
The shorn and parcell'd Oxus strains along
Through beds of sand and matted rushy isles—
Oxus, forgetting the bright speed he had
In his high mountain-cradle in Pamere,
A foil'd circuitous wanderer—till at last
The long'd-for dash of waves is heard, and wide
His luminous home of waters opens, bright
And tranquil, from whose floor the new-bathed stars
Emerge, and shine upon the Aral Sea.

99

THE PRAYER

(The Real Experience of a French Gunner)

1914

Amelia Josephine Burr

You say there's only evil in this war—
That bullets drive out Christ? If you had been
In Furnes [1] with me that night . . . what would you say,
I wonder?
　　　　　It was ruin past all words,
Horror where joyous comfort used to be,
And not clean quiet death, for all day long
The great shells tore the little that remained
Like vultures on a body that still breathes.
They stopped as it grew dark. I looked about
The ghastly wilderness that once had been
The village street, and saw no other life
Except a Belgian soldier, shadowy
Among the shadows, and a little group
Of children creeping from a cellar school
And hurrying home. One older than the rest—
So little older!—mothered them along
Till all at once a stray belated shell
Whined suddenly out of the gloom, and burst
Near by. The babies wailed and clung together,
Helpless with fear. In vain the little mother
Encouraged them—"But no! you mustn't cry,
That isn't brave, that isn't French!" At last
She led her frightened brood across the way
To where there stood a roadside Calvary
Bearing its sad, indomitable Christ—

---

1. **Furnes.** A city in western Belgium.

Strange how the shells will spare just that! I saw
So many. . . . There they knelt, poor innocents,
Hands folded and eyes closed. I stole across
And stood behind them. "We must say our prayer—
Our Father which art in heaven," she began,
And all the little sobbing voices piped,
"Hallowed be Thy Name." From down the road
The Belgian soldier had come near. I felt
Him standing there beside me in the dusk.
"Thy kingdom come—"

            "Thy will be done on earth
As it is in heaven." The irony of it
Cut me like steel. I barely kept an oath
Behind my teeth. If one could name this earth
In the same breath with heaven—what is hell?
Only a little child could pray like this.
"Give us this day our daily bread—" A pause.
There was no answer. She repeated it
Urgently. Still the hush. She opened wide
Reproachful eyes at them. Their eyes were open
Also, and staring at the shadowy shapes
Of ruin all around them. Now that prayer
Had grown too hard even for little children.
"I know—I know—but we *must* say the prayer,"
She faltered. "Give us this day our daily bread,
And—and forgive—" she stopped.

                "Our trespasses
As we forgive them who have trespassed against us."
The children turned amazed, to see who spoke
The words they could not. I too turned to him,
The soldier there beside me—and I looked
Into King Albert's [2] face . . . I have no words
To tell you what I saw . . . only I thought
That while a man's breast held a heart like that,
Christ was not—even here—so far away.

   2. **King Albert.** King of Belgium (1918).

TRANCLATEIN OWN WIRDS

100

VITAÏ LAMPADA [1]

HENRY NEWBOLT

There's a breathless hush in the Close [2] tonight—
   Ten to make and the match to win—
A bumping pitch [3] and a blinding light,
   An hour to play and the last man in.
And it's not for the sake of a ribboned coat,
   Or the selfish hope of a season's fame,
But his Captain's hand on his shoulder smote,
   "Play up! play up! and play the game!"

The sand of the desert is sodden red,—
   Red with the wreck of a square that broke;—
The Gatling's jammed and the colonel dead
   And the regiment blind with dust and smoke.
The river of death has brimmed his banks,
   And England's far, and Honor a name,
But the voice of a schoolboy rallies the ranks,
   "Play up! play up! and play the game!"

This is the word that year by year
   While in her place the School is set
Every one of her sons must hear,
   And none that hears it dare forget.
This they all with a joyful mind
   Bear through life like a torch in flame,
And falling fling to the host behind—
   "Play up! play up! and play the game!"

---

1. **Vitaï Lampada.** The torch of life.
2. **Close.** Enclosed field used for athletic purposes.
3. **Bumping pitch.** In cricket the "pitch" or "crease" is the ground between the wickets. If this ground is uneven it causes such a bounding of the ball as to make its location at any moment uncertain.

INDEX OF TITLES

INDEX OF AUTHORS

APPENDIX

(Prepared by George L. Marsh, author of *Manual for the Study of English Classics*)

HELPS TO STUDY

GENERAL CONSIDERATIONS

Make lists of the poems which you consider particularly good examples of the following qualities mentioned in the editor's "Foreword" (pp. 3-5):

(1) Dramatic power.
(2) Presentation of excellent pictures.
(3) Presentation of vigorous and admirable characters.
(4) Strong appeal to the heroic.
(5) Concrete expression of human emotion.

Choose favorite poems, and favorite heroes or heroines, and formulate the best reasons you can for your choice in each case.

Consider together the poems by each author who is represented in the volume by more than one specimen. See whether you can come to any general conclusions as to the main characteristics of his work. If, after dealing with several different poets in this way, or with all of those who are extensively represented, you can come to a conclusion as to a favorite narrative poet, state your choice with reasons.

Which of the poems read are humorous? Which are pathetic? Which deal with romantic adventure? Which are brief love stories? How many deal with war or combat? Make a classification on the principles suggested by these questions, with addition of such other classes as you find represented.

The first seven poems in the volume are ancient ballads. Which of the poems by known authors do you find in any way imitative of the ancient ballads, in versification, in manner of narration, in style and spirit? (For explanation of ballad

437

characteristics see *English Popular Ballads,* edited by Hart, in the Lake English Classics.)

See pages 447-450 below for a general explanation of English versification, which may be applied at pleasure to poems in the volume.

THE SPECIFIC POEMS

Robin Hood and Little John. How is good sportsmanship shown in this poem? What passages are humorous? What important customs of Robin Hood and his band of outlaws are indicated (p. 16)? Examine some of the interesting words in the poem, such as *thorough* (p. 11), *good b'w'ye* (p. 12—its etymology and present form?), *gillore* p. 16—its present form?).

Robin Hood's Death and Burial. What chivalric quality does Robin show? Do you think the poem would be more effective if a motive for the cousin's act were given?

Johnie Armstrong. How is sympathy roused for the hero in spite of the fact that he is said to be "a bold outl⟨aw⟩" ⟨and⟩ Su "robbed all the north country"? What historical ba⟨sis⟩ for this ballad (p. 20)? Note the repetition, with slight variations, of a stanza on page 22. This device is very frequent in ballads and should be watched for.

Sir Patrick Spence. It has been said of this poem that it has "precisely the artistic qualities which we look for in the best modern verse." Try to decide what characteristics are meant by this and cite examples. Note resemblances between this poem and "The Wreck of the Hesperus" (pp. 42-45); specific stanzas, for example, that are similar.

Young Waters. Note the effect of introducing quotations without specifying the speaker (p. 26). Can there be any doubt who is meant? This poem is an excellent example of suppression of all but the most essential details and telling by suggestion. It also contains some unusually good examples of repetition— find them.

The Dowie Dens of Yarrow. Work out a careful statement as to the speakers of the different quoted stanzas. Why did the hero go to the banks of Yarrow, and why did he fight when he found himself so outnumbered?

The Battle of Otterburn. Who are the speakers on page 31?

Sir Philip Sidney said of this and another ballad about the same event: "I never heard the old song of Percy and Douglas that I found not my heart moved more than with a trumpet"; and Addison wrote two *Spectator* papers on the ballads (one of which is to be found in the Lake Classics edition of *Selections from The Tatler and The Spectator*). How do you account for such estimates of the ballad?

The Bell of Atri. How is the fact that the horse could ring the bell accounted for (p. 36)? Do you think it necessary or important that the "moral" should be stated so plainly as on p. 38? A clever student might find it interesting to try rewriting this in the suggestive style of the older ballads.

God's Judgment on Hatto. Do you find the effectiveness of this injured by its grotesqueness in some particulars? Is the Bishop's act accounted for in any way?

The Wreck of the Hesperus. Work out all points of resemblance between this poem and "Sir Patrick Spence" (pp. 23-4). In what ways is the tragedy of the wreck made especially bitter?

Lochinvar. This poem appears in *Marmion* as a song sung by Lady Heron (see Lake Classics edition of *Marmion*). How do you account for the great popularity that it has attained?

Lady Clare. Find ways in which this poem imitates the old ballads; give specific examples. Note points of resemblance (for example, in a certain democracy of spirit) between "Lady Clare" and "The Lord of Burleigh" (pp. 61-63).

Lord Ullin's Daughter. What good qualities of the ballad does this illustrate? Is the pursuit by Lord Ullin accounted for? His forgiveness of his daughter?

Amy Wentworth. Tell in plain terms the story implied in this poem, and mention other poems in the book to which it is related in idea.

Maud Muller. Both the idea and the method of treatment of this poem are very simple, almost commonplace, yet it is probably as widely known, at least in America, as anything else in the book. Why? Would you criticize the conclusion in any way?

The Lord of Burleigh. Compare "Lady Clare" (pp. 47-50). Is it the intention to imply that the "trouble" which "weigh'd upon her" caused the death of the lady (p. 63) "before her time''? Do you think this indicates any undemocratic views on Tennyson's part?

Lucy Gray. A characteristic idea of Wordsworth was that poetry required no artificial vocabulary; but that "incidents and situations from common life," presented "in a selection of language really used by men," would make as great poetry as any other sort of material. Point out ways in which this poem illustrates his theory. Do you find it unpleasantly commonplace in any particular?

The Singing Leaves. To what preceding poems is this related in idea? What ballad characteristics does it have? Is it plausible that there should be no further mention of the father in III? What did he probably think of the pretensions of "Walter the page"?

In School-Days. Does this seem natural and child-like? Do you think the last stanzas add anything important?

We Are Seven. This poem is a very simple expression of an important idea of Wordsworth's "Ode on Intimations of Immortality." Look up the ode (which may be found in *The Golden Treasury,* Lake Classics edition) and formulate this idea. Does "We Are Seven" contain any examples of Wordsworth's carrying his theory as to poetic diction too far? Answer specifically.

The Inchcape Rock. Is there any statement of a "moral" here? What do you think as to the need of one? Show how this poem illustrates "dramatic irony" and "poetic justice."

The Witch's Daughter. What fact does this poem indicate as to the way in which old ballads and songs (*folk* ballads and *folk* songs) are preserved (p. 79)? Defend the digression of three stanzas on page 80. Does it seem plausible that popular murmur should subside? That such a marriage should be happy?

Skipper Ireson's Ride. How and why is the refrain varied? What attitude on the poet's part do you think the whole poem indicates? Would the poem have been as effective if it conformed to the facts explained on page 86 (note 1)?

Bernardo del Carpio. Does this seem sufficiently complete? Why is there no discussion of revenge? Where was the "haughty king" at the time of the discovery that the father was dead?

The Baron's Last Banquet. Compare Baron Rudiger's defiance of Death with that of the three rioters in Chaucer's "Pardoner's Tale" (Lake edition of *Selections from Chaucer*). See also Poe's "Masque of the Red Death" (*Poems and Tales*, ed. Newcomer, Lake Classics). Note the freedom from comment (p. 96).

Spanish Waters. Who is speaking in this poem? Note ways in which the language is made appropriate to him. Recall all the stories or poems about buried treasure that you know; see especially books by Hawthorne, Irving, Poe, and Stevenson in the Lake English Classics.

How They Brought the Good News from Ghent to Aix. How much of the scene of this poem figured in the Great War? Point out some of the best examples of galloping movement in rhythm. How long did the ride last?

Paul Revere's Ride. Compare this in narrative spirit and speed of movement with "How They Brought the Good News" (pp. 99-101). In reading this, as well as all other patriotic poems of the American Revolution, students should keep in mind what British king and cabinet were responsible for the oppression of the colonists. For the view of the most enlightened British public opinion at the time, see the new Lake Classics edition of Burke's *Speech on Conciliation* (1919).

The Ballad of East and West. Was the Border raid presented here anything like the one in "The Battle of Otterburn" (pp. 30-35)? How do you account for the action of Kamal and the Colonel's son? Find some of the best examples of rapid movement. Of internal rimes in the long lines.

John Gilpin. Find a striking error in grammar on page 111. Why was it used? In what way are humorous effects secured in this poem?

Tam O'Shanter. Carlyle, in his *Essay on Burns*, called this "not so much a poem, as a piece of sparkling rhetoric" (p. 79, Lake edition of the *Essay*). What do you think he meant? Do you agree with him in depreciating this poem among Burns's works? What do you think of the bits of digression, as on pages 122-3? What is the effect of the Scottish dialect?

Jock of Hazeldean. Who is the speaker in the quoted parts? Why should the lady be weeping, in view of what finally happens (p. 130)?

The Glove and the Lions. Compare and contrast the narrative methods of this poem and the next (pp. 132-38).

The Glove. What peculiarity in the rimes do you notice? What is the effect? Do you like it in a poem essentially serious? What devices of style are there to make the poem seem appropriate to a French poet of the sixteenth century? What is the essence of the lady's defense (p. 136)? What finally happens?

The Courtin'. What notably poetical bits do you find amid the homely colloquialisms of this poem? In what ways is it humorous? What do you think of its effectiveness, on the whole?

The Pied Piper of Hamelin. Study the variations of meter to fit the sense; the peculiar and ingenious rimes (how are they effective, and are they always effective?); the rapid movement of the narrative. Does the last brief division really add anything to the poem (p. 152)?

The Well of St. Keyne. How does this poem indicate the prounciation of the name "Keyne"?

The Deacon's Masterpiece. Note how curiosity and interest are aroused in the first stanza. What do the minute technical details as to parts of the vehicle contribute to the poem? Why should there be such emphasis on "logic"?

How the Old Horse Won the Bet. What incidental bits of social satire are there in this poem? What is its relation to the preceding? Do you think the old horse's winning is made plausible?

The Ballad of the Oysterman. What do you think of treating a tragedy so humorously? Choose some of the most effective bits in the poem.

The Yarn of the Nancy Bell. Why should one stanza be repeated several times (with some variations)? By what devices is cannibalism made humorous?

The Eve of St. John. How does the poem show the pronunciation of "Buccleuch"? What has the particular time—St. John's eve—to do with this story?

Arnold von Winkelried. In just what way did the sacrifice of Winkelried result in success for the Swiss cause?

The Defense of the Alamo. Does the last stanza add anything proper to the poem (p. 183)? Do you find all the lines rhythmical?

The Battle Flag at Shenandoah. Note how the last line of each stanza is practically a refrain, though regularly varied in harmony with the thought of the preceding three lines.

The Song of the Camp. What universal characteristic of human nature does this poem illustrate? Do you know a song popular in the recent war that illustrates the same characteristic?

Marco Bozzaris. Do you think this poem would be any more effective if it dealt more with events and less with comments? Why have we the contrast in the two stanzas on page 189?

Little Giffen. Note the compression of this poem—how the barest facts are given, or hinted at, in almost a laconic manner.

Music in Camp. Did the ''Federal band'' play ''Dixie'' (p. 193)? Does this poem seem natural and reasonable?

Agincourt. Note an important later use of the peculiar stanza form of this poem (pp. 204-5). Compare Shakspere's treatment of Agincourt in his *Henry V* (Lake Classics edition). This has often been called one of the greatest battle poems in English—would you agree? Give reasons for or against.

The Battle of Blenheim. What keen, ironic criticism of wars is implied in this poem? Is it entirely just?

Incident of the French Camp. What good qualities of narration are here illustrated? Study the little flashlight of Napoleon—what important characteristics are made prominent?

The Charge of the Light Brigade. To what preceding poem is this related metrically? Does the use of the dactylic meter result (either in this poem or in the related one) in unnatural or strained accentuation?

The Battle of Naseby. In what ways is the language of this poem made appropriate to the pretended narration by a Puritan? Is it over-partisan and bigoted?

The Burial of Sir John Moore. What lines or phrases in this poem have passed into the common stock of those who speak or write English?

The Soldier's Dream. What view of war is implied here?

Destruction of Sennacherib. What is the effect of the meter of this poem? Note the striking figures and the vividness of the pictures suggested.

The Revenge. Do you find the rime and rhythm of this poem well suited its spirit? Illustrate your conclusions. Sir Walter Raleigh's account of the last fight of the ''Revenge'' may be found in Newcomer and Andrews, *Twelve Centuries of English Poetry and Prose,* pages 208-11.

Hervé Riel. Are the variations in meter aids to the smooth flow of the narrative? What is to be said of this poem in the matter of vividness? Does the small reward Hervé Riel receives increase or decrease the effectiveness?

The Defense of Lucknow. Note the accumulation of vivid details to show the difficulties and horrors of the defense.

The Pipes at Lucknow. What is the relation of this poem to the preceding one as to subject matter?

Fight. Note the naturalness of the dialogue, even though it is fitted into a rhythmical scheme. What is the purpose of the stanza of description at the beginning of II? And of the repetition of some of it at the end of that part? Of the mention of the cricket in the next stanza (p. 240)? What bearing has the last part of the poem on the war begun in 1914?

Arnold at Stillwater. Who is the narrator of this poem? Is it fitting to commemorate thus the brave deeds of a man who became a traitor?

Keenan's Charge. Are any essential details omitted? Could any details now found in the poem be spared?

Greencastle Jenny. Why did Pickett's men act as they did? Is the psychology of the poem sound?

Vive la France. Note the skillful variations in the refrain. What merits has this poem in choice of details, suppression of non-essentials, etc.?

The Hell-Gate of Soissons. How is the style of this made appropriate to the narrator? Note the vividness and vigor and rapidity.

The Italian in England. Why did the woman (pp. 267-8) act as she did? What is the narrator's attitude toward her? Does such a poem as this throw any light on the present feeling of Italians regarding Austrians?

The Prisoner of Chillon. Note the monologue form of this poem. Is it particularly appropriate to the material? What is the main idea of the poem? Does it aim to tell a story, or to present and account for a state of mind? Trace the gradual changes in the Prisoner's feeling. Observe how a cumulative impression of the horrors of the dungeon is given. Compare Poe's "The Pit and the Pendulum." Compare also the story of Ugolino in Dante's *Inferno*, Canto XXXIII. Chaucer's version of the same story is to be found in the Lake Classics edition of *Selections from Chaucer*, pages 183-5. What is the purpose of the episode of the bird (p. 279)? Compare the influence of other living creatures on the Ancient Mariner.

Horatius. In what ways is the fundamental eight-line stanza varied in this poem? Note the extensive use of proper names— is it effective? Does the poem gain by being spun out to such length?

Rizpah. Who is the narrator? Is the language appropriate? What elements of tragedy and pathos are there in the poem? It has been said of this poem "that if all the rest of the author's works were destroyed, this alone would at once place him among the first of the world's poets." Discuss this judgment briefly and give whatever reasons you find for it.

King Robert of Sicily. Is this merely the story of a dream, or a miraculous legend? How is the change in the spirit of the king to be accounted for?

Juggling Jerry. Note the important ways in which this is kept appropriate (in language, figures of speech, etc.) to the speaker. What were the main characteristics of Jerry and the principal articles in his philosophy of life?

Pan in Wall Street. In what contrast does the effectiveness of this poem lie?

Fleurette. What bearing has this upon Wordsworth's theory that true and effective poetry may consist of simple and ordinary language such as is "really used by men"? Is there anything in the least unnatural or out of tone?

Grand-Père. How much is told of the speaker? Can you imagine much more being crowded into so little space?

How Oswald Dined with God. What application of this poem can you make to conditions in many parts of the world today?

How the Great Guest Came. What relation does this bear in idea to Lowell's *Vision of Sir Launfal* (see the Lake Classics edition)?

The Fool's Prayer. Why was the king so affected by the fool's prayer?

Opportunity. State in plain terms the keen and forceful idea of this poem.

The Reverie of Poor Susan. A stanza of moralization originally concluded this poem. Do you consider it in need of explanation or comment? State its meaning in bald prose.

Columbus. Is it natural that relief—success—should come when things look darkest? Note resemblances between the spirit of Columbus and that of Ulysses in Tennyson's poem (*Selections from Tennyson* in Lake Classics edition).

Abou Ben Adhem. This is one of the few poems by its author that have lived in popular esteem—how do you account for that fact?

The Legend Beautiful. In what way is this poem a concrete expression of the preceding one (pp. 342-3)? Mention other related poems in this volume, or mentioned in these "helps."

"He Fell Among Thieves." Who is the hero of this? What has happened to him, and what happens? Is the psychology in the stanzas that begin "He saw" natural?

The Boy and the Angel. Explain how this poem illustrates the idea mentioned in the note on page 349. Just what happens to Theocrite?

Tithonus. This has been pronounced "perhaps the most perfect specimen of artistic workmanship in all Tennyson." What characteristics tend to justify this judgment? What does Tithonus wish for, and why?

The Angels of Buena Vista. Does this poem indicate an attitude of condemnation of the Mexican War? Of war in general? What kind of rime is the second one in the middle stanza on page 359?

The Host of the Air. Here the language is very simple, but there is a mystical suggestiveness about the poem. Can you explain how it is secured?

The Lady of Shalott. This is an early presentation of substantially the story of Elaine in *Idylls of the King* (see *Selections from Tennyson* in the Lake Classics). Enumerate the points of resemblance between Tennyson's two treatments of the material; the differences. Discuss the matter mentioned on the note on page 362.

La Belle Dame sans Merci. Study the plan of this poem; note, for example, that though no quotation marks are used, there are different speakers. Who are they? To what famous class of stories does this belong?

The Haystack in the Floods. Do you see any special reason for this title? What course of events have preceded the action of this poem?

Vigil Strange I Kept on the Field One Night. Do you find this rhythmical? What do you think of its sentence structure?

Shameful Death. Who is the narrator? What relation did he bear to Sir Hugh? What had happend to Sir Hugh, and why? What revenge was taken?

The Highwayman. Does this poem tend too much to exalt the highwayman and his trade? Explain the way in which repetition is used at the end of each stanza. Is it effective?

The Singer in the Prison. What general principles as to crime and punishment are implied here? Does Whitman seem capable of using rime effectively when he wishes to do so? Which part of this poem is more effective—the regularly rimed part, or the irregular part?

The White Ship. Is there anything particularly effective in having Berold, the butcher's son, made narrator of this poem? Why does so much of it deal with events after the ship struck the rock?

Sohrab and Rustum. Critical details as to this poem may be found in the Lake Classics edition of *English Poems,* edited by Miss Scudder. Arnold said that poetry should be "a criticism of life." Does this apply to "Sohrab and Rustum?" Apply in detail Arnold's analysis of the chief characteristics of Homer (*English Poems,* p. 514)—that is, the chief characteristics of the best epic narration. Note some of the best examples of long Homeric similes. Do they all seem effective? What other conventional epic devices are there? What is the effect of beginning with "and" and of the frequent use of that word at the beginnings of lines? What is the effect of so many and such odd proper names? What impressions do you get as to the amount and accuracy of the local color? Do you find too much of the Greek tone? Is Rustum's refusal to admit his identity adequately accounted for? Why should not Sohrab sooner indicate that Rustum is his father? Is the tragedy heightened by such blindness? How does the last paragraph return to the note of the beginning? What symbolism may be found?

The Prayer. How is the presence of the king accounted for? Note the effective suspense and surprise.

Vitaï Lampada. Is this really a narrative poem? Has it any special appropriateness at the end of this book?

ON ENGLISH VERSIFICATION

For purposes of analysis the names given metrical "feet" in Greek and Latin have been taken over into English, and some of them are so commonly used that the student should be familiar with them.

The commonest foot in English is the *iamb* (or iambus), consisting of an unaccented syllable followed by an accented syllable, which may be marked as follows:

ălóne

A familiar line consisting of iambic feet is the following:

Ĭ cóme | frŏm haúnts | ŏf cóot | ănd hérn.

The *anapest,* consisting of two unaccented syllables, followed by an accented syllable ($\cup \cup \,'$), is often used in connection with the iamb, and gives a more tripping effect to the line. The following is an anapestic line (though the first foot is an iamb):

Ĭ gál | lŏped, Dĭrck gál | lŏped, wĕ gál | lŏped ăll thrée.

The *trochee,* consisting of an accented syllable, followed by an unaccented syllable ($'\cup$), is the opposite of the iamb. The following is a trochaic line:

Í ăm | Mérlin.

The *dactyl,* comprising an accented syllable followed by two unaccented syllables ($'\cup\cup$), bears the same relation to the trochee that the anapest bears to the iamb. The following is a dactylic line (though the last foot is a trochee):

Hálf ă leăgue; | hálf ă leăgue; | hálf ă leăgue; | ónwărd.

Most English verse can be "scanned" as consisting of these four kinds of feet. A few other terms are occasionally used, but so rarely as not to require attention here.

Verse lines in English have been commonly given names according to the number and kind of feet, or the number of stresses or accents and the prevailing metrical movement.

Thus a line of two dactyls is *dactylic dimeter:*

Táke hĕr ŭp | téndĕrlў.

A line of three trochees is *trochaic trimeter:*

Whére thĕ | ápplĕ | réddĕns.

A line of four anapests is *anapestic tetrameter:*

Ĭ spráng | tŏ thĕ stír | rŭp, ănd Jó | rĭs, ănd hé. (The fact that the first foot is an iamb does not affect the prevailing movement of the line.)

A line of five iambs is *iambic pentameter:*

Sŏ áll | dăy lóng | thĕ nóise | ŏf bát | tlĕ rólled.

A line with six accents is *hexameter;* a line with seven accents, *heptameter;* a line with eight accents, *octameter;* but these last two terms are not very much used. Of course, the adjective indicating any kind of foot may be prefixed to any one of the nouns indicating the number of feet, or accents (which is the same thing).

It must be understood, in applying the foregoing material, that English metre does not demand rigid uniformity. On the contrary, the better the poet, usually, the more variety in distribution of stresses there is likely to be. Word accents and metrical accents must and do fall on the same syllables. Therefore, if at the beginning of what is otherwise an iambic line we find a word that is accented on the first syllable—a trochee, we do not make an iamb of this word by giving it an unnatural and improper accent on the second syllable. Instead, we recognize that there is a shift of stress in the first foot—a trochee is substituted for an iambus. Such a line is the following:

Wálkĭng | ăbóut | thĕ gár | dĕns ánd | thĕ hálls.

Such shift of stress, or the substitution of one kind of foot for another, occurs very often and in different parts of the line. It is not an objectionable irregularity, but a device intentionally used to secure rhythmical variety. In formal scansion lines should be marked according to the actual fall of the stresses; and calling a line iambic, or trochaic, or anapestic, or dactylic, should never be taken to mean that all its feet must somehow or other be twisted into the one kind named. These terms often mean only that the prevailing metrical movement is of the kind specified.

Analysis of a brief passage from Tennyson's "Merlin and the Gleam" will indicate how varied the metrical movement of a poem may be:

Yóu thăt ăre | wátchĭng (dactyl and trochee).

Thĕ gráy | măgí | ciăn (iambic, with extra unaccented syllable at end).

With éyes | ŏf wón | dĕr (iambic, with extra unaccented syllable at end).

Í ăm | Mérlĭn (trochaic).

Aňd Í | ăm dȳ | iňg (iambic as above).

Í ăm | Mérlĭn (trochaic).

Whŏ fól | lŏw thĕ Gléam (iamb and anapest).

The only uniformity in these lines, obviously, lies in the fact that each has two stresses. They are dimeter, but infinitely varied as to the kind of feet, or the distribution of accents. Most poems are not so varied as this one, but students must remember that great variety in this regard is thoroughly compatible with effective rhythm and irreproachable poetic technique.

The description of verse form is by no means complete when the prevailing foot and the length of line—the number of stresses—are named. It must be noted whether *rime* is used, and if it is used, how the rimes are arranged.

Blank verse is unrimed iambic pentameter—the metre of *The Idylls of the King, Paradise Lost,* the unrimed verse of Shakspere's plays, etc. The term blank verse is not usually applied to unrimed verse that is not iambic pentameter.

The *heroic couplet* is iambic pentameter rimed in pairs—the metre of most of the work of Dryden and Pope, of Goldsmith's *Deserted Village,* of Chaucer's Prologue to *Canterbury Tales,* etc. The following is an example:

> Know then thyself, presume not God to *scan;*
> The proper study of mankind is *man.*

(Rimed words are italicized.)

The *octosyllabic couplet*—iambic or trochaic tetrameter—is also common—the metre of the main parts of Milton's *L'Allegro* and *Il Penseroso.* Example:

> Come, and trip it as you *go,*
> On the light fantastic *toe.*

Of course, there may be various other kinds of *couplets,* according to the number of stresses and the prevailing feet; and there may be *triplets*—groups of three riming lines.

Stanzaic forms may be almost infinitely varied, as to length of lines, kinds of feet, and rime-schemes. The method commonly used for indicating rime-schemes is to give the letter *a* to the first rime in a stanza, *b* to the second, *c* to the third, and so on. Thus, all the lines marked *a* rime together; those marked *b* rime (and, of course, are different from *a*), etc. For example, turn to "The Lady of Shalott" (p. 362); the rime-scheme of the first stanza is *a a a a b c c c b.* All the lines have four stresses (are tetrameter), except the second one marked *b,* which has but three stresses. The movement in this stanza is mainly iambic, but many lines of the poem are trochaic.

A *quatrain* is any combination of four lines. Tennyson's *In Memoriam,* for example, is written in iambic tetrameter quatrains with the rime-scheme *a b b a.* Two particular kinds of quatrains have been given special names of some importance, as follows:

The *ballad stanza* ("common metre" in the hymn-books) is a very simple quatrain with the rime-scheme *a b a b* or *a b c b;*

the *a*'s (or *a* and *c*) with four stresses, the *b*'s with three stresses.

The *elegiac stanza* (as in Gray's "Elegy") also rimes *a b a b*, but the lines are pentameter. Other stanzaic forms are very numerous and need not be discussed in detail, since the means of making metrical analysis have been indicated above.